THE MENDOCINO COAST
GLOVE BOX GUIDE

*ON THIS WILD AND ROCKBOUND COAST,
the everlasting surf has carved out
strange and fanciful forms — of
satyrs and genii; of great black giants,
who stand in the spray with dripping
beards of seaweed, ready to devour
ships and their crews; of ruined
temples and 'cities by the sea' which
loom with an alluring beauty.*

— J. Ross Browne
The Coast Rangers
Harper's New Monthly Magazine,
Volume 23–24, 1861–1862.

THE MENDOCINO COAST
GLOVE BOX GUIDE

LODGINGS, EATERIES, SIGHTS,
HISTORY, ACTIVITIES & MORE

BOB LORENTZEN

BORED FEET PRESS
www.boredfeet.com
MENDOCINO, CALIFORNIA
THIRD EDITION, 2003

©1995, 1997, 2004 by Robert S. Lorentzen
Third edition, October 2003
Printed in the United States of America on 30% recycled paper

Edited by Jim Fullan
Maps by Beca LaFore
Design and production by Elizabeth Petersen, Petersen Graphics
Production on the third edition by Wendy Blakeway of Design Xperts
Sasquatch Books has generously given permission to use the Sharon Doubiago
    quotation on page 119, excerpted from the anthology *Edge Walking on the
    Western Rim*, ©1994 One Reel.
Emmy Lou Packard illustrations on pages 3, 5, 105, 110, 117 and 210 used by
    permission of the artist.

Published and Distributed by
Bored Feet Press
www.boredfeet.com
Post Office Box 1832
Mendocino, California 95460
(707) 964-6629, (888) 336-6199
Fax: (707) 964-5953

Library of Congress Cataloging-in-Publication Data
Lorentzen, Bob, 1949-
        The Mendocino coast glove box guide: lodgings, eateries, sights, history, activities & more, third edition, Bob Lorentzen.
            pp. 256
        Includes bibliographical references and index.
        ISBN 0-939431-29-7
        1. Mendocino County (Calif.)—Guidebooks.   I. Title.   II. Series.

                                                        CIP

ISBN 0-939431-29-7

10 9 8 7 6 5 4 3

To Liz Petersen, who believed in this book
through all the chaos, and who brought
joy, hope and balance to my life.

ACKNOWLEDGMENTS

I offer a robust thank you to the hundreds of people who helped create this book. In particular I thank Elizabeth Petersen for her elegant design, meticulous production, and just for putting up with this monstrous project as long as she did; Jim Fullan, who got on the bus back at the first stop, guided the journey and kept it on track through chaos and darkness into the light; Beca LaFore for her graceful maps; Robert Lee and Bill Wagner for special help with the historic photographs; John Biaggi for his generosity with the priceless photo of the coast road at Flumeville; David Springer for his help guiding all of us through the fault zone so we might better understand it; John Birchard for taking all those great shots of the Mendocino Headlands; and Emmy Lou Packard for generously sharing her wonderful block prints of Mendocino to grace this book.

Thanks to my marvelous and masterful proofreaders both out loud and silent Donna Bettencourt, Bruce Levene, Wilma Tucker, Don Tucker, John Skinner, Kate Dougherty, Ron Bloomquist, Sarah Flowers, Lenora Shepard, Celeste Bautista, Katy Tahja, Dan Kozloff, Johanna Bedford, Randy Bancroft, Honey Fortney,, Linda Brown, Lily Parsons and Anne Kissack.

For moral and technical support I thank Judy Tarbell and Jim Tarbell of Black Bear Press; Crescent Dean Tarbell for sharing his modem; Sally Grigg for her encouragement and support early on; Kate Lee and Rebecca Jarrett for their help at the end; Gene Barnett and Julian at Eel River Redwoods Hostel for feedback on the Leggett Valley; Ruth Dobberpuhl for help putting together the many changes for the second edition; and Donna Bettencourt and Howard Martin for their invaluable help with the third edition.

With particular thanks to all the people who work together to run the little museums and libraries that help make this community more whole, and especially to the greater community of the Mendocino Coast.

CONTENTS

PREFACE TO THE THIRD EDITION

In a guide book you want the most recent and accurate information available. When we first published this book in December 1994, it encompassed a wealth of local knowledge gathered during my two decades in Mendocino County, combined with the wisdom and expertise of hundreds of other local folks. We published the Second Edition in 1997.

Now after six years, I am pleased to present the completely revised and updated Third Edition of *The Mendocino Coast Glove Box Guide*. We've added dozens of new listings for you to investigate. Equally important, we at Bored Feet have personally contacted each of the book's hundreds of entries so that we continue to present the most up-to-date and thorough information available to the cornucopia of great destinations along the Mendocino Coast.

Inside you'll find the latest details on 129 lodgings and 128 places to eat, listed in each community from the most to least expensive, choices to fit the tastes of every traveler. I've chosen 68 of those as my personal favorites, and marked them with a star (☆) so you can find them at a glance. I've fully updated and expanded the information about all the parks, campgrounds, performing arts, wineries, galleries, museums and gardens, plus the shops, activities and sights that make the Mendocino Coast unique.

The spectacular natural beauty and intriguing local history remain mostly as I described them in our first edition, but I've added a few choice bits of new information to the history. That dramatic natural grandeur and the story of its interface with human endeavors is the true story of any guide book with a heart.

Enjoy your journey,

Bob Lorentzen
September 2003

*S*OME OF THE MOST PICTURESQUE COUNTRY *in California lies on or near the coast north of San Francisco. Least visited by strangers, it contains a very great deal of wild and fine scenery.*

In such a journey the traveler will see the famous redwood forests of this state, whose trees are unequaled in size except by the giant sequoias. He will see in Mendocino County one of the most remarkable coasts in the world, eaten by the ocean into the most singular and fantastic shapes.

The roads are excellent, and either a public stage or a private team is always obtainable. In a country where every body is civil and obliging, and where all you see is novel to an Eastern person, the sense of adventure adds a keen zest to a journey which is in itself not only amusing and healthful, but instructive.

— Charles Nordhoff, 1874
*Northern California, Oregon
and the Sandwich Islands*

Wherever You Go on the Mendocino Coast, There You Are

ONE HUNDRED TWENTY-NINE YEARS AGO, when Charles Nordhoff, grandfather of the author of *Mutiny on the Bounty*, visited the Mendocino Coast, the journey from San Francisco took 24 hours or longer, whether you traveled by stagecoach or steamship. This spectacular and gorgeous coast was truly remote then, but people nonetheless braved danger and discomfort to see it.

You may still consider the Mendocino Coast remote, especially by Eastern or European standards. But now you can drive to this stunningly beautiful coast in about four hours from the San Francisco Bay Area or Sacramento, a trip short enough to make Mendocino an ideal destination for a weekend or a week. You will be rewarded with scenery that will linger in your memory for a lifetime.

Not only is the marvelous shore Nordhoff described still intact, but you can also skip the stagecoach careening over twisting dirt roads and drive the excellent, though still winding, pavement yourself. Nordhoff's "somewhat rude" accommodations have been supplanted by a full range of refined lodgings and eateries, from first class to budget, in most every town.

You'll also encounter a dazzling array of other amenities and activities, whether you crave excitement or relaxation, pampering or roughing it: gorgeous parks with room to ramble, live music from symphonies, operas and chamber concerts to rock, folk, blues and jazz, superb live theater from drama to musical comedy and melodrama, hot tubs beneath infinite stars, whale-watching or sport-fishing trips, horseback rides to deserted beaches and remote forests, guided sea kayak adventures to hidden sea caves and coves, scenic plane flights, paddling on placid tidal rivers through bird-filled estuaries. If you want to relive the nineteenth century, you can even ride in a horse drawn carriage around an historic town.

Whenever you travel the Mendocino Coast with your *Glove Box Guide,* wherever you go, there you are, with all the details you need to plan your special escape, whether it's a three-star retreat or a family camping trip. So don't leave home without it!

How This Guide Works for You

The Glove Box Guide flows from south to north along the coast, from Sea Ranch and Gualala to Mendocino, Caspar, Fort Bragg, Westport and the end of Highway One at Leggett. We follow this with separate

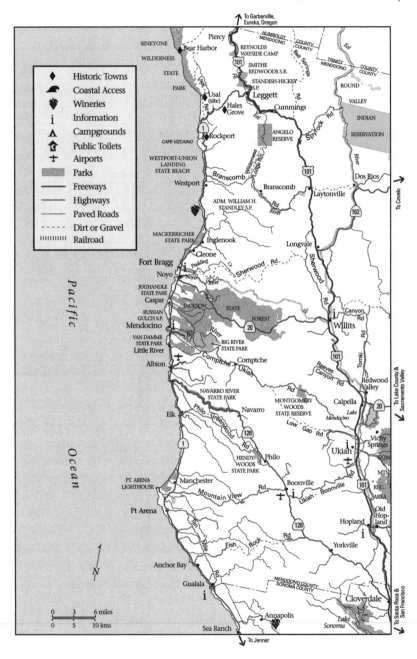

Historic Towns
Coastal Access
Wineries
Information
Campgrounds
Public Toilets
Airports
Parks
Freeways
Highways
Paved Roads
Dirt or Gravel
Railroad

sections on quicker routes: from the Bay Area via Anderson Valley's wine country on Highway 128 and from the east via Highway 20 through Jackson State Forest. Each town has its own section, located in the book exactly where you will find the town in the lay of the land. The section for each town provides comprehensive listings of the accommodations, the most extensive and up-to-date information currently in print, plus the varieties of sights and activities the town offers. So, wherever you go on the Mendocino Coast, you have the facts you need in hand.

The listings for each town run from most to least expensive, so you can quickly find the price range you want. Lodging prices show each inn's full range, while eateries indicate price per person. For restaurants and lodgings we've marked our favorite choices with a star (✩), denoting exceptional quality and/or value. Accommodations without a star may also be excellent, we just don't know them as well.

Whether you've never been to the west coast or have lived here for years but never taken the time to discover the place, we've designed *The Glove Box Guide* to allow you to explore and savor all the flavors, to get acquainted with the quiet corners and hidden treasures. We put the essential information and the juicy and odd tidbits at your fingertips, so that you can design a journey of substance, one that will let you say, upon returning home, "Wow! What a great trip!"

You might find it helpful to look at your visit to the Mendocino Coast like life itself. You can rush through it, never stopping to smell the flowers or contemplate the little joys and mysteries, and when you're done it'll just be over. Or you can approach it as an adventure, exploring each new bend in the road, stopping to savor the flavor and ask why it is the way it is.

Planning Your Visit

We know spontaneous travel can be a joy, but on the Mendocino Coast it can be a difficult way to approach things. It might work for you during midweek in the off season, but it can lead to nightmares most of the year.

You'll do best to reserve your lodging or campground as soon as you know when you're going. The best accommodations fill up fast, especially on weekends and holidays and all through the summer.

Likewise, while this book is designed to locate the information you need with a quick turn through the pages, you will enjoy your trip even more if you take time to read through it before you go, perhaps marking the places, sights and activities that look especially intriguing or appealing to you. Spontaneity is an excellent spice for your trip, but a little planning pulls it all together.

Each season on the coast has its own character. If you have the luxury of deciding when to go, here's a summary to guide you.

SPRING starts out roaring like a lion, sometimes with pouring rain, more often with strong northwest winds that can be cold and persistent. Soon the season of renewal quickly works its magic, bringing glistening green hillsides, sparkling wildflowers and calming seas. This is when the coast shows off its most vibrant beauty, not to mention the whales parading north and the hummingbirds, swallows and ospreys returning to their Mendocino Coast summer homes.

SUMMER brings sunny days that soon alternate with thick fog. The winds of spring may linger, but they usually turn more gentle and warm. Along the shore where the fog visits most often, the wildflowers carry on their flashy displays of color. Inland the hills turn brown, but may offer you a refuge from the damp, chilly fog. Of course summer also brings capacity crowds, especially in July and August when the highways sometimes slow to a crawl.

AUTUMN brings fine Indian summer days with a new chill in the nights and mornings. An occasional storm may bring rain but most days are warm, with fog less common. As the temperature lessens, so do the crowds. October and November (before Thanksgiving) are among the least crowded times of year.

WINTER in Northern California starts when the big Pacific rainstorms arrive, not necessarily in sync with the calendar. Recent droughts make this less predictable, but while October and November may bring a few good storms, December through March is the truly rainy time. The rain may last for days or may blow through overnight, bringing a crisp, chill morning with sparkling blue skies. Even in winter the coastal temperature seldom drops below 30 degrees Fahrenheit. Snow is rare, but may drape the coast briefly in alabaster.

Visitor traffic dwindles to a minimum except during Thanksgiving week and the week between Christmas and New Year's Day when the

Driving with the Zen Mind

Driving can be as natural as walking. As drivers we all possess the innate abilities required to handle a car safely and efficiently. Just put your natural-self — your innate ability — behind the wheel, without cluttering it with your personality and other daily burdens.

Take your clear, quiet mind and head up the road. Meditation is single-minded attention to what you're doing, and Zen Driving is being with the car, the road, and the river of traffic without letting your personality and feelings get involved. Allow yourself to do it as a moving meditation, keeping your mind free to be here now, at one with the road.

As K.T. Berger asks in the pithy book Zen Driving, *"Wouldn't it be a joy if driving was actually a means of enhancing our destinations?"*

Driving with the Zen mind can make you a better driver, and it also allows you to more fully enjoy the driving experience.

When you drive with the inner mind, you feel your car as a part of your body, the road flowing under your tires.

entire Mendocino Coast is usually booked far in advance. After that, almost no one comes in January and February (except on the holiday weekends), a perfect opening if you like solitude, winter storm- and surf-watching, and long, cozy nights beside the fire.

As you head off into the wilds of Mendocino County, keep in mind one more thought. The roads here are without a doubt difficult and slow, but they are the routes to the treasures and, in some cases, the treasure themselves. Let them unfold naturally like a treasure hunt. Don't force or rush the journey; unwind along with it, stopping often to breathe deeply of the sparkling air, absorb the peace or drama of the scenery before you and let the rushing traffic hurry on. Just be sure you use your turn indicator, pull fully off the pavement, then look carefully before reentering traffic. Your journey, and your life, will become the richer for the care you take.

Getting to the Mendocino Coast

Getting here can be tough. No commercial airline flies into Mendocino County. The only train to the coast runs just 40 miles from the inland town of Willits on Highway 101. Jeez, the Greyhound Bus doesn't even come to the coast anymore! Your best bet is to drive yourself, although public transportation options have improved recently (more about that at the end of this section).

If you don't live in Northern California, you'll probably want to hop on a flight to San Francisco or Oakland in the Bay Area, or Sacramento to the east, where you can rent a car. All three airports are about four hours drive from the Mendocino Coast. While it costs more to fly into Santa Rosa, it would cut more than one hour from your driving time. You'd pay a lot more to charter a plane to the Mendocino Coast's airport at Little River, but with flight time just one hour from the region's major airports, it might be worth it for a group. Call **COAST FLYERS** 937-1224, for a quote. (**All phone numbers in this book are** AREA CODE-707, **unless noted.**)

Driving to the Mendocino Coast on the region's squiggly but scenic highways offers the most common, and for most people, the most fun way to discover the coast. Many people opt to drive the most direct routes — Highways 101 and 128 from the San Francisco Bay Area or Highway 20 from the Sacramento Valley and points east. This book discusses those routes in detail in Chapters 9 and 10, then refers you to the proper place in the text.

Our main text follows California Highway One up the coast from San Francisco simply because it's the most scenic route to discover California's north coast in general and the Mendocino Coast in particular. In fact the 200 miles of Highway One from the Golden Gate Bridge north to the highway's end at Leggett in redwood country provide one of the most spectacular, breathtaking and

Rules of the Road

1. Always drive alertly, considerately, calmly and defensively. Signal your intentions, use turnouts to pull over for faster traffic, and when you stop, pull fully off the road.

2. Watch for bicyclists, deer, pets and other living things darting into your path.

3. Please don't litter, and especially don't throw burning objects from your car.

4. Keep your valuables safe and secure. Don't tempt the desperate. You're here to relax, not fall apart!

5. Remember to be polite and considerate to the locals … you're a guest in their country. We hope they always remember to be considerate to you.

romantic road journeys in the United States, a trip listed among the most beautiful drives in the world.

How long will it take to drive up the coast? Well, how long do you have? It's truly a shame to rush by some of the world's greatest scenery, and depending on the traffic, it may be impossible to rush at all. A good rule of thumb is to anticipate an average speed of 30 miles per hour, meaning the whole 200 miles can be driven in about seven hours. But we strongly recommend you plan plenty of extra time to stop — to look, eat, walk, savor the view, sit on a beach, spend the night in some tiny town or out in the middle of nowhere, to stay over an extra day in Mendocino, the "Jewel of the North Coast." If you absolutely must, you can rush along the entire north coast in a long day's drive — I saw a van full of Europeans doing it just the other day — but one full week is not too long for your journey, especially if you want to savor the cornucopia of treasures this coast holds.

There is one more way to explore the coast — from the north to the south. If you are driving down from far Northern California, Oregon or Washington, you'll probably prefer to turn off U.S. Highway 101 at Leggett and discover the Mendocino Coast heading south. In this case you should practice the art of reading backwards. You'll still find this book useful; just turn to the end of Chapter 8 and follow the road text backwards to the beginning, remembering to look, turn and think left when we say right, and so on.

Public Transportation To and Around the Mendocino Coast

If you can't drive, won't drive or prefer to leave the driving to someone you've never met before, Mendocino County does have an efficient, though somewhat bare bones, public transportation system led by the **MENDOCINO TRANSIT AUTHORITY** 1-800-696-4MTA, with service on the coast between Fort Bragg and Navarro Junction (where Highways One and 128 meet) by **MENDOCINO STAGE** 964-0167. While most lines have only one or two buses daily, they run year round (some lines shut down for five major holidays), make their required connections (so you won't be left in the middle of nowhere), and offer competent, affordable service.

This little network even makes connections with major

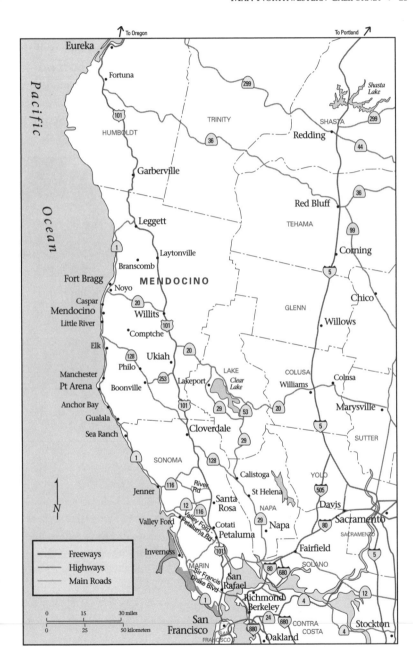

transportation from outside the county: **AIRPORT EXPRESS** 837-8700 via Santa Rosa; **AMTRAK** 1-800-USA-RAIL from Martinez via Ukiah and Willits; **GREYHOUND** 1-800-231-2222 from Portland, Eureka and San Francisco via Ukiah and Willits. Most services are wheelchair lift equipped, but call to be sure.

In addition to these intercity services, the Fort Bragg area has on-call van service with **MENDOCINO LIMOSINE** 964-8294 and **DIAL-A-RIDE** 964-1800.

ANCIENT HISTORY OF THE
MENDOCINO COAST
100 Million B.C. to 1852 A.D.

HE MASSIVE BULKS OF TWO CONTINENTAL
plates grind slowly and inexorably against
each other. The thick North American plate
creeps westward about an inch each year,
colliding with the thinner Pacific plate
drifting north. The collision of these two
immense bodies folded and lifted the ocean
sediments along the continent's western
edge, creating the California Coast Ranges.
The uplifting that began around 100 million
years ago put most of the Coast Ranges in
place by 25 million years ago, recognizable
as the shapes we find on the California
coast today.

Climatic forces of rain, wind and ocean
waves eroded and shaped these new land
forms, carving streams and channels and
building soils. The earth's climate cooled,

bringing glaciation to the Coast Ranges and much of the world beginning about two million years ago and continuing until relatively recent geological time, around 10,000 years ago.

The Mendocino Coast was formed during the last half million years as the combined forces of continuous plate collision and glaciation uplifted and shaped marine sediments into wave cut terraces and steep ocean bluffs. The uplifting process continues today along the San Andreas Fault, the next marine terrace slowly lifting above sea level after constant shaping by waves at the edge of sea and continent.

Ocean levels dropped 300 feet during the most recent ice age, exposing a land bridge between Asia and Alaska. Major migrations of Mongolian peoples walked this land bridge around 12,000 years ago, spreading out to populate the North American continent.

Camping at Caspar, 9500 B.C.

Archaeological evidence confirms human habitation near the present town of Caspar 11,500 years ago. When these early settlers hunted here, sea level was 250 feet lower than it is today and the shore almost two miles west. Today's grassy headlands were largely covered with Bishop pine forest.

The Casparites prospered and spread along the shore, developing a sophisticated, intricate culture centered around village life and

extended family. Seasonal migration grew into trade and cultural exchange with neighboring people. In the last thousand years these diverse cultures reached their most complex development, a stage anthropologists call the "California Culture." Tribal groups produced refined and diverse baskets, shared intertribal ceremonies, expanded trade, and furthered commerce by exchanging clam-shell and magnesite beads for goods and services.

Who Are Those Pale People?

Beginning in the sixteenth century, large wind-powered ships sailed along the coast with increasing frequency, no doubt causing the north coast's native Pomo people to wonder and worry. Around 1587 the Spanish captain of one such galleon coined the name Mendocino for the westernmost point in California in honor of his boss the viceroy of New Spain, Antonio or Suarez de Mendosa. Not until the late eighteenth or early nineteenth century did the coastal Pomo have any contact with the mysterious travelers.

The first onshore visitors were probably Russians who came to hunt the valuable pelts of the sea otter around 1800. The amicable Russians traveled with native Alaskan Aleut hunters who impressed the Pomo with their hunting abilities and sea-going skin boats.

By this time the Pomo trade network brought news of hostile encounters between the men of the ships and native people to the south. At the same time, the Spaniards were pushing their missions farther north into California trying to convert the natives to Catholicism and forcing them to labor on mission farms. As European interest in the coast north of San Francisco grew, whaling ships and English naval expeditions joined the parade of Spanish galleons offshore.

The first overland European explorers along the Mendocino Coast were apparently the party of Englishman John Work, who visited in 1833 seeking beaver for the Hudson's Bay Company. The Pomo helped the visitors while the Coast Yuki to the north ran and hid. The rugged terrain and lack of beaver gave the local natives almost 20 more years of life free from disruption.

The Trickle Becomes a Flood

People from the far corners of the world caught gold fever in 1849, and the rush for California was on. The Pomo accepted the first settlers. Then, after 1852, the trickle became a flood even on the remote Mendocino Coast. Within five years the Pomo and all native people on the north coast had their world turned upside down, their resources usurped by the white invasion, and their pride stung by every injustice. Miraculously the native people survived, although their honorable and abundant ways of living were subverted by the invaders.

Beyond such tragedies so ingrained in the history of our continent, there is a subsequent history of resourcefulness and worthy toil, of hardships and their transcendence, the story that lies behind this wondrous wild coast and the friendly little towns this book is about. But while you are exploring the corners of this verdant coast, remember that the native people stewarded the land for millennia, using it and respecting it without depleting its grandeur and bounty.

The lessons of the long native stewardship of the land and its resources today more than ever offer the most important lessons for western civilization to learn. Nothing less than survival of our world is at stake.

1. HIGHWAY ONE NORTH TO THE MENDOCINO COAST

THE ROUTE

CALIFORNIA HIGHWAY ONE DANCES ALONG the ragged edge of our continent for 711 miles. Nowhere along this fantastic route is the scenery more tremendous than at its northern end. Often called America's most romantic road, the Pacific Coast Highway originated in the Southern California land and oil booms of the 1920s, although the National Automobile Club stumped for a "shoreline highway" from Santa Barbara to Eureka in the early 1910s. When the state of California completed the coast road in 1937, building the final segment on the Big Sur coast, they dubbed it California Highway One.

For the purposes of this book the romantic road has three sections:

◆ Dana Point (south end, near Los Angeles) to San Francisco: This 511 miles offers plenty of traffic, some great twists and turns, and a whole 'nother state of mind, not to mention geography, than we're concerned with here.

◆ San Francisco to Gualala: It's 94 miles from the great City by the Bay, up along the increasingly wild coasts of Marin and Sonoma counties. The traffic generally thins and the buildings have more wide open spaces between them until the Sonoma-Mendocino County line at the Gualala River. This chapter summarizes these 94 marvelous miles.

◆ Gualala to Leggett (end): This is our coast of Mendocino County and we're darned proud of all 106 miles. If you stick with this book, you're gonna learn all about it.

The 94 miles from the Golden Gate Bridge to the Sonoma/Mendocino County line at Gualala take about three hours to drive without stopping. But driving this grand stretch of road without stopping is like going to Rome without visiting the Colosseum — a waste.

The most scenic route north from San Francisco follows Highway One. After the romantic road joins with Highway 101 to cross the Golden Gate Bridge, the combined routes climb over Waldo Grade, then descend to the bay shore at the north end of Sausalito.

THE DRIVE

Highway One splits from Freeway 101 only 4½ miles from the Toll Plaza. The coast road skirts the village of Mill Valley, then ascends corkscrew turns over the flank of Mount Tamalpais (2586 feet) to Tam Junction, where famed Muir Woods National Monument and 6218-acre Mount Tamalpais State Park beckon on the right.

Highway One picks up the name Shoreline Highway, which it bears to its northern terminus, as it spirals down and around numerous tight curves to reach the Marin Coast at Green Gulch. Head north past Steep Ravine and alongside the popular white sands of Stinson Beach.

At sleepy Bolinas Lagoon, where the San Andreas Fault comes ashore, the Shoreline Highway turns inland to follow Olema Valley north. While all of Highway One north of San Francisco dances along near the fault, never straying more than eight miles from it until north of Westport when the highway turns inland, the next 28 miles show the rift zone most clearly as you follow fault-formed Olema Valley and Tomales Bay. The Shoreline Highway crosses the fault at least six times in 117 miles, and actually straddles the fracture for dozens of miles.

This is the edge where the continent has been growing westward for the last 100 million years, and where it continues growing today. Rest assured that most of this growth occurs very slowly in tiny increments, averaging one inch a year. Only when pressure created by the friction of the massive North American and Pacific plates builds to a certain threshold do major earthquakes, like the recent 1989 quake or the big 1906 temblor, occur. Then the opposing sides of the fault move as much as 20 feet in moments, like they did at Olema in 1906.

East of the fault, the local geology consists of sandstone and shale of the Franciscan formation. This dark gray rock lends itself superbly to sculpting by ocean waves into marvelous shapes: arches, tunnels, blowholes, sinkholes and coves. Geologists don't favor Franciscan rock, it being so mauled by the continental collision that it holds few coherent layers or fossils. (It makes climbing hazardous too — ask any rock climber!)

West of the fault you are on the Pacific Oceanic plate, a block of light Salinian granite and granitic sandstones thoroughly different from the neighboring rock across the fault. Geologists have matched Salinian rock at Point Reyes and Bodega Head with similar rock 350 miles south, east of the fault in the Tehachapi Range south of the Sierra Nevada. Being generally softer and more consistent in texture than Franciscan rock, Salinian stone erodes into more uniform shapes, de long beaches of light sand like those at Bodega and Jenner.

As you drive north, notice that the continental collision forms a steep jagged edge where the colliding force is greatest (like on Meyers Grade beyond Jenner), and a gentle, consistent uplift where the force is most evenly distributed, as on the terraces of the Mendocino Coast near Fort Bragg. When you

Rogues & Killer Waves:
Never Turn Your Back on the Ocean!

The northern Pacific Ocean is not only bone-chilling at its usual 50 degrees Fahrenheit, but it holds other nasty surprises as well. Freak waves known as rogues periodically swamp unwary beachcombers, breaking on the beach from otherwise puny surf and occasionally washing people out to sea. While nobody knows their cause, they usually occur with the outgoing tide and may be linked with storm activity far offshore.

The urgent message is — **NEVER turn your back on the Pacific while walking on north coast beaches.** *The worst of these, called killer waves, may run up onto a beach as much as 100 yards beyond the normal foam. The mouth of the Gualala River, Manchester and the Lost Coast present the greatest danger, but sneaker waves can happen anywhere.*

return to the North American plate, notice also that the beaches are of dark sand, coarser than the blond Pacific-plate beaches.

As you ascend Olema Valley, part of Golden Gate National Recreation Area lies on your right, with Point Reyes National Seashore on the left. Tiny Olema was the epicenter of the devastating 1906 earthquake.

At Olema or Point Reyes Station you can detour left to explore the National Seashore, or you can continue on Highway One, winding north with views over fault-line Tomales Bay, home of oyster farms and a breeding ground for great white sharks. After passing more state park lands, the Shoreline Highway leaves the fault, veering inland to ford the Estero Americano and enter Sonoma County near the tiny crossroads called Valley Ford, where you merge with a more direct route from the Bay Area; see time-saving options below. The Shoreline Highway returns to the coast at Bodega Bay, home to a large fishing fleet, several parks and plenty of visitor-serving facilities. Alfred Hitchcock filmed *The Birds* around here in 1963.

Then Coast Highway One follows the Pacific shore northwest with gusto, hugging the edge of Sonoma Coast State Beaches all the way to the Russian River, where you meet Highway 116 from Rohnert Park and Santa Rosa, another shorter route with less glorious scenery.

Time-Saving Options

You can compromise, traveling some of winding Highway One and seeing the most gorgeous part of the Sonoma Coast by cutting through Sonoma County via several routes, all scenic and each quicker than tracing the entire Shoreline Highway, but none nearly as spectacular or dramatic. You can leave Highway 101 at Petaluma — on Bodega Avenue and Petaluma-Valley Ford Road — to reach Highway One at Valley Ford. Or you might try departing Highway 101 north of Santa Rosa on River Road and Highway 116 to meet the coast road at Jenner. Numerous twisting back roads offer other routes through rugged country to reach Coast Highway One, but the two routes above are relatively quick and painless.

Up the Wild and Rugged Northern Sonoma Coast to Gualala

From the Russian River, the Shoreline Highway passes through tiny Jenner (gas, food, lodging), then runs north up the coast, twisting and turning over steep headlands and down through coastal watersheds. The romantic road traverses such wild, rugged country between Jenner and Salt Point that it remained an oiled gravel surface until the late 1960s.

As you travel the coast from the Russian River north to Fort Bragg, remember that this is the land of the Pomo people. They still live here and are the spiritual guardians of the land, even if they do not "own" it by law.

Pomo ancestors settled the coast at least 11,000 years ago, just as the last ice age was ending. Pomo oral history goes back far enough to corroborate what geologists now surmise transformed the area in the past ten or twelve millennia. Over the centuries the Pomo ancestors prospered, spreading their settlements over nearly 5000 square miles, from Clear Lake to the Pacific and 80 miles along the coast. They developed one of the most sophisticated cultures in North America, making a wide array of refined baskets (now world famous) and practicing extensive trade and cultural exchange with neighbors. Pomo population density was among the highest in North America.

Not that Pomo culture was homogeneous. In fact the name Pomo encompasses six distinct language and cultural groups, each comprising dozens of autonomous villages, each one speaking a different dialect.

Black Bart's Most Famous Robbery

Today's Shoreline Highway mostly follows the old stage road north from Jenner and Russian Gulch, making the twisting ascent to Meyers Grade summit 600 feet above the Pacific. The original stage route preserved as Meyers Grade Road climbed even higher than today's Highway One to meet the Fort Ross-Cazadero Road. That's where Black Bart, the West's most notorious stage robber, pulled off his most famous heist.

The stage left Mendocino City on August 2, 1877, racing along the crooked coast road to Point Arena where driver and passengers spent the night. At dawn the coach resumed its journey to Duncan's Mills on the Russian River. The steep 12 miles south of Fort Ross usually took 2½ hours but on this day there was a hold up.

At a sharp bend atop Meyers Grade, a man with a flour sack over his head used his shotgun to force an unscheduled stop. He ordered the driver to turn his back or be shot down, then asked politely for the express box. He probably thanked the coachman and ordered him on his way.

When lawmen reached the robbery scene and recovered the broken cash box, they found a Wells Fargo waybill on a nearby tree stump. Scribbled on the back, each line in a different script, the bandit proclaimed:

Along the coast the Southwestern or Kashaya Pomo territory lies from the Russian River to Stewart's Point, the land of the Southern Pomo is south of the Gualala River mouth, the Central Pomo north of the river mouth, and the Northern Pomo north of the Navarro River. Trade among groups was once common, using an intricate trail system covering several hundred miles. Of course the Pomo suffered greatly as Europeans came to settle their lands, as did all Native American cultures.

The Pomo people survive, still comprising two to four percent of the population in Mendocino and Lake counties, with all Pomo tribal groups represented. Several Pomo communities remain along the Mendocino/Sonoma coast.

You soon climb steeply over Meyers Grade, one of the most magnificent (scary for some) stretches of the coast road. At the summit, take the turn off on the left for the **VISTA TRAIL**, a short, wheelchair-accessible loop with picnic tables and a breathtaking, bird's eye view of this sheer shoreline.

Highway One descends to the historic Russian settlement of **FORT ROSS**, a marvelous footnote to California history now protected in a 3000-acre state park. You meander up the coast past Timber Cove, where San Francisco sculptor Benaiamino Bufano's tall totem-pole-like statue towers over the knotted shore. The highway twists north through **SALT POINT STATE PARK**, a 7000-acre enclave of natural splendor. Then, amidst the beautiful rock-studded coast and rolling headlands held by the large Richardson Ranch, you pass the historic settlement of Stewart's Point, still anchored today by the intriguing **STEWART'S POINT STORE**, established 1868.

The Shoreline Highway wiggles north up the coast into the contemporary planned community of **SEA RANCH** (POP. 280, EL. 40). This 5200-acre residential development, begun in the 1960s by Castle and Cooke Company of Hawaiian pineapple fame, stretches nine miles along Highway One to the far northwest corner of Sonoma County. Lawrence Halprin created the original land use plan of clustered development enveloped by extensive open space. Architect Charles Moore designed many of the early buildings in a style complementing the

I've labored long and hard for bread/For honor and for riches/But on my corns too long you've tred/You fine haired Sons of Bitches
s/Black Bart, the Po8

This was Bart's fourth of 29 stage robberies from 1875 to 1883. The masked highwayman had never given a name before, nor left a poem to catch the imagination of news-hungry editors. Gentleman bandit Black Bart became an overnight sensation and folk hero.

Mendocino and Sonoma County stages were among Bart's favorite targets, with four robberies in each county, including a second heist on Meyers Grade in 1880. Bart was always polite, chivalrous to the ladies and never robbed or harassed the passengers.

Bart's capture in 1883 revealed his true identity. Charles Boles, Civil War hero, lived in a respectable San Francisco boarding house and was known as a quiet mining investor. His 'holdings" actually were all over the north state in Wells Fargo express boxes.

coastal environment without dominating it, creating a new movement of organic architecture. Sadly, the dynamic original concepts of planning and design have been watered down in recent years.

Sea Ranch offers a lodge, restaurant, post office and small store near its south end, about six miles of public trails with coastal access ($3 day use), and an award-winning, ocean-view golf course along its northern boundary. If you rent a vacation home here, you can walk or ride many miles of private trails through the community. Other facilities for residents and guests include air strip, tennis courts, heated pool and riding stables.

The original parcel of land, Rancho de German, was a 20,000-acre Mexican Land Grant to Ernest Rufus, a German captain in John Sutter's company. The Mexican government granted the land to Rufus in the 1840s. The Rufus family operated a sheep ranch here for many years. Before the republic of Mexico granted the land to Rufus, the native Pomo people lived here for millennia. The Kashaya (Southwestern) Pomo claimed the coast and adjacent hills from the Russian River to around Stewart's Point; the Southern Pomo lived in the hills around where Sea Ranch is today.

Adjacent to Sea Ranch on the north end, **GUALALA POINT REGIONAL PARK** occupies a spectacular 75-acre site along the lower Gualala River, extending out to a windswept promontory between Sea Ranch and the river mouth. The delightful park offers hiking, biking, camping and picnicking in a glorious setting.

After winding along the Sonoma County coast for 58½ miles, the Shoreline Highway crosses a sweeping bridge over the Gualala River and enters Mendocino County. The tidal flats of the river present a striking natural setting where today you might see abundant bird life. In yesteryears it was the site of the Gualala Redwood Mill from 1862 through 1906.

You immediately enter the town of Gualala, the largest town on the coast between Bodega Bay and Fort Bragg. The historic lumber town has been enjoying a mild revival since the Sea Ranch opened in the 1960s. The landmark **GUALALA HOTEL**, established 1903, appears quickly on your right.

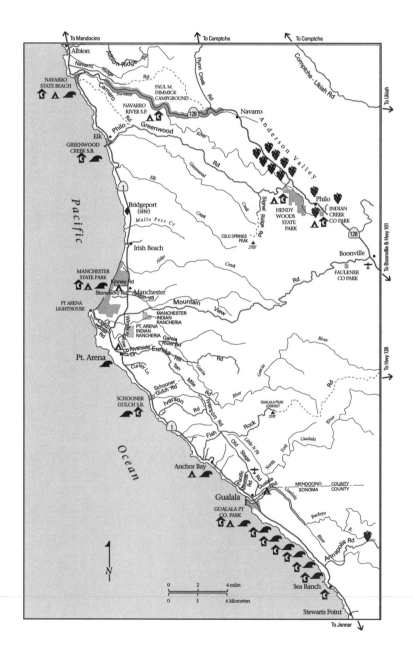

Gualala Ferry c.1890

GUALALA
(POP.585, EL. 67)

PRONOUNCED WAH-LAL'-AH, THIS TOWN, LIKE MANY ON
the north coast, has a split personality. Its rough and tumble lumber
town roots extend right into the second half of the twentieth century,
with some people still making their living in logging. Gualala's modern
side looks California chic, a result of the affluent presence of Sea Ranch
and the nearness of urban Santa Rosa.

Evidence of the rough and tumble mill town has become scarce in
the last 20 or 30 years. Today it is represented primarily by the homey,
old-fashioned atmosphere of the Gualala Hotel, where loggers used to
literally climb the walls of the barroom in their spiked calk
(pronounced cork) boots.

Gualala's modern side offers casual sophistication somewhat alien to
its origins. Numerous pleasant restaurants offer fine fare, plentiful
lodgings offer a broad range of elegance and comfort, and several
galleries add refinement and culture, providing an atmosphere far
different from the town's wild west origins. Sufficient services keep
most of the locals from having to leave more than once a month. Some
folks never leave, and after a bit of time here, you'll understand why.

It all adds up to a pleasant vacation or holiday town, especially since
the natural beauty of the coast provides the perfect setting. As a bonus
Gualala sits in an area known as the "Banana Belt," mostly protected
from fog and icy northwest winds by the protrusion of Point Arena
into the Pacific Ocean to the north.

History

Three distinct tribes of Pomo people lived within ten miles of
today's townsite. The Central Pomo had a seasonal village beside the
river here, with their main village at the headwaters of the river's
north fork. Beginning in 1857, many local Pomo people were
forced onto the Mendocino Indian Reservation at Fort Bragg.

When Cyrus and Elizabeth Robinson arrived from
Pennsylvania in 1858, only one cabin had been built where
Gualala stands today.

What's in a Name?

Even residents can't agree on how to say the town's name, let alone agree on where it came from.

Actually the local Pomo people called the place at the mouth of the river "walala," meaning "where the waters meet." The Russians probably got their term for the locals, "Wallalakh," from the people themselves.

When German Ernest Rufus received his Mexican land grant in the 1840s, he dubbed his spread "Valhalla," the name of the place in northern European mythology where brave warriors went after they died in battle. Undoubtedly Rufus had heard the native name for the land and was struck by its similarity to this mythical place in his Germanic heritage. But the mixing of the German name with the original native terms led to a century of confusion, further complicated by Hispanic variations.

Apparently the original town post office was designated "Walalla," until a postal bureaucrat in San Francisco "corrected" the spelling to "proper Spanish," changing it to Gualala. Attempts by the local residents to change it back went unheeded.

Most old timers say "Wall-all-ah" but you'll undoubtedly hear the "g" sound tacked on front if you stay for long.

Cyrus came to California for gold in 1849. Like most forty-niners he didn't stick with prospecting. After mining in the Sierra Nevada and Trinity Mountains, he logged in the Humboldt woods, then started a store in San Francisco. In 1854 he brought Elizabeth to California. The couple ran a hotel and a ferry at the Russian River, then moved to Gualala to do the same.

When the Robinsons filed their homestead claim in 1861, their first rudimentary hotel, the Gualala House, may have already been operating. Their claim encompassed all of what would become Gualala. Within a year they sold the south portion of the claim to Rutherford and Page so the newcomers could build a sawmill. The deed stipulated that the buyers or their heirs could not allow any hotel or bar on those lands. The Robinsons retained possession of the ferry crossing beside the mill.

They quickly formed the monopoly on local transport and accommodations that would last for nearly 50 years. They also contracted to run the post office and Wells Fargo Express office. The Robinsons built a slide chute landing north of the river in 1865 on what is today called Robinson Point.

A man named Heywood bought the mill in 1868 and improved its efficiency. Single workers boarded at the Gualala House or on nearby farms. Workers with families got the company houses.

In cutting season the woods workers moved to temporary camps upriver where the logging was. Railroad ties and other split goods — shakes, fence posts, grape stakes — were cut during the wet winter months when the woods were mired in mud or raging with flood. In spring farmers and woodsmen could boost their income collecting tanbark for use in California's booming leather industry.

In 1872 the Robinsons built a better hotel to replace their first. The new Gualala House perched on a knoll at the north end of town, representing what little refinement was available at the time. Women were not allowed in the bar. Neither were rowdy loggers, although they could purchase take-away liquor at the bar's door.

Ships were an important part of local commerce. Not only did they carry the manufactured goods to market, mostly in San Francisco, they also brought in most of the goods not produced locally. They carried passengers and the mail too.

Regular stagecoach lines provided competition for the schooners beginning about 1870, but their freight and passenger capacity was minimal compared to ships. Whether by land or sea, the trip required a rough, long ride. The schooners characteristically had two masts and a crew of four. In the 1880s the ships' sails were augmented with steam engines. Steamship lines ran along the north coast into the late 1930s.

Morton Bourn built a chute to compete with Robinson's before 1870. Though it was two miles north, the word soon spread among doghole captains that, while Robinson's had hidden rocks, rough seas and a shifting sand bottom, Bourn's was excellent in any weather. Bourn's new chute made loading ships much easier.

Gualala Redwood Company built a wide gauge railroad to Bourn's Landing in 1872. It was one of the widest rail lines ever built, 68H inches track-to-track, apparently so that the two draft horses that did the early hauling had room to walk side-by-side.

Also in 1872, the North Pacific Railroad planned a line all the way from Sausalito to Gualala, 115 miles. By 1877 the railroad was completed to Duncan's Mill on the Russian River. They abandoned the effort to push the line north, calling the rest of the north coast "a complete wilderness, entirely unfit for civilization." Thanks to the NPRR, stage lines soon ran six days a

Gualala House c.1872

week between Duncan's Mill and Mendocino City, by way of Gualala. The first real bridge across the Gualala River replaced the rickety ferry in 1892.

Gualala got its first school in 1883. Before then a teacher would board at a ranch house to teach the neighborhood children. Dance halls in Gualala and surrounding communities provided weekend entertainment. Baseball was very popular, and an occasional rodeo or boxing match provided variety.

A substantial Chinese community gave the name to China Gulch on the edge of town, with its residents doing many of the dirtiest jobs in the woods. Chinese people also became cooks and launderers due to an ongoing shortage of women laborers. A Chinese school was established in 1889 due to resistance to integration in the main school.

Lumber man Tom Moungovan told of a Gualala logging crew finding a redwood 36 feet in diameter, too big to cut. They had to dynamite it to put the tracks upriver. By 1894 only second-growth trees were left around Gualala.

By 1903 the fast steamship Pomo made regular weekly runs between Point Arena and San Francisco, with scheduled stops at

Gualala. While the Pomo made fast trips from the City, the ship would often sit offshore for days waiting for the sea to calm enough to land passengers and cargo. The Gualala House burned down in 1903. Cyrus had a new hotel built closer to the mill. You can still find accommodations, and one of the only bars in town, at the Gualala Hotel today.

The mill burned in September 1906, bringing economic depression to the area. The voting population shrank from 92 to 30. In 1911 when Englishman Smeaton Chase rode through on his noble horse Anton, the town was still reeling. Chase found Gualala "depressed and depressing, most of its buildings closed and decaying." The barber-postmaster-shoemaker with whom Chase had business observed that "he had 'had enough of this derned place,' and was going to 'light out for some liver burg.' He guessed he would go to Greenland." Jack London visited Gualala frequently in its sleepy years, enjoying the great steelhead fishing on the river.

New investors built a small sawmill in 1914. They soon brought in the parts for a large electric sawmill, but it rusted on the river bank and was never built. By 1925 only 25 people called Gualala home.

While times were tough around Gualala during the Great Depression, it was easier to scrounge a living in this lush country than in the cities, so the 1930s brought city refugees to the area. They camped by the river or squatted in deserted buildings. The fishing was good, the berries bountiful in season, and if there was no work for money, one could often earn a meal chopping firewood. Most of Gualala had burned down or otherwise collapsed by 1937.

New sawmills went up in the lumber boom after World War II, and Gualala started growing again. The town only gained electricity hook-ups in 1952, with most outlying areas following over the next four years. This belated development is perhaps the most telling commentary on how long it took the little town to grow out of its economic doldrums. Perhaps this is why Gualala has been growing so rapidly in recent times, trying to catch up from years of arrested development.

Gualala Lodging

Listings are organized from the most expensive to the least expensive

SEA RANCH LODGE $144–395
60 Sea Walk Dr/Box 44
Sea Ranch 95497
785-2371/800-732-7262

www.searanchlodge.com

Perched on a lovely, wild stretch of coast, award-winning architecture and subdued elegance enhances the peacefulness that nature provides, offering a great getaway. Walk secluded beaches and trails, followed by a soothing hot tub or massage.

20 rooms; full breakfast; res. advisable; phones, computer ports, in-room coffee; min. stay summer wknds, holidays; V/MC/AE; midweek rates; family units; adj. restaurant; ocean views; some bathtubs, hot tubs; golf/tennis; families welcome; adj. to hiking

THE OLD MILANO $140–210
38300 Hwy One, Gualala
884-3256

Established in 1905 and listed in the National Registry of Historic Places, the cottages are located on three private acres of ocean front property.

5 rooms; full breakfast; min. stay 2 nights wknds/ holidays; V/MC/checks; winter mid-week disc.; all rooms private baths; jacuzzi/hot tub by appt; ocean views; fireplaces; gardens; golf/tennis nearby; adj. to hiking

☆ **SEACLIFF ON THE BLUFF**
$100–160
39140 S. Hwy One/Box 1317
Gualala
884-1213/800-400-5053 (Ca only)

www.seacliffmotel.com

Modern suites designed for guest's privacy and comfort, each room with king beds, gas-burning fireplaces, spa, after-spa robes, private observation deck and unequalled view of beach, fishing boats, whales and other ocean life.

16 rooms; res. advisable; min. stay 2 nights holiday wknds; MC/V, checks; compl. champagne or cider; coffeemaker & supplies, refrigerator, fireplaces, jacuzzi tub, tvs; ocean views; gardens; smoking rooms; adj. restaurant; golf/tennis/fishing nearby; &

GUALALA COUNTRY INN
$105–179
S. Hwy One/Box 697, Gualala
884-4343/800-564-4466

www.countryinn@gualala.com

Modern comfort and country charm with morning coffee, continental breakfast, ocean views, and parlor.

20 rooms; continental brkfast; res. essential wknds; min. stay 2 nights holidays; all CC; winter mid-week disc.; compl. coffee; some private jacuzzi/hot tubs; all fireplaces; bathtubs; phone/tv in room; pets ok; &

BREAKERS INN $95–275
39300 S. Hwy One/Box 389
Gualala
884-3200/800-BREAKERS

www.breakersinn.com

Beautiful blufftop location has luxurious oceanfront rooms individually decorated in a regional theme. Romantic rooms have fireplaces, two-person whirlpool spas, wet bars, king beds and private decks with panoramic views. Walk to shops, galleries, dining, secluded beaches.

27 rooms; deluxe continental breakfast; res. advisable; min. stay on wknds; winter specials; V/MC/

Disc/AE/checks; adj. restaurant; phone, cable tv in room; fireplaces; ocean views; sauna; bathtubs; meeting room; smoking rooms; &

SERENISEA OCEAN CABINS
$95–250
36100 S. Hwy One, Gualala 95445
884-3836/800-331-3836

www.serenisea.com

One of the coast's most intimate small resorts sits dramatically on an ocean bluff. Fully equipped cottages offer a fine getaway any time of year.
3 cottages plus 23 nearby vacation homes; res. advisable; min. stay 2 nights; V/MC/checks; family units; pets ok; jacuzzi/hot tub; fireplaces; bathubs; ocean views, gardens; phone/tv/refrig/cooking in room; beach access

SURF MOTEL AT GUALALA
$95–179
S. Hwy One/Box 651, Gualala
884-3571

Right in town on bluff overlooking the ocean. Newly remodeled, modern, comfortable rooms.
20 rooms; all CC; smoking rms; winter mid-week disc.; suites w/full kitchen; all rooms w/microwave & frig; pets ok; compl. coffee/tea/hot chocolate; fireplaces; bathtubs; adj. to hiking; phone/tv in room; &

☆ ST. ORRES $80–250
36601 S. Hwy One/Box 523
Gualala
884-3303 or 3335

A Russian style inn built in 1976, with individual cottages on 42 acres. Choice of eight rooms sharing three baths or thirteen cottages with private bath. Some have a fireplace, some a wood stove, and two a soaking tub. Full breakfast served in dining room or cottages. Near hiking, golf, and fishing.
8 rooms/13 cottages; full breakfast; res. essential;

min. stay 2 nights wknds; V/MC/checks; small family groups only (3–6 persons); adj. restaurant; jacuzzi/sauna; ocean views; bathtubs; gardens; adj. to beach; &

SECRET GARDEN B&B $80–115
38201 S. Hwy One
Gualala
884-3302

www.gualalasecretgarden.com

Large room decorated in coral and green a mile north of Gualala on 1.6 acres has its own rose garden and redwood grove. Helpful hosts are happy to tell guests about local activities.
1 room; breakfast; res. advisable; min stay 2 nights on holiday wkends; checks; mid-week disc; tv/refrig/ microwave in room; gardens

GUALALA HOTEL $50–120
39301 S. Hwy One/Box 508
Gualala
884-3441

The spirit of bygone days lingers in this historic inn built in 1903. The hotel retains the charm and atmosphere that made it a favorite of Jack London, each room furnished with period antiques, and oak or wrought iron beds.
19 rooms, 5 w/private bath; res. advisable; MC/V/ AE/checks; adj. restaurant; ocean views; bathtubs; adj. to hiking

Eateries

☆ ST. ORRES

36601 S. Hwy One, Gualala 95445
884-3335
D: $40 prix fixe

Creative California "North Coast" cuisine served in a dramatic hand-hewn dining room with an ocean view. They utilize local produce, herbs from the St. Orres garden, and specialty meats such as wild boar, venison, lamb, quail, mussels and salmon in celebratory presentations served by an attentive staff.
Sun–Fri 6–9:15 pm, Sat 5:15–9:45 pm; res. essential; checks; beer/wine; seats 55; &

TOP OF THE CLIFF

39140 S. Hwy One, Gualala
884-1539
L: $9–15, D: $20–25

Intimate oceanfront dining in casual elegance. The cuisine is continental with an emphasis on seafood, plus vegetarian dishes.
Lunch Fri-Sun 11:30-2, dinner Thur-Sun from 5:30; V/MC/checks; full bar; seats 50; &

CYPRESS BAR & GRILL

Cypress Village, 39102 Ocean Dr.
Gualala
884-1835

L: $6–13, D: $17–23

Continental cuisine with fresh seafood daily. Ocean views from every table in a casual, friendly atmosphere.
Daily from 11 am –9 pm, lunch and dinner; V/MC/Disc; full bar; seats 80; take-out; &

☆ PANGAEA

39165 Hwy One, Gualala
www.pangaeacafe.com
884-9669

$10–24

Global, eclectic cuisine presented in an art-filled room. Chefs use fresh, natural and local ingredients to prepare festive and distinctive food, with vegetarian, fish, and free-range organic meat dishes. Exquisite desserts. No limitations.
Wed–Sun at 6 pm, from 5:30 on wkends; call ahead for seasonal hours; res. advisable; V/MC/ checks; beer/wine; seats 50; &

GUALALA HOTEL RESTAURANT

39301 S. Hwy One, Gualala
884-3441
WB: $6–12, L: $6–12, D: $14–19

Modern, eclectic American cuisine served in the oldest building in town. Saloon-style bar serves libations and bar menu (11 am–closing) in a convivial atmosphere.
Daily lunch 11 am–2 pm, dinner 5–9:30 pm, shorter hours mid-winter; res. advisable; all CC/ checks; full bar; seats 75; banquet room seats 55; take-out; &

OCEANSONG PACIFIC GRILLE

39350 S. Hwy One, Gualala
884-1041
L: $7–10 D: $8–45

Modern food with an international touch served in an ocean view dining room on the bank of the Gualala River. Seafood, meat and poultry specialties.
Daily; res. advisable; V/MC/Disc/ATM; full bar; seats 80; &

SEA RANCH LODGE

60 Sea Walk Dr, Sea Ranch 95497
785-2371/800-SEA-RANCH
SB: $25, B/L: $5-21, D: $7–30

Coastal cuisine with daily menus emphasizing the bounty of local ingredients, served overlooking a dramatic shoreline. Wine list assembled to enhance dishes offered. Bar menu available too, $5–11.

Daily 8 am–9 pm; Sun brunch 9–2:30; res. advisable; V/MC/AE/checks; full bar; seats 64; take-out; ё

UPPER CRUST PIZZERIA

39331 S. Hwy One, Gualala 95445
884-1324
D: $8–14

Gourmet pizzas and salads to eat here or take out.

Sun–Thur 4–8, Fri, Sat 4–9; checks; beer/wine; take-out; ё

☆ THE FOOD COMPANY

Hwy One at Robinson Reef
Gualala
884-1800
$8–12

Specializing in interesting and excellent food for people to eat here or to take home, to the beach or holiday getaway. Everything is prepared by hand using only what is fresh and best.

Daily 8–6, one hour later in summer; V/MCchecks w/guarantee card; beer/wine; seats 41; take-out; early arrival for picnic food is advised (food sells down later in day); catering; ё

CAFE LALA

Cypress Village, 39102 S. Hwy One
Box 1241, Gualala
884-1104
B: $4–8, L: $6–9

An intimate bistro setting with a beautiful ocean view. Featuring daily breakfast and luncheon specials, soups and salads. Sit outside when weather allows.

Daily 8 am–4 pm; checks; seats 40; take-out; catering; ё

SANDPIPER RESTAURANT

39080 S. Hwy One, Gualala
884-3398
B/L: $6 avg.

Home style breakfasts, espresso drinks, lunches fast and reasonable, from burgers to fish, all with a beautiful view.

Mon–Sat 6 am–2:30 pm, Sun 7 am–1 pm; CA checks; full bar; seats 60; take-out

SMOKEHOUSE GRILL

Clubhouse at Sea Ranch Golf Links
Sea Ranch
785-9696
$3–14

Good food at affordable prices. Ribs, chicken, smoked salmon, fish & chips, burgers, hot dogs.

Daily 7–6, longer in summer, beer,wine; seats 42; ё

SURF SUPERMARKET

39250 S. Hwy One/on the oceanside
Gualala
884-4184

Full service market with hot deli, bakery, fresh fish and meat. Wine tasting on weekends.

Daily at 7:30 am; ATM/V/MC/local checks; beer/ wine/liquor; ё

Outdoor Activities

SEA RANCH GOLF LINKS

785-2467, has an oceanside 18-hole course designed by Robert Muir Graves. Driving range, course, and Smokehouse Cafe at clubhouse open daily.

ADVENTURE RENTS 884-4386, 1-888-881-4386, offers rentals of canoes and kayaks, plus guided trips, including moonlight flotillas. At the Cantamare Center behind Century 21 Realty. Open daily, weather and river permitting.

NORTH COAST SCUBA 884-3534, 38820 Hwy One, offers scuba gear rentals for exploring the underwater side of this rugged coast.

ROTH RANCH 884-3124, 37100 Old Stage Road, provides horse rentals and equestrian excursions.

SEA RANCH PUBLIC ACCESS TRAILS 785-2377. Fee. Seven public trails cross the immense private development of Sea Ranch, providing access to beaches and headlands. Each is marked with the coastal-access symbol, with a parking area west of the highway.

ANNAPOLIS WINERY 886-5460, www.annapoliswinery.com. Visit this small family winery in the sun belt above the wind and fog. Picnic supplies available, so picnic with a bottle of their wine as you enjoy the view. Tasting room open daily 12–5, from 11 a.m. on weekends. From Highway One, go 7 miles on Annapolis Road.

Parks

GUALALA POINT REGIONAL PARK 785-2377. Fee. The pristine public enclave of 75 acres encompasses rolling coastal grasslands crossed by cypress windbreaks in the day-use area west of Highway One, plus a pleasant campground (to reserve, call 565-2267 at least 10 days ahead) in redwood forest

along the river east of the road. Hiking, biking, camping and picnicking in a glorious setting beside the river winding to its outlet at the Pacific. Most facilities are wheelchair accessible. Several trails explore river canyon and headlands, with a paved trail for bikes and handicap access. Park open daily, Visitor Center Fri–Mon, 10:30–3:30.

BOWER COMMUNITY PARK. Pleasant park with tennis courts and playgrounds in the redwoods on the sunny ridge above town, 3 miles up Old Stage Road from Gualala.

Indoor Activities

Galleries & Shops

Gualala Arts Center 884-1138, 46501 Old State Hwy, www.gualalaarts.org. Gallery of regional artists, concert series, art classes for adults and kids, lecture series and more in a gorgeous new facility.

Noma 884-1320, just north of Surf Supermarket. A carefully chosen selection of contemporary crafts and handpainted clothing.

The Dolphin 884-3896, 39225 Hwy One. This co-operative gallery of the Gualala Arts group features the works of north coast artists in many media.

Gualala Sport & Tackle 884-4247, 39225 Hwy One, Sundstrom Mall. Daily.

Redwood Floral Arts 884-4233, Sundstrom Mall. Full service florists.

Clutterbug 884-3611, 39150 Hwy One. Crowded with home and personal accessories.

Gualala Sea Spa 884-9262, Hwy One. Face and body treatments by appointment.

Velvet Rabbit 884-1501, Seacliff Center. Works by selected artists and craftspeople.

Celebrations 884-1920, Seacliff Center. Gifts.

The Cotton Field 884-1836, Seacliff Center, Hwy One. Clothing and jewelry for women.

Artsea 884-4809, 39140 Hwy One. Posters, prints and framing.

Dragon Wings 884-9447, 39111 Hwy One. Kites, dragons and other fun things.

Village Bootery 884-4451, 38951 Hwy One. Fine leather goods and footwear.

SK Gallery 884-3549, Cypress Village. Paintings, sculptures and other art and crafts. Thurs-Mon.

Stewart/Kummer Gallery 884-3581. Open by appointment. Sculpture, paintings and crafts primarily by North Coast artists.

Blue Moon 884-3152, Cypress Village. Fine lingerie, beads and gifts.

Spindrift Gallery 884-4484, Cypress Gallery. New paintings and 3-D art by Northern California artists. Thurs-Sun.

The Sea Trader 884-3248. 38640 Hwy One. Cards, New Age and childrens book, toys, jewelry, crystals.

Massage

Healing Arts & Massage Center. Cypress Village, Hwy One. 884-4800.

Paula Gordon 884-3823. Therapeutic bodywork massage and integrated awareness by appointment.

Mari Sue Haris 884-1159. Massage by appointment, in studio or your location.

Gualala Events

For more information call the Chamber of Commerce 800-778-5252 or go to www.redwoodcoastchamber.com

MARCH: Redwood Coast Whale & Jazz Festival

MAY: Soroptimists Annual Architectural Tour & Wine Tasting

JULY: Pacific Community School Barbecue, Bower Park Sand Castle Contest, Anchor Bay Beach

AUGUST: Arts in the Redwoods Festival 884-1138

SEPTEMBER: North Coast Artists' Guild Annual Studio Discovery Tour 785-9513

OCTOBER: Scarecrow Country

NOVEMBER: Wine & Mushroom Days

DECEMBER: Holiday Hospitality Nights

*B*EFORE THE STAGE SETS YOU DOWN AT *Mendocino, you will have noticed that the coastline is broken at frequent intervals by the mouths of small streams [where] sawmills are placed. Not easily accessible, these little sawmill ports are rarely visited by strangers, and the accommodations are somewhat rude, but the people are kindly and the country is wonderfully picturesque, and well repays a visit.*

As you travel along the coast, the stage road gives you frequent and satisfying views of its curiously distorted and ocean-eaten caves and rock. It has a dangerous and terrible aspect to mariners, but it is most wonderful viewed from the shore.

— Charles Nordhoff,
1874 in *Northern California, Oregon, and the Sandwich Islands*

2. GUALALA TO POINT ARENA
15 MILES

THE ROUTE

WHILE THE COAST ROAD NORTH OF GUALALA WAS once so rugged that stagecoaches climbed more than 1000 feet along the ridge to avoid it on their way to Point Arena, the road today flows smoothly along, mostly within sight of the Pacific. Numerous wayside inns offer overnight accommodations in the four miles to Anchor Bay. Then the route winds through a wooded residential area, finally traversing open coastal terraces where large ranches still dominate on the final leg into Point Arena. The entire stretch presents a tame loveliness that obscures the rugged harsh wilderness that greeted the first settlers. The traffic is fairly heavy so expect the 15-mile journey to Point Arena to take 30 minutes.

Smeaton Chase described this lovely coast as he saw it on his horseback ride north in 1911: "Castellated islets and peninsulas alternated every mile with romantic little bays." Chase went on to describe the commerce of the day.

Here and there along the cliff tan-bark and railway ties were piled. The map of the coast was thickly marked with names, but most of them relate to lumbering settlements that have vanished with the marketable timber of the immediate locality.

The evocative names included Nip and Tuck, Hard Scratch, Rough and Ready, Slick Rock, Buster's, and Schooner Gulch between Gualala and Point Arena. As you travel along the coast you'll still find some of these names, while others washed away with most of the evidence of their existence.

Today you may hardly notice the eleven gulches the coast road crosses in the four miles to Anchor Bay, but they were a formidable barrier to early travelers. When bridges were built to cross these brush-choked streams, the builders became local heroes. At one time there were seven bridges averaging 60 feet in height in these four miles. Early roads connected one homestead to the next rather than moving traffic swiftly up the coast. Most early roads were privately built and maintained by the homesteaders or the local community. Many settlers kept locked gates and charged tolls to pass. Even after the tolls faded, coast travelers had to stop at each property boundary to open and close the gate, a routine that persisted even into the 1940s.

Mendocino County had no road into Gualala until 1915. The county built the route because the coast road in Sonoma County had been completed, bringing heavier auto traffic from the urban areas. Cattle and sheep drivers loved the improvements. They seldom yielded the road to autos willingly. Cars were still rare on the coast in the 1920s and 1930s. Most everyone stopped to look when one passed.

In 1935 the state got involved in this part of the coast route, first coating the road with dust oil, later with a thin layer of asphalt. The pavement was so thin, locals joked about tracking cars by the wheel ruts left in the asphalt. Most of the wooden bridges were torn out, the gulches bulldozed to bedrock so that modern steel-reinforced concrete bridges could be built. Coast Highway One was being born. Only in the mid-1950s did modern pavement finally replace the oiled surface north to Mendocino.

THE DRIVE

Today the Shoreline Highway runs straight and wide northwest from Gualala, dipping briefly to cross Big Gulch. The commercial enterprises yield reluctantly to a wooded coast. After a long straightaway the ocean glimmers on your left. You cross Bourn's Gulch, where a small pioneer cemetery is hidden on the right, then climb slightly over the promontory that held Bourn's Landing, an important shipping point into the twentieth century. The coast road dips quickly across Glennen Gulch, then St. Orres Creek. It is hard to miss the spectacular onion-dome architecture on the right that marks **SAINT ORRES INN & RESTAURANT** (see Gualala Listings for inns on this page).

Highway One swings through gentle curves along a wooded shore. You pass Collins Landing where on the left sits **SERENISEA OCEAN CABINS**. At Collins Landing the two St. Ores brothers built the first wire chute on the north coast in the 1870s, replacing the primitive slide chute. Today, at the north edge of the Serenisea facilities, a steep trail and stairs descend to the beach. You must ask permission of management first.

Collins Landing c 1875

Doghole Ports

Sailing ships that plied the Mendocino Coast found an inhospitable place where challenging weather hid submerged reefs and offshore rocks, tall cliffs and shallow coves and bays.

The narrow, storm-exposed harbors required small two-masted schooners that could maneuver into such tight spaces. The larger three- and four-masted schooners could only load at the best anchorages, even then only in calm seas. Every ship needed a sea captain with nerves of steel, a devil-may-care approach, or both.

To get into position to load, the captain . . . had to sail straight toward the cliff, then, less than 100 yards from disaster, bring the schooner about in virtually her own length like a dog settling into its hole, and finally . . . get out four moorings to buoys and iron rings in the rocks.

— Wallace Martin,
Sail and Steam

ANCHOR BAY
(POP. 176, EL. 145)

The romantic road dips through two wooded gulches and arrives at the small community of Anchor Bay. The marvelous and wooded coast here is in the heart of the Banana Belt, protected from prevailing winds by the jutting coastline to the north. Fish Rocks offshore provide nesting sites for tufted puffins and other sea birds.

During Prohibition rum runners took advantage of the secluded cove at Anchor Bay to unload bootleg Canadian whiskey, delivering it by wagon to local buyers.

In addition to small shops and a laundromat the town offers **ANCHOR BAY VILLAGE MARKET** 884-4245. Their deli uses organic food for sandwiches, soups, salads & desserts, plus patio seating, large wine & beer selection, organic food, fresh produce, daily 8–8, 'til 7 on Sunday. **ANCHOR BAY CAMPGROUND** 884-4222, Box 1529, Gualala 95445, has 52 sites, hookups, hot showers, small boat launching, and fish-cleaning facilities, plus day-use access to beach, $27–38.

FISH ROCK CAFE
35517 Hwy One, Anchor Bay
884-1639

Burgers, sandwiches, pasta and seafood dishes.

Daily except Monday, 11 am–9 pm; res. advisable for large groups; MC/V/checks; beer/wine; seats 60; take-out; ♿

TAQUERIA BRIZA DEL MAR

35501 Hwy One, Anchor Bay

884-1735

B: $3-9 L/D: $6-10

Authentic Mexican cuisine with regional specialties like chicken mole, spinach enchiladas, tamales, chile rellenos, posole, menudo, carnitas, and fish tacos. Food made fresh daily using family recipes and freshest ingredients.

Wed–Mon, 7 am–9 pm, 'til 8 in winter; MC/V/Disc/checks; beer,wine; seats 40; take-out; ᕯ

After winding sharply through Fish Rock Gulch, Coast Highway One meanders through a residential neighborhood where the woods grow dense with Bishop and shore pines, madrone, pioneer eucalyptus and scattered redwoods. You pass **FISH ROCK ROAD** on the right which climbs over Signal Ridge and turns to dirt before ending at Highway 128 near Yorkville in about 30 miles (See CHAPTER 11. BACK ROADS).

The Shoreline Highway straightens out to cross the top of Havens Neck, a tall promontory rich with wildflowers in spring and summer. The site of the doghole port called Nip and Tuck was just south of the Neck. A final string of lodgings line your route, the last before Point Arena ten miles north.

☆ WHALE WATCH INN BY THE SEA

$180–300

35100 Hwy One, Gualala 95445

884-3667/800-WHALE42

www.whalewatchinn.com

A special getaway, offering luxury, privacy, ocean views and personal service in a dramatic contemporary setting. Surrounded by incomparable scenic beauty, the inn blends romance and drama on two cliffside garden acres overlooking Anchor Bay, with a private staircase to beach and tidepools.

Thus the ships became known as doghole schooners, the anchorages as doghole ports. The worries of the captain and crew were unending. The skipper always had to be ready to drop moorings at the hint of bad weather and run back out to the relative safety of the storm-churned sea. Many captains learned the hard way that you couldn't wait long to run from a storm.

Storm waves dashed many schooners on the rocks. One ship moored at Mendocino Bay was sucked into a wave tunnel during a storm. Though the crew jumped to safety in time, nothing of the ship was left to salvage. A single storm on November 10, 1865, wrecked two schooners at Mendocino, three at Little River, one at Caspar and another at Noyo.

When steam began to power the ships around 1880, they could maneuver more easily in the tight doghole ports and operate without waiting for a favorable wind. But the sails were kept as back-up for many years, often proving to be life savers.

18 rooms; gourmet breakfast delivered to room; res. essential; min. stay 2 nights wknds, 3 nights holidays; MC/V/AE/checks; suites; family units; cooking facilities; private jacuzzi/sauna; private decks, some w/ hot tubs; fireplaces; bathtubs; ⓑ

NORTH COAST COUNTRY INN
$175–215

34591 S. Hwy One, Gualala 95445

884-4537/800-959-4537

www.northcoastcountryinn.com

The inn comprises a cluster of redwood buildings nestled into a forested hillside overlooking the Pacific. Large rooms have antiques and comfy furniture, wood-burning fireplaces and private decks. Guests can relax in the garden gazebo and private hot tub.

6 rooms; full breakfast; min. stay 2 nights wknds; V/MC/AE/checks;refrig/fireplace in rooms; gardens; hot tub; some bathtubs, cooking facilities

MAR VISTA COTTAGES $140–200
35101 Hwy One, Gualala

884-3522/877-855-3522

www.marvistamendocino.com

Housekeeping cottages on land side of Hwy One with beach access across the highway; most have ocean views, some decks, some fireplaces; one and two bedroom cottages with kitchens; children and pets welcome.

12 cottages; min. stay 2 nights wknds; MC/V/checks; full kitchens; soaking tub; adj. to hiking; BBQ area; org. garden avail. to guests; ⓑ

CONTINUING ON...

Highway One crosses Triplett Gulch and Roseman Creek, then

Nip and Tuck slide chute

passes the sites of another historic doghole port, Steens Landing, alias Hard Scratch. The road angles west briefly, then turns northwest again to cross Slick Rock Creek and Morrison Gulch near where they empty into small rocky coves.

Shoreline Highway then dips and twists through Walker Gulch, named for local logging folk hero Long Walker, who lived here beside the coast road. Walker was known as the best and fastest axe man in the woods. Legend says he chopped trees all week in a long row without falling a single one, then felled one on Saturday afternoon that knocked each of them over one by one until they all lay neatly on the ground.

Beyond the gulch the coast highway breaks out of the forest onto the grassy headland called Iversen Point. Iversen Point had a water-powered sawmill in the days of early settlement. Ships loaded wood products from a chute called Rough and Ready in the cove south of the point until around 1900.

As the road descends from Iversen Point, the marvelously striated blond cliffs stretching north to Point Arena come strikingly into view. A short frontage road on your left provides a place to stop and admire the scene. Shoreline Highway dips across Hearn Gulch, at the mouth of which Saunders Landing served an early sawmill. The barely submerged rocks of Saunders Reef offshore claimed numerous ships in the early coastal trade.

The coast road turns north right along the shore, passing the site of Slick Rock, or Scoutt's Landing, before it reaches wooded **SCHOONER GULCH**, a site for early ship building and a shingle mill. Today a small parcel of state park land provides access to the pretty, wind-sheltered beach at the mouth of the gulch. Be warned that you can only stop here by parking facing south, on the west side of the road. If you want to stop, continue north to a safe turn around (perhaps Moat Creek), then return. At low tide this public land also provides access to spectacular **BOWLING BALL BEACH** to the north, between Galloway and Ross creeks. The intriguing, straight coastal rock strata there are accentuated by sandstone concretions, spherical rocks ranging from the size of perfect bowling balls on up to 12-foot weathered discs. It's a great walk at low tide, less accessible when the tide is in.

The Shoreline Highway carries you northwest across rolling grassy headlands. Where the road dips to cross Ross Creek, a coastal access trail descends to a tiny cove popular with surfers. The adjacent bluffs are known as Whiskey Shoals, another unloading point for rum runners during Prohibition.

Where the road dips nearly to sea level to cross Moat Creek you can turn left into a dirt parking area for two coastal access trails. The **MOAT CREEK** access leads ⅛ mile to a small rocky beach and tidepools, while a new blufftop trail heads south along the Whiskey Shoals bluffs to Ross Creek. No dogs allowed please.

The Pacific Coast Highway quickly ascends a high grassy hill for a view of the surrounding pastoral countryside backed by high, wooded ridges. As your road drops into a brushy canyon, please slow to 25 miles per hour to suddenly enter the historic and congested downtown of Point Arena, Mendocino County's smallest incorporated city.

Point Arena
(pop. 440, el. 220)

*P*oint Arena offers amenities greatly exceeding its tiny posted population. It has plenty of accommodations, some worthwhile shops, and even boasts its own movie theater. A steep, straight span of Highway One serves as the town's downtown district and Main Street. A mixture of twentieth century art deco and boxy buildings mingle here with the few nineteenth century Victorians that survived the 1906 earthquake.

To sample the saltier side of Point Arena, turn west onto Port Road from the town center and drive to its end where you will find **ARENA COVE** sandwiched between rocky cliffs. As well as being the site of the original wharf, Arena Cove was once a whaling station and the Coast Guard maintained a station here for years. Today Point Arena's fanciest accommodations cluster in this sheltered canyon. The cove also offers some of the best surfing on the Mendocino Coast.

Point Arena c.1890

In January 1983 huge high-tide-driven storm waves roared in one after another at Arena Cove, destroying the pier and fish house and severely damaging the historic boat house and cafe. Not the first of such incidents, it was the worst since the original wharf was built.

The rebuilt steel and concrete pier, completely wheelchair accessible, is 322 feet long, fifteen feet higher than its predecessor. No fishing license is required to fish from this public pier. Arena Cove offers the only all-tide boat launching facility between Bodega Bay and Fort Bragg. Pier facilities include public rest rooms, fish-cleaning tables, cold showers, a hoist and offshore mooring.

History

After a rudimentary store was built in 1859, a small settlement sprang up around it. Andrew Hall built the first complete store in 1865. Business improved after the town's first wharf was built in 1866, but only after the Garcia Mill was established in 1869 did Point Arena truly start to prosper. It had a paper mill, tannery and several dairies in its heyday. A whaling station at the cove processed the valuable whale oil then preferred for lamps, extracted from the immense mammalian carcasses hunted off the coast.

The lumber mill was seven miles upriver in a deep, rugged canyon.

Point Arena after 1906 earthquake

Lighters, Wharves, Slide Chutes, Wire Chutes & Trapezes

The various doghole ports used several methods to load the schooners that squeezed into their rocky coves. Lighters were small boats used to haul lumber to ships anchored in deep water. These shallow-draft crafts could land right on a beach, but since the wood had to be loaded twice, they proved too costly. Many lumber ports built wharves in the early days, but they seldom withstood more than a few winters of the voracious storm surf.

Slide, or apron, chutes simply used gravity to send boards one by one down a wooden trough to the deck of a ship. The clapper, a sort of brake at the bottom end, slowed the board so a deck hand could grab it. Even then the clapperman had a dangerous job. Slide chutes,

the most common loading method in the nineteenth century, extended only 200 or 300 feet offshore. Many a slide was ripped away by a winter storm only to be rebuilt in spring.

The wire chute proved to be the best of the old loading systems. This innovation, introduced in the 1870s, allowed ships to moor as

The owners planned to build a railroad to the town's schooner landing, but a rancher demanded too much money for the right-of-way. In an ingenious innovation, the owners built a flume of virgin redwood along the river flats to Flumeville. Then a series of rollers driven by a water wheel raised the lumber 300 feet up a 45-degree grade. The boards were then hauled to the harbor, dropping down a steep grade called the Devil's Cutoff. In 1892, 5000 railroad ties were flumed to the port in one day. Adventuresome youths sometimes rode the railroad ties along the 30-inch-wide, 16-inch-deep flume. The challenge was to jump off before the water wheel.

Though fire destroyed the mill in 1894, the flume was kept in service until the 1910s. Traces of the flume could still be found many years later.

The fog-shrouded, reef-bound coast at Punta de Arena (Sandy Point) has always been dangerous for ships. Ten ships ran aground here one stormy night in 1865. This disastrous evening led to the building of the Point Arena Lighthouse in 1870. The 1906 earthquake shook, swayed and finally cracked the original brick tower, which was soon rebuilt as the present structure.

The great earthquake also devastated much of the town. Although most of it was rebuilt, the town never regained its former prosperity. When Smeaton Chase rode through in 1911, he passed signs for six hotels before he found one open for business. A resident who had been in Point Arena 40 years reported that the town had fewer residents than when he had arrived.

Point Arena Hot Springs opened in 1904. Several miles up the Garcia River, the resort billed itself as a "first-class summer resort" and offered lodging for 150 people. Developers of the resort tried mightily to attract a fashionable clientele like Calistoga had (and still does) 60 miles southeast. Hot Springs pamphlets described Point Arena as a place "where the lover of nature can always find his gentle mistress in her most delightful moods." Room and board at the deluxe hotel cost $8 to $12 a week. Round trip fare from San Francisco by fast steam schooner ran another $8, including stage fare to the resort.

In 1927 a huge fire ran amok and destroyed even more of the old town than the 1906 earthquake.

Pacific Gas & Electric proposed building a nuclear power plant near Point Arena in the early 1970s, despite the town's proximity to the San Andreas fault. The utility had been halted from a similar proposal at Bodega Bay only a decade before because of earthquake danger. PG&E eventually withdrew the Point Arena plan.

much as ¼ mile offshore. A heavy wire cable was stretched from land to a buoy in the sea. The cable was

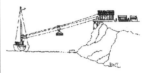

connected to the ship's mast and slings moved back and forth along the cable, carrying bundles of lumber to the ship, and passengers and goods back to shore. The cables and slings were powered by a steam-powered drum on shore. Women passengers got to ride a trapeze or chair, but men usually had to climb the rigging.

Point Arena Lodging

Listings are organized from the most expensive to the least expensive

☆ COAST GUARD HOUSE HISTORIC INN $125–245

695 Arena Cove/Box 117
Point Arena 95468
882-2442/800-524-9320

www.coastguardhouse.com

Restored Coast Guard life-saving station in 1901 Cape Cod-style house, listed in National Register of Historic Places. Fine old home overlooking Arena Cove offers gracious hospitality with turn-of-the-century Arts and Crafts decor, with each room having a unique flavor.

5 rooms, 2 deluxe cottages; deluxe full breakfast; min. stay 2 nights most wknds; V/MC/Disc/checks; 2 bdrm suite w/large bathroom; adj. restaurant; jacuzzi/hot tub; ocean views; fireplace in LR; 3 rms w/wood stoves; bathtubs; gardens; adj. to hiking/beach

POINT ARENA LIGHTHOUSE HOME RENTALS $175-190

882-2777/877-725-4448
End of Lighthouse Road/Box 11
Point Arena
www.pointarenalighthouse.com

Rent an historic lighthouse keepers' home, vintage 1939, within a stones throw of the historic light. Each home has three bedrooms, two baths, wood-burning fireplace, full kitchen, and spectacular views. From the house you might see migrating whales, river otters, harbor seals, and migrating birds like tundra swans, cormorants, pelicans and swallows. Outside are abundant wildflowers.

3 houses; V/MC; res. essential; ocean views, gardens; full kitchen, fireplace, satellite tv, bathtub; adj. to hiking; families, pets welcome; ₺

☆ WHARF MASTER'S INN $75–250

785 Port Road/Box 674
Point Arena
882-3171/800-932-4031

www.wharfmasters.com

Modern lodging surrounding a beautiful old house overlooking Arena Cove.

25 rooms; continental breakfast; coffeemakers in rms; min. stay 2 nights holiday wknds; V/MC/AE/Disc/checks; ocean views; suites; private jacuzzi, fireplace, phone, tv, four-post feather beds, computer port in rms; families,pets welcome; ₺

SEA SHELL INN $50-90

135 Main/Box 393, Point Arena
882-2000/877-733-7435

Clean, friendly, inexpensive with a wide range of accommodations — same family ownership since 1976. Most rooms have direct dial phones, complimentary fresh ground coffee and cable tv. Good restaurants nearby. Close to wharf, ocean, and good fishing.

32 rooms; MC/V/Disc/AE; 2-bdrm units; 12 rms w/microwave & frig.; adj. to hiking; fax in office

Eateries

ARENA COVE BAR & GRILL
790 Port Rd, Point Arena 95468
882-2100
L: $6–16, D: $8–20

Overlooking Arena Cove and harbor, food blends California cuisine with Latin fusion, specializing in fresh seafood. Bar fare available, too, at one of the biggest bars on the north coast.
Daily 11 am–9 pm,'til 10 on summer wkends; res. advisable; V/MC/AE/Disc/checks; full bar; seats 150; take-out; ♿

OLD HOUSE CAFE
at Rollerville Junction, 2 miles north of Hwy One. Point Arena
882-1733
B: $5–11, L: $4–11, D: $10–14

Good home cooking: burgers, hot dogs, salads. Barbeque dinners with ribs and chicken.
Sat, Sun 8-2, dinners Fri, Sat in summer. V/MC/checks; beer/wine; seats 36 plus outside deck; families welcome; take-out; ♿

PALMER'S GRILL
405 School St, Point Arena
882-2360
B: $2–6, L: $4.50–9, D: $7–9

Family-owned local gathering place.
Tue–Sun 11:30–7:30 winter, daily 8–8 summer; local checks; seats 30; take-out; ♿

THE RECORD
265 Main, Point Arena
882-FOOD
B: $3–5, L: $4–12, D: $5–12

Deli, cafe and market. Light fare—breakfast, sandwiches, salads, soup. Espresso drinks. Local and organic produce, fresh breads, organic meats and cheeses cut to order.
Mon-Sat 7-6, til 8 in summer, Sunday 9-5, in summer 8-5; V/MC/checks: beer/wine; seats 24 plus outdoors; take-out; ♿

CARLINI'S CAFE
206 Main St, Point Arena
882-2942
B: $2.50–9, L: $5–9

Delicious, delightful, charming favorite with locals and return visitors. Standard breakfast - lunch menu with unique daily specials, all made to order with highest quality ingredients. Specials include salmon patties, home-made corn beef hash, crab omelettes, shrimp melt, spinach crepes and eggs benedict.
Mon, Tue, Thurs, Fri 6:30 am-2:00 pm. Sat & Sun 7:30 am-2:00 pm. Closed Mid Jan to Mid Feb. Local checks; seats 28; take-out; ♿

EL BURRITO ORGANIC TAQUERIA
165 Main St, Point Arena
882-2910
$4.50-7

Organic Mexican food, burritos the specialty, but also quesadillas, tacos, taco salads, huevos rancheros and breakfast burritos. Organic drinks too.
Daily 11:30–7, plus breakfast from 8 am Mon-Fri; Mendo Cty checks; beer; seats 20; take-out; ♿

COSMIC PIZZA
Arena Cove, Point Arena
882-1900

Pizzas, calzones and delicious salads.
Daily: 12–9; beer/wine; seating or take-out

Campground

ROLLERVILLE JUNCTION
882-2440, 22900 Hwy One, has 55
sites with hook-ups, camping cabins
with lights and tv, 2 cottages with
private bath. Hot showers, hot tub,
heated pool, cable tv, store, cafe,
espresso bar, laundry and propane.
$26–99. &

Outdoor Activities

POINT ARENA LIGHTHOUSE
882-2777. End of Lighthouse Road
about 5 miles northwest of downtown.
Fee. Open to the public 10–4:30 daily,
'til 3:30 in winter. On a clear day the
view is spectacular, as is the whale
watching in season. When it's foggy the
antique Fresnel lens at the top of the
spiral-staired tower, the starkly
picturesque headlands, and the fine fog
signal building museum are still worth
a trip. For the full experience, stay
overnight in their guest houses (see
listings).

SURF THERAPY 882-3176,
150 Main St, Surfboard sales and
rentals.
DOUBLE D RETAIL 882-2746,
415 School St. Skindiving, boating
and fishing equipment and supplies.

Indoor Activities

Arena Theatre 882-3020, 214 Main.
Movies and live concerts in an
extensively renovated art deco theatre.

Arena Renaissance 882-3272, brings
occasional music, theater and other
cultural events to town.

Galleries & Shops

City Art Museum 882-3616, 284
Main St. Gallery showcases interesting
local artists.

Everything Under the Sun 882-2161,
211 Main. Third world and local crafts.

DuPont's Mendocino Mercantile
882-3017, at the pier. Gallery and gift
shop with locally made crafts and art.

P. J.'s Billiards at Giannini's 882-2146,
174 Main. Two tables. Mon–Sat, 7:30
am–8 pm.

Point Arena Dance Studio 882-2125,
340 Main. Focus on children's dance,
plus yoga, tai chi, belly dancing for
adults.

Arena Pharmacy 882-3025, 235 Main.
Natural and homeopathic remedies as
well as standard in a bright modern
pharmacy.

Point Arena Events

MAY: Redwood Coast Fire & Rescue
Wild Pig Barbecue & Dance

JULY: Independence Day Parade &
Fireworks
Point Arena Lions Greco Barbecue
Pacific Community School Barbecue

AUGUST: Harbor & Seafood Festival

DECEMBER: Christmas Celebration

3. POINT ARENA TO ELK
19 MILES

THE ROUTE

*T*HIS SECTION OF THE COAST, ALTHOUGH DOTTED with small communities, offers a remote, wild feeling that makes it easy to recall the days of early settlement in this challenging wilderness. The road varies between straight, easy legs and tortuous curves, so be prepared for sudden changes as you drive. Plan at least thirty to forty minutes to traverse this rugged area of the coast.

THE DRIVE

The Shoreline Highway turns west to exit Point Arena, passing historic St. Aloysius Church, then providing a glimpse down to hidden Arena Cove on the left. After a cluster of commercial establishments on your left, the highway heads north across a nearly level plateau 200 feet above the nearby harbor. The highway aims toward the promontory of Point Arena, the nearest point to Hawaii in the continental United States, although the climate here shares little with the islands 2000 miles offshore. This is truly one of the foggiest places on the west coast.

After two pioneer cemeteries on the left, look for Lighthouse Road. A left turn on the latter leads 2¾ bumpy and beautiful miles across a windswept peninsula to the point itself, where the historic **POINT ARENA LIGHTHOUSE** still functions, offering tours daily from 10 to 4:30 (see Point Arena Listings).

The intersection of Lighthouse Road and Highway One marks the site of Flumeville. Today the intersection offers **ROLLERVILLE JUNCTION**, a privately run campground with cabins, a cafe and a small store.

Highway One makes a crooked descent to the flood plain of the Garcia River, crossing Hathaway Creek at the base of the bluff, then wandering through rich farm land. In winter you might look northwest across the field on the left. From November to March tundra (or whistling) swans winter here, enjoying the mild 50-degree weather before flying back to their Arctic nesting grounds. These elegant white birds have a seven-foot wingspan and weigh up to 20 pounds. In flight tundra swans make an ethereal whistling sound, thus their second name.

The highway crosses the Garcia River, a small stream even by north coast standards except when it fills this flood plain in a wet year.

The Garcia is named for an 1844 Mexican land grant to Rafael Garcia, brother-in-law to Stephen Smith of Rancho Bodega. The Mexican government awarded Garcia about 40,000 acres, bounded on the south by the Garcia River and on the north by Mallo Pass Creek. Garcia already had two big land grants in Marin County so he built a second home (a Mendocino Coast first!) and ranchero where Mountain View Road meets Highway One today. Garcia cattle grazed on the rich bottom lands beside the river. He erected a guardhouse on the river's north bank, where a caretaker lived to look after Garcia's "grante del norte." This guardhouse still stood in 1904 according to one report. While Garcia's northern grant was denied by the California State Land Commission in 1854, he still left his name and other marks on the land.

The Shoreline Highway winds past the dairy farms long held by the Stornetta family. You soon pass **MOUNTAIN VIEW ROAD** on the right. This paved but extremely steep and winding road will take you to Boonville in 25 miles (see CHAPTER 11.BACK ROADS). Soon on the left is Stoneboro Road, offering coastal access to trails in the southern portion of Manchester State Park, a beachcomber's paradise, and the easiest way to reach the mouth of the Garcia River.

In another half mile Highway One enters the sleepy town of **MANCHESTER** (**POP. 462, EL. 120**). **S & B MARKET**, 882-2805, the general store here since 1945, offers grocery, hardware and deli items daily from 8 to 7. While the town claims to be a bit larger than Point Arena, other than S & B, the services here are minimal. It is most remarkable today for the outstanding topiary display on the right, just before the post office and store. The tiny community also has a very large heather garden and an immense Monterey cypress tree. In early days Manchester was renowned for the large population of grizzly bears living along Brush Creek, north and east of town.

Among the first settlers here were Awasa and Jane Saunders, who left Maine in 1856. Awasa came west with his own lumber mill equipment, traveling with it around Cape Horn while his wife took the new railroad across the Isthmus of Panama. They intended to go to Eureka, but their ship foundered off Point Arena on what is now known as Saunders Reef. So they settled at Brush Creek instead, opening the south coast's first lumber mill there in 1857. They left Mendocino County in 1879 when the Northern California lumber market collapsed.

As you leave downtown Manchester, consider a stop at spacious **MANCHESTER STATE PARK**. For the main access to the park and its campground, turn left on Kinney Road about a mile north of town, just beyond Home Sweet Home Ranch. Walk to the beach, stay in the park's 46 primitive campsites, nestled in dunes a half mile from the shore, or walk a level mile to sleep in the peaceful environmental

Diving for the Elusive Haliotis

They arrive by the thousands every year to search for it. They come in every shape, from muscled to portly to petite. They bring pry iron, size gauge, zodiac or inner tube, wet suit, face mask, snorkel, and fins, and they better bring a license. When they find it, they shell it, clean it, pound it, bread it, then fry or barbecue it, saute or boil it, chop it for chowder or fry it as fritters. (Do anything but poach it!) When they've eaten it, they go back out for more.

It has two eyes, one gill, many tiny tentacles, one big foot and iridescence inside its shell with red, green, pink, black or white on the outside, depending on the species.

"It" is the delectable univalve abalone, the slow-moving denizen of Pacific subtidal waters and primeval cousin of the snail. It thrives along the Mendocino Coast, especially the red abalone, Haliotis rufescens, largest of the breed. Each year the divers who seek it have a little harder time finding their limit of three (24 per year). Still, more divers join the throngs each year.

While abalone is commercially harvested in Mexico and Japan, on the north coast it's supposed to be strictly a sport fishery. I say supposed because thousands are poached, that is, illegally collected or stolen each year, despite stiff fines and jail terms.

camps. For more sophisticated camping, try **MANCHESTER BEACH KOA,** 882-2375, Box 266, Manchester 95459, just east of the state park, www.manchesterbeachkoa.com. They offer 77 sites, plus cottages and cabins, a heated pool, hot tub, showers, playground, laundry, propane and store. $30–150. ♿. For the higher price you can rent one of their cottages, which have bathroom, kitchenette, gas fireplace and tv. The owners know the area well and can direct you to other sights to see.

The Shoreline Highway dips through a tiny canyon, climbs over a small rise, then descends toward the lush, green canyon of Alder Creek. On the left Alder Creek Road provides beach access at the northern end of Manchester State Park.

Highway One crosses the San Andreas fault where it follows Alder Creek out to sea. The 1906 temblor destroyed the old bridge and offset one fence six feet. Welcome back to the North American plate!

In the days of early settlers, the farms along Alder Creek nearly precipitated the local equivalent of a range war. The homesteaders had arrived in 1891 before the land was surveyed, and therefore technically open to settlement. In 1893 the land was declared open and all the men went to San Francisco together to file their claims. The State Land Office informed them that the land had a prior claim by a timber company. The homesteaders brought suit to clear up the issue. Eighteen years later the suit still was undecided. During that time the farmers continued working their land, refusing even to be shaken off by the great 1906 quake. In 1911 the timber company, whose railroad had recently reached the disputed lands, hired 20 gunfighters to evict the settlers. While the company called them guards, they were in fact ex-convicts hired after their release from San Quentin. The settlers requested a federal marshall to come to their defense, but none ever arrived. Though the company instructed the guards to stay on the timber claims and avoid people, trouble soon developed. A fight broke out during a drunken poker game and one guard shot and critically injured another. The thugs threatened to come into Greenwood and shoot up the town. The local constable brought an armed group of townsmen out to the lumber camp by train. They disarmed the thugs, paid them off, escorted them to the wharf and loaded them on a schooner bound for San Francisco. The timber company eventually bought the timber claims from the settlers, typically paying $400 for 160 acres of virgin redwoods.

The Shoreline Highway continues its push north, crossing a high, level headland before winding through wooded Irish Gulch and passing through the modern subdivision of the same name. To truly explore this isolated coast you might consider renting a vacation home here (see APPENDIX: VACATION HOME RENTALS).

The north coast sport season for abalone opens April 1, runs through June, closes for July and resumes August through November. The legal limit of three (24 per year) abalone must be kept in their shells (no smaller than seven inches) and in the possession of the licensed diver who collected them until they're cooked up or taken home. No scuba gear is allowed.

If you'd like to brave the coast's icy waters for abs, contact a local dive shop for the necessary equipment and lessons. The sport isn't so easy as some make it look, and each year divers drown or require rescue from the tricky Pacific currents.

If you see poaching or suspicious abalone gathering, please call 1-800-952-5400.

A bit farther along is deluxe:
☆ VICTORIAN GARDENS
14409 S.Hwy One
Manchester CA 95459
882-3606

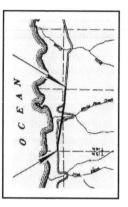

www.innatvictoriangardens.com

A B&B and restaurant in a grand 1904 Victorian, where four elegant rooms on 92 acres overlook the sea and a wooded wilderness. Room rates ($180–250) include casually elegant rooms filled with antiques plus a lavish breakfast.

The restaurant offers impeccable five-course dinners of historically authentic Italian regional dishes lovingly prepared and served by the owners, Luciano and Pauline Zamboni, in their charming home. Enjoy the rare opportunity of savoring the endangered art of unrushed, elegant dining. The menu changes nightly, using fresh and seasonal ingredients from their garden, farm and elsewhere. Luciano takes pride in not serving returning guests the same dish twice. Be sure to call ahead for reservations if you plan to visit.

Dinners Thursday through Sunday, one seating only at 7:30pm; $75 prix fixe includes wines and all other beverages; V/MC/AE/Checks; reservations essential for dinner or lodging; families welcome; seats 16.

Just north of the access road for Victorian Gardens is a **VISTA POINT** on the left. It overlooks a rocky shore indented by the deep cove at the mouth of Mallo Pass Creek. To the east the view looks into the lush streamside forests of the deep and narrow canyon. Where the highway today dips to cross the creek, the broad, straight road offers not a hint of the canyon's impact on early day land traffic up and down the coast, although you can spot the old highway twisting up the hill to the north.

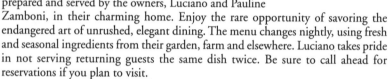

This rugged canyon, fully 200 feet deep where the highway spans it today, seriously impeded travel between Point Arena and towns to the north. Today's moniker is actually a derivation of the original Spanish name of Gran Mal Paso, meaning Great Bad Pass. Mal Paso splits the earth from far back in the woods to the ocean. The gulch was so rugged even the strongest travelers dreaded the crossing. Even at its best in good weather, the chasm required a long, steep detour. When the track was muddy or washed out, wagons had to be dismantled, the pieces lowered one by one with block and tackle to the ford, then hoisted up the other side. The last tree that had supported the block and tackle was cut in 1965 when the modern crossing was built. Sometimes a pulley was employed to shuttle people across one by one. Even this method could be deadly — a woman and her infant once fell from the pulley, plunging into the deep gorge below. The

crossing of this natural barrier did not become routine until the 1930s, when an all weather bridge was built thanks to the advances of modern technology.

If you want a closer look proceed north ¼ mile to a wide spot in the road just beyond the chasm, where the old highway parallels the canyon's north rim briefly. It's difficult to see much through the dense growth. Don't try to descend into the ravine, you might never get out! If you had worked for the L. E. White Lumber Company of Greenwood around the turn of the century you might have ridden their logging railroad across Mallo Pass Creek and on up the coast to Greenwood, but this was not an option for the public.

A mile up Highway One from Mallo Pass, a hand painted sign on the left that warns of "vicious bulls" is actually a warning to those disreputable folks who might consider trespass on the rancher's property. The landscape here consists of a gradually sloping marine terrace of deep loamy soil 200 to 400 feet above the ocean, backed by steep ridges cut by deep, wooded stream canyons.

Swerve across wooded Mills Creek, then pass an inconspicuous sign for Bridgeport Ranch. Marked by a small cluster of outbuildings and houses today, this was the site of the nineteenth century town called Bridgeport, which flourished from 1860 to 1900.

While the first settlers in the early 1850s didn't stay long, in 1857 Irishman Thomas Walsh settled in with his stake from the Sierra gold fields. He was the biggest fish in this little pond for many years. Orso Clift, a sailor from New England, settled here around 1860, eventually moving five miles north to Clift Ridge.

Early supplies were brought ashore by rowboat, then hoisted up the 200-foot cliff. In 1862 A. J. Irish built an apron chute near the mouth of Mills Creek. In 1868 the chute collapsed and was rebuilt, the same year a road pushed north to the big town of Cuffeys Cove. History didn't record when this place was first called Bridgeport. Its settlers cut railroad ties and peeled plenty of tanbark oaks, but farming and ranching held sway, outlasting a boom in wood products.

Fred Helmke bought Fisk's Mill at Salt Point, moving it to Bridgeport in 1872. By then Bridgeport already had a store and a school (11 years before Gualala had one), but prosperity was right around the corner. The new mill shipped four million board feet of lumber its first year and had 70 workers at its peak. When a post office opened in 1873, another California town already claimed the label Bridgeport. The name Miller may have been chosen for the U.S. Mail after the stage driver who delivered it.

The town soon boasted a hotel, two stores, two blacksmith shops, wagon building shop and carpentry shop. One of Bridgeport's two midwives attended every birth from 1870 to 1895. Disastrous shipwrecks at Bridgeport spurred construction of a wire chute two miles south at New Haven as the main port, but wrecks continued.

Bridgeport's bust came as quickly as its boom. The mill closed in 1886 when the handy timber was gone. Diseases and competition devastated local potato farming in 1888. Even before the last ship was loaded in 1898, Bridgeport became the sleepy ranching community it remains today.

During the 1906 earthquake the deafening clamor of sea birds on the ocean cliffs broke the quiet. Numerous cracks disrupted the coast road, with one stretching inland for five miles. Huge mudslides rearranged the hills over the next winter.

Today a good, straight ribbon of asphalt carries you quickly across the lush green marine terrace that once held the town. At the terrace's north end, just before you start to descend toward Elk Creek, a remnant of an ancient sea stack just west of the highway is vaguely reminiscent of an unexcavated Mayan pyramid shrouded in dense coastal vegetation.

North Fork Bridge, Elk Creek

Get ready to brake and shift into low gear. The Shoreline Highway curves sharply left, then right and descends steeply through its crookedest stretch since Salt Point 50 miles south. Known affectionately as "dramamine drive," the road snakes sharply through hairpin turns stacked one upon another, then levels to meander through the canyon of Elk Creek. The rugged and wild canyon, dappled with the white-barked trunks of alder trees, seems appropriately named. It is easy to envision a herd of majestic elk grazing along the placid creek. As you'd expect, elk herds were once abundant in the area. They were hunted to extinction to provide meat and hides for the early settlers.

While Elk Creek is notable today for its natural beauty, what is also remarkable is the dearth of signs of the extensive commerce which occurred here from 50 to 120 years ago. When Smeaton Chase rode his horse through here in 1911, he noted, "A mill and railway were in full operation, and the wide stream was blocked with logs awaiting their turn under the screaming saws." Lest you should want to stop and explore, be forewarned that this is all private property, jealously guarded by the owner.

Highway One writhes out of the deep canyon and passes the remains of a 1940s sawmill as it zips quickly along the high ocean bluff. The road winds and descends across Bonee Gulch and Greenwood Creek in rapid succession, then twists up a short hill into the little but lively burg of Elk. On the east side of the highway is the tiny, well stocked **ELK STORE**. A rustic, hand-painted mileage post outside the store orients coastal travelers to the remote town's place in relation to the greater world. According to the locals, Bezerkeley is 264 kilometers, Sedona, AZ is 487 miles, Beijing is 8193 miles and Bathrooms are across the street 133 yards.

ELK/GREENWOOD
(POP. 250, EL. 140)
Sleepy Town with Two Names

S- CURVES CLIMBING FROM GREENWOOD CREEK URGE you to slow down as you enter Elk. Your first impression is likely to be one of a sleepy town with limited services, but this has to be one of the liveliest, most pleasant little towns hiding along the Mendocino Coast. This tiny former logging town and doghole port offers a pleasantly diverse mix of lodgings and eating establishments which are among the best on the Mendocino Coast. While the town's other businesses are few in number, their quality and diversity are also notable. The old-fashioned, small town atmosphere may be the perfect antidote for the stress of modern urban life.

Elk's dramatic natural setting makes it feel more isolated than it actually is. Mendocino lies just 30 minutes up the road, and Anderson

Valley's wine region nestles amidst the coastal hills to the east, not far away by another short, scenic drive.

Elk provides numerous seasonal events and celebrations. The local Catholic community has celebrated **ST. PATRICK'S DAY** for more than 100 years. And you can count on the **FOURTH OF JULY** to provide traditional local festivities. Other dances and community events revolve around the Greenwood Community Center throughout most of the year. The community's biggest party falls in mid-August when **GREAT DAY IN ELK** turns the entire area out for a Saturday filled with home grown festivities culminating in an evening dinner and dance which, while thoroughly modern, also harks back to the isolated town's golden days when three dance halls and several outdoor platforms provided weekly entertainment. A **CHRISTMAS CRAFTS FAIR** in early December brings many talented residents down from the hills.

When you first arrive in this placid little town, sitting snugly atop its ocean cliffs and looking out upon a dazzling sea bejeweled by immense sea stacks, it is difficult to imagine all the history and changes wrought by the 150 years since its first settlers arrived. But Elk's history lies close to the surface, perhaps because the town never became too large to forget, but especially because its natural beauty caused some of the settlers to stay on, allowing them to pass the history on to the new arrivals.

History

A town called Cuffeys Cove one mile to the north actually took hold first, although both places were settled in the early 1850s. The four Greenwood brothers settled in 1852 along Greenwood Creek. They were sons of Caleb Greenwood, an early mountain man and guide known as "Old Greenwood," who died in California's gold country at age 87 after leading many pioneers into Oregon and the Golden State. The Greenwoods worked as trappers and hunters, supplying the mills and logging camps around Mendocino City with venison, elk and bear. While three of the brothers moved on after 20 years when the game became scarce, Britt stayed on as a cattle rancher and is buried in Fort Bragg. After the brothers gave their name to the town, the name Elk was chosen for the new post office in 1887 because California's other Greenwood, founded by father Caleb, already had a post office. Greenwood remained the name of this coastal town despite the Elk mailing address.

Other settlers came and went in these early days, when tie splitting, tanbark gathering, ranching and potato growing drove the local economy. Fred Helmke opened Greenwood/Elk's first sawmill in

Mill at Greenwood,
Mendocino Co., Cal

Greenwood from the south

1875, relocating from Bridgeport to the south. A small redwood shingle mill started in Laurel Gulch. Another mill ground tanbark for shipment to San Francisco tanneries.

A man named Lorenzo White eventually put Greenwood/Elk on the map, but he worked all over Northern California before settling here. He mined in the Sierra in 1849, then bought a ranch in Marin County. He drove a herd of cattle to a relative's ranch near Greenwood in 1858. In the 1860s White owned a store in Albion. By 1880 he established a mill at Whitesboro, south of Albion, with his brother.

Union Hotel Bar

In 1883 Lorenzo White bought most of the land where Elk stands today. He first built a wharf out to Wharf Rock to make ship loading easier. Then he built a large sawmill, a railroad and an entire company town. All of it was operating by 1890, plus a fleet of four ships to haul timber products to San Francisco and bring back supplies for the booming town. Passengers paid $5 to make the 12- to-16-hour trip to San Francisco.

The mill operated continuously from 1890 through 1929, perhaps the only large sawmill on the Mendocino Coast that never suffered a fire. Businesses relocated from Cuffeys Cove to share in Greenwood's prosperity. In its heyday Greenwood had 10 hotels, 14 saloons, several dance halls, three general stores, butcher, creamery, jewelry store, candy store, barber shops, blacksmith shops, livery stable and a population around 1000. In addition to the daily stages along the coast, another line ran over Greenwood Ridge to Philo to connect with the Cloverdale stage. After the turn of the century came a garage and auto dealer, movie house and trailer court.

White's Greenwood mill had 500 men on the payroll for 20 straight years during its prime. His Greenwood and Elk River Railroad was one of the most innovative and dangerous of the many early lumber railways. It crossed 101 bridges in 19 miles of track, two of them more than 400 feet long and 100 feet high. Grades reached 4% or more, dangerously steep for the primitive equipment of the day. More train crewmen lost their lives on this line than on all the other north coast railways.

The 36-inch narrow gauge line ran south to upper Alder Creek east of Manchester, with a spur climbing 12 miles up Greenwood Creek. On its way to Elk Creek the railway ran on a trestle hugging the cliff above the crashing surf 200 feet below. They said if one looked seaward while crossing this trestle, it felt much like flying.

Jack London visited Greenwood repeatedly in the early 1900s, renting an upstairs room in the hotel that later became the hospital. London wrote at a desk beside a window looking out to sea. When Smeaton Chase rode into Greenwood in 1911, he stayed at the Elk Hotel, run, like most of the town, by the local timber company.

After the big mill at the mouth of Greenwood Creek closed down in 1930, smaller mills and timber enterprises kept the local economy afloat, but Greenwood's heyday had passed. When the last two mills closed in 1966, the town's timber era ended and the local economy went bust. But Greenwood had always been a proud town. The locals who stayed on joined forces with the wave of new settlers who arrived in the '60s and '70s. They kept the town alive and kicking until modest prosperity came to Greenwood/Elk once again.

Elk/Greenwood Lodging

Listings are organized from the most expensive to the least expensive

☆ HARBOR HOUSE INN $325–475

5600 S. Hwy One/Box 369
Elk 95432
877-3203/800-720-7474

www.harborhouseinn.com

Harbor House Inn, located in a spectacular setting and built entirely of virgin redwood in 1916, offers luxury lodging, discriminating dining and magnificent seaside gardens. All rooms and cottages have been refurbished with antiques and classical furnishings.Enjoy a walk down a wildflower edged path to a private beach or relax with a dramatic ocean view, hot beverage in hand.

10 rooms & cottages; full breakfast & dinner included; res. advisable; min. stay wknds, holidays;V/MC/AE/ checks; closed 1st 3 weeks of Dec; winter rates; adj. restaurant; fireplaces; bathtubs; ocean views; gardens

SEA ESCAPE/SEA ESCAPE TOO

$235–300
7400 & 7426 S.Hwy One/Box 337, Elk
877-3331/888-732-4677
www.seaescape-elk.com

Ocean front, blufftop home and suite south of Elk with the comforts of home.

2 lodgings; res.essential; 2 night min stay, 3-4 night holiday wknd; V/MC/checks; kitchen, phone, satellite tv, fireplace, hot tub in lodging; ocean view, gardens

☆ SANDPIPER HOUSE INN

$140–260
5520 S. Hwy One/Box 189, Elk
877-3587/800-894-9016

www.sandpiperhouse.com

Built in 1916 on a rugged bluff above the sea and tastefully furnished in European country style, the inn offers stunning ocean views over perennial gardens and private beach access. Guest rooms are beautifully appointed with antiques and comfortable furnishings, each one a special private retreat.

5 rooms; full breakfast, wine & hors d'oeuvres at 5; res. advisable; min. stay 2 nights wknds, 3 nights most holidays; MC/V/AE/checks; weekday and winter rates; sitting areas; fireplaces; bathtubs; guest phone in living room

☆ GREENWOOD PIER INN

$130–300
5926 S. Hwy One, Elk
877-9997

www.greenwoodpierinn.com

Ocean bluff cabins, rooms and suites in a colorful garden setting with many artistic touches. Adjacent to state park with large beach — beauty abounds! A place for ceremonies and celebrations.

14 rooms; continental breakfast; res. advisable; min. stay 2 nights wknds, 3 nights holidays; V/MC/AE;

smoking ok on decks; winter mid-week rates; adj. restaurant; hot tub; suites available; ocean views; fireplaces/wood stoves, bathtubs, refrig in rms; gardens; microwaves in some rms; jacuzzi & decks most rms; adj. to hiking; children, pets welcome; &

ELK COVE INN $100–350
6300 S. Hwy One/Box 367,
Elk 95432
877-3321/800-275-2967
www.elkcoveinn.com

Nestled in peaceful seclusion atop a bluff overlooking a mile of dramatic beachfront, the inn's Victorian mansion was built in 1883 as an executive guest retreat for the White Lumber Co. Enjoy refined relaxation in a romantic setting surrounded by native trees, a creek and the ocean.

15 rooms; full gourmet breakfast; 4 1-BR suites w/ spa tubs, fireplaces, balconies; res. advisable; min. stay 2 nights wknds; MC/V/AE/Disc/checks; ocean views; bathtubs; gardens; phone in lobby; port & chocolates in rooms; adj. to hiking

GRIFFIN HOUSE $98–200
5910 S. Hwy One/Box 190, Elk
877-3422

This cozy, informal bed and breakfast inn offers seven cottages, three with spectacular views of Greenwood Cove. A hearty breakfast is delivered to the cottage door each morning. Cottages and main house (now Bridget Dolan's Pub, dinner nightly) were built between 1890 and 1920.

7 cottages; full breakfast; res. advisable; V/MC/AE/Disc/checks; seasonal rates; suite; some cottages w/ parlor; adj. restaurant; ocean views; wood stoves; bathtubs; gardens; adj. to hiking; tv in pub next door; limited &

ELK GUEST HOUSE $75–300
1990 Hwy One, Elk
877-3308
www.elkguesthouse.com

Situated on 60 acres of whitewater ocean front bluffs, all rooms offer spectacular ocean views, feather beds, and fireplaces. Casual and secluded, with a private blufftop hot tub.

Two guest houses, 1 guest room; fully equipped kitchen in houses; res. advisable; min. stay holiday wknds; checks; smoking on decks; reduced winter rates; pets ok; private hot tub; ocean views; fireplaces; wood stoves; gardens; gymnasium; river canoes & kayaks; private beach; families welcome

Eateries

☆ **HARBOR HOUSE**
5600 Hwy 1, Elk
877-3203
B: $12 prix fixe, D: $45 prix fixe

Incomparable ocean view dining. Fresh California cuisine prepared daily, offered in a four course menu that changes nightly. Wine Sectator Award of Excellence. Excellent wine and beer list.

Daily; closed 1st 3 weeks of Dec; res. essential; V/MC/AE/checks; seats 30

☆ **GREENWOOD PIER CAFE**
5926 S. Hwy One, Elk
877-9992
B/WB/L: $8-12, D: $15–22

A pan-Pacific approach to creative cookery, specializing in seafood and garden-grown salads and herbs. Tables look out to gardens and beyond to the sea.

Summer: brkfst & lunch daily, dinner Wed-Sun; winter: brkfst & lunch Sat, Sun, Tues-Thur, dinner wkends only; res. advisable; V/MC/AE/checks; beer/ wine; seats 30; take-out; &

☆ BRIDGET DOLAN'S

5910 S. Hwy One, Elk 95432
877-1820
$7–20

A traditional village pub, welcoming families and animated conversation. Full pub menu most nights using only the freshest ingredients available. Great food, friendly folks, fair prices. *Daily at 5 pm; res. advisable; MC/V/AE/Disc/ checks; beer/wine; seats 21; take-out; &*

QUEENIE'S ROADHOUSE CAFE

6061 S. Hwy One/Box 73
Elk
877-3285
B/WB: $5–10, L: $6–10

Serving breakfast all day. For lunch, dine indoors or out with fabulous ocean view. Menu features organic food with vegan, vegetarian, or good ol' bacon 'n' eggs Mendocino. Microbrew beer and local wines. *Thur–Mon 8–3; closed Jan 5-Feb 13; MC/AE/V/ checks; beer/wine; seats 40; take-out; &*

ELK STORE

6101 S. Hwy One, Elk
877-3411

Country grocery store with a full service deli and extensive selection of gourmet cheeses. Local organic produce in season. *Daily 8–6, till 7 pm summer wknds; checks; local beer/wine*

Outdoor Activities

GREENWOOD STATE BEACH

provides spectacular short walks along the headlands or down to a breathtaking beach, the site of early Greenwood's largest sawmill. Low tide there reveals excellent tide pools.

FORCE TEN 877-3505, Box 262, Elk 95432, offers ocean kayak tours for beginners to advanced, lessons in ocean safety and survival. (Elk is home to some of the most renowned sea kayakers around, the Tsunami Rangers—not affiliated with Force Ten—who prefer kayaking in big storms when the ocean is raging.)

Indoor Activities

ELK/GREENWOOD STATE BEACH VISITOR CENTER is located in the historic post office building. Sat 10–1, Sun 10–12.

Greenwood Pier Country Store and Garden Store 877-3440, 5928 Hwy One, offer a wild range of goods spiced with flavors and colors of local artists and artisans: clothing, jewelry, toys, music, books, candy, plants and much more. Why go to a mall?

Erna's Enchanted Cottage, 877-1618, 6141 Hwy One. Browse their eclectic mix of local arts and crafts, antiques and books for sale. Daily 10-5, &

Judith Hale sells art from her studio/home by appointment, 877-3404.

Ross Ranch, 877-1834 Private horseback riding on Manchester Beach and in the Elk mountains.

Massage

Rosemarie Acker 877-3474. Massage and acupressure by appointment.

Donna Call, The Body Works 877-3430. Therapeutic massage and herbal facials by appointment. Donna serves the coast from Sea Ranch to Fort Bragg, plus Anderson Valley.

4. ELK TO ALBION
9 MILES

THE ROUTE

THIS SHORT STRETCH OF THE ROMANTIC ROAD offers a winding route along a magnificent shoreline of tall cliffs and sea stacks, one of the most spectacular sections on the entire coast. This rugged landscape will likely remain unspoiled since three parcels encompass nearly all the land here. Many of the weathered old ranch buildings remain unpainted and 1000 acres of these glorious hills have recently been deposited in the Sonoma Land Trust.

As wild and lonely as the coast north of Elk is, you can soon be in the heart of local commerce. Fort Bragg is only 27 miles distant, Mendocino just 15 miles. Enjoy the lovely coast here before the traffic doubles when you hit the Highway 128 junction only six miles ahead.

THE DRIVE

As you head north out of Elk, the western end of Greenwood Ridge towers a thousand feet above the coastal terraces. Farms, ranches and homesteads put the few acres of level land on the terraces to good use. Within a mile the land steepens and level ground becomes the exception rather than the rule. As you cross Laurel Gulch the many offshore rocks and sea stacks between Elk and Cuffeys Cove break the glistening surface of the Pacific below.

During the 1880s a shingle mill operated at the head of Laurel Gulch. When a sign reading "No Irish need apply" was hung at the entrance, some leprechaun scrawled beneath it, "You will find the same sign on the Gates of Hell."

Cuffeys Cove was the first non-native settlement north of Fort Ross, beginning before Elk/Greenwood, Gualala or Mendocino.

Cuffeys Cove c.1885

Frank Farnier and Nathaniel Smith were already operating a farm here when Jerome Ford stopped by in spring 1852. Ford was driving oxen and mules north to Big River to be used in the new logging operation soon to be developed there. This rough-and-tumble era was a time of prejudice and bigotry, and Farnier and Smith were more often called Portuguese Frank and Nigger Nat because of their origins. In fact the most plausible story of the naming of the settlement stems from Nat's ethnicity. It seems a New England whaling ship put in at the cove for food and water. When several Australian members of the ship's crew came ashore and found Nat in charge of the homestead, they called the place Cuffey's, the common Australian slang for a black person. Nat often joked that he and Frank were the first white men on the coast.

How the pair landed along this wild coast is uncertain. Frank claimed to have seen the north coast from a whaling ship in 1822. (Nat, who was Frank's companion for many years, said Frank was the biggest liar he ever knew.) Frank said he left the ship and joined the Mexican Army, which sent his troop to Pomo country, where he deserted and went to live with the natives. So Frank and Nat may have walked to the coast with the Pomo, or they may have come alone. They may have settled at Cuffeys Cove on their own or they might have been encouraged by Captain William Richardson, who received a Mexican land grant to the land in 1844. One source places Farnier at the cove in the late 1830s or early 1840s, but information is scarce and subject to dispute.

We do know that Frank Farnier lived in three centuries. Born in 1799, Frank died in 1905 at his home eight miles east of Mendocino, where he ran a saloon for 40 years. For more about Nathaniel Smith, read the history of the town of Mendocino.

The homesteaders soon sold out to empire builders. One of them, James Kenney, built a three-chute landing at Cuffeys Cove around 1868, used to ship split timber and red potatoes. Later John Kimball, Lorenzo White's brother-in-law, built schooners and barges here. Violence was reportedly common and life cheap in the town's heyday. They say death sometimes visited every night. The town's post office opened in 1870, but closed in 1888.

Cuffeys Cove prospered until White built the big mill at Greenwood. Then activities suddenly shifted south. The school and livery stable moved to

Frank Farnier in his saloon

Greenwood in 1890. Fires struck in 1886 and 1892, accelerating the town's demise. By the time the last fire struck in 1911, mostly abandoned buildings were destroyed.

Today the town site of Cuffeys Cove offers only two well-kept cemeteries, on the highway's left shoulder at the 35.6 milepost. They are worth a stop since there are so very few good places to pull out and admire the coast along this treacherous span of highway. If you stop, pull fully off the road and use extreme caution crossing the road.

The Shoreline Highway winds north through wooded Sartori Gulch, crosses a terrace with stunning views seaward, then dips through Cavanaugh Gulch. The coast road twists tightly as it climbs Cavanaugh Grade along the top of precipitous cliffs. At the top of the grade, the Pacific churns 300 feet directly below.

After winding across two forks of an unnamed creek, Highway One straightens briefly across a narrow coastal terrace. You cross another creek where it plunges 200 feet into the ocean on your left. If passengers keep their eye on the ocean side of the road, they might catch a glimpse of Devil's Basin at milepost 37.89. This mind boggling natural feature is a decadent (meaning no longer active) blowhole of gargantuan proportions. Its north wall rises 240 feet from the sea, its south wall 150 feet. The ocean churns furiously at the bottom of this immense pit, though you will not see it from the road. Ocean spray often streaks the windshields of passing cars. Private property prevents a closer look.

The Coast Highway dances along the edge of cliffs studded with breathtaking views seaward, soon crossing another creek. If you'd like to stop and savor this rugged landscape for an extra day or two, look on your left for a tiny 3-unit lodging situated at the old Dearing ranch, **ELK GUEST HOUSE** (see Elk Listings).

Shoreline Highway straightens out to pass Saddle Point, then climbs over one more hill as it approaches the mouth of the Navarro River. The steep Navarro Bluffs are directly left of the road, with a few homes clinging tenaciously to their top edge. Navarro Head juts out to sea beyond the river mouth.

Highway One bends to the right and descends to the Navarro River. Just before the river bridge, a road on the left provides access to **NAVARRO RIVER STATE BEACH**. The ¾-mile access road leads past now

Navarro c.1899

closed Navarro-by-the-Sea resort and comes to a broad, wild beach at the mouth of the river. Navarro Beach can be a placid place of sparkling beauty or a windswept, storm-flooded strand depending on the weather and season. Recently acquired by the state, the beach offers picnicking, primitive camping, a pit toilet, beach walking and a short but dramatic trail climbing along the pre-1960 version of the Shoreline Highway.

The word Navarro was probably a Spanish rendering of the Central Pomo name for this place. The northern limit of Central Pomo territory was marked by Navarro Ridge, which towers over the last mile of the river. The town of Navarro was built around the sawmill here in the early 1860s. Another part of the town grew up on Navarro Ridge, where two hotels put up visitors as early as 1860.

Navarro suffered through the boom-and-bust cycle of most north coast settlements. Smeaton Chase found the setting "beautiful — a deep valley with a wide, winding river; the eucalyptus trees and dracaena palms in the gardens showed the owners' expectations of remaining." But the only visible residents Chase found were a few pigs and chickens. "Most of the buildings were out of plumb; the church leaned at an alarming angle; a loon swimming leisurely in

No Offshore Oil!

Imagine, as you travel north on Highway One, looking out over the Pacific and seeing ten oil drilling platforms. That's what Big Oil wants and the U.S. Department of Interior has proposed in Lease Sale #53, currently on hold thanks to intense public opposition. But as long as our society is dependent on oil or until a permanent ocean sanctuary is established here, the danger of oil development on the pristine Mendocino Coast remains a threat.

If you think offshore oil isn't a bad trade off for unlimited use of the family car, imagine further, as you pass scenic north coast hamlets, onshore service bases with 30 acres of tanks, pipes, towers, buildings and pavement blotching the landscape. Consider the visual effect of pipeline right-of-ways paralleling the road and spanning the canyons, walls of concrete riprap disrupting sweeping sets of surf.

Ponder dozens of helicopter flights daily shuttling supplies and crews between land and platforms. But worst of all, imagine a major oil spill devastating abundant coastal marine life, clogging estuaries

the middle of the stream seemed to certify the solitude of the place."

The resort Navarro-by-the-Sea prospered here during the 1950s, but faded to oblivion again when the lodge closed. The beach became a place of controversy in the 1970s, then again in the 1990s.

Until 1994 Navarro Beach was known as the last free beach in California, a place where one could camp or live without paying a fee. But county officials, who had long managed the beach, grew short of maintenance funds and patience as the free beach attracted more and more impoverished people living in broken down campers and trailers. The county gave the beach to the State Parks Department, who agreed to evict the homeless. The eviction process dragged on, with emotions raging on all sides. Finally the community found places for some of the squatters to live and encouraged others to move on. While you can still camp here, each of the 10 sites now costs $5 a night. You'll have to move on after the two-week limit. Day use is still free.

Another controversy centered around Navarro Beach about thirty years ago. A new owner acquired Navarro-by-the-Sea resort in 1970, then tried to block public access through his property. The Sierra Club filed suit to keep the beach open, resulting in a landmark decision by the California Supreme Court. The court ordered the beach opened, ruling that, since the road had been open to the public for more than five years, "implied dedication" had established the route as public access.

The owner was still trying to regulate who used the beach in 1973. The sign at the parking lot read:

Casual attire is acceptable provided it is clean. Bare feet, patches, torn undershirts, faded clothing and untidy appearance NOT ACCEPTABLE.

No bare feet allowed on the beach? This story offers more than meets the eye, as is often the case with local politics.

When the utopian dreams of the hippie community in San Francisco's Haight-Ashbury came crashing down in a haze of drug abuse and crime after 1967's "Summer of Love," many counter-culture city residents began an exodus to the quiet, unpopulated and affordable life along the north coast. New left politicos and war resisters were attracted to the coast too. Some of the immigrants came with enough money to buy the cheap land then available. Others came only with bedroll and backpack. In those days many a new arrival to the Mendocino Coast spent their first winter camping in a "stump house" — plastic or boards thrown across the top of a goose pen redwood stump — along the Navarro River and elsewhere.

Some old-timers saw these long-haired immigrants in tie-dyed and tattered clothing as undesirable aliens, taking any

and beaches with tarry goo, reducing bird populations and wreaking mayhem on this enthralling shoreline.

In 1988 thousands of coast residents testified for two days before a Department of Interior panel in Fort Bragg, voicing their opposition to oil development through anger, tears, humor, song, poetry and dance, bringing the attention of national media and politicians to this quiet area. Rachel Binah, owner of Rachel's Inn at Little River, who spearheaded the opposition, proposed a National Ocean Sanctuary to protect the unspoiled coast from oil and other industrial threats.

In 1989 Congress established the permanent Cordell Bank National Marine Sanctuary off the Sonoma/Marin coast. In 1992 protection was won for California's central coast in the Monterey Bay National Marine Sanctuary. But Congress has failed as of this writing to provide permanent protection for the Mendocino Coast.

Big Oil wants the Mendocino Coast. If, after spending some time here, you'd prefer we all owned it and kept it safe, get an Ocean Sanctuary or No Offshore Oil! bumper sticker for your car. And when you get home, tell your elected representatives how you feel about oil development on the Mendocino Coast!

step possible to keep them out. While many urban dropouts moved on or returned to the city, many more found a way to stay.

The test of time proved that many of these counterculture people fit very well into the independent, self-sufficient lifestyle for which Mendocino County residents were known. The new arrivals became fishermen, shop keepers, teachers, journalists, even loggers; they established theater companies and inns, fought for political power, built houses (some to code and some not), bore and raised children, fought for better schools. In short they lived their dreams and made their compromises, but they found in Mendocino County a land where they could survive, a land that made their hearts sing.

While far from everyone who settled here in the late '60s and early '70s considered themselves hippies (the term has little meaning today anyway), most everyone came seeking refuge from the rat race, bringing high ideals and expectations about what country life offered.

Highway One crosses the Navarro River on a sturdy bridge and comes to a stop sign as it meets Highway 128, a main route from the Bay Area (see Chapter 9). Expect traffic to double at the junction.

The Shoreline Highway twists up a steep hill with breathtaking views of the river at its mouth. Round the next bend to overlook the promontory called Navarro Head, now owned by the Mendocino Land Trust, with the spectacular coast sweeping north beyond.

Navarro Ridge Road on your right offers a lodging perfect for travelers seeking a dramatic setting in a secluded atmosphere, yet only a five or 15 minute drive to shops and restaurants: **FENSALDEN INN**, built around 1860 as the Navarro Ridge Inn, was an important stage stop and transfer point. (See Albion Listings.)

Shoreline Highway sweeps down a hill and blasts across Salmon Creek where the stream empties into Whitesboro Cove, site of the village of Whitesboro.

Whitesboro was an early enterprise of Greenwood's Lorenzo White, who built the mill here before 1880. Nothing remains of that tiny town's business district along the creek, though the Whitesboro Grange up Navarro Ridge recalls the days of prosperity. When Smeaton Chase passed through Whitesboro in 1911, he noted "the two or three rickety shacks, the wreck of a wharf, the former store, now a dirty saloon with two profane old men loafing on the porch."

The Coast Highway climbs to a broad terrace at the base of Albion Ridge. Don't blink or gaze at the gorgeous coast line now. You might miss the village of Albion. Its low profile center is east of the highway. The post office and **ALBION GROCERY** are only 100 yards up Albion Ridge Road. Two private campgrounds and another inn lie across the bridge.

ALBION

(POP. 398, EL. 178)

MODERN ALBION, SOMETIMES REFERRED TO AS THE ALBION Nation in deference to the independent spirit of its residents, offers an eclectic mix of visitor facilities and local commerce in a setting distinguished by the deep canyon of the Albion River and the towering wooded ridges. As you roll into town from the south, look left for the **LEDFORD HOUSE** restaurant and bar. On the right Albion Ridge Road leads to the old part of town just up the road, where you will find a hardware store, post office and **ALBION GROCERY** 937-5784, featuring groceries, gas, delicatessen, sporting goods. Up the ridge are two fine specialty nurseries. **ALBION RIDGE NURSERY** 937-1835, specializes in collector rhododendrons, rambling roses, dwarf conifers and bonsai; open Thur, Sat & Sun or call for appointment. **DIGGING DOG NURSERY** 937-1130, features grasses, vines, trees, perennials and shrubs; open Monday through Saturday, call for directions.

The modern center of Albion perches on the high bluffs south of the Albion River. Residential neighborhoods stretch east along Albion Ridge, where several ranchers and farmers settled after 1870. Other portions of the little town lie north across the river bridge and down along the tidal flats of the river, where Albion first began and a small commercial fishing fleet operates today.

The Albion River bridge spans the steep canyon at the river's mouth. The historic bridge, constructed in 1944, crosses 120 feet above the placid river. Steel and reinforced concrete were unavailable during World War II, so the bridge was built of salvaged wood. This is the last wooden bridge remaining on the Shoreline Highway.

Immediately north of the bridge, look to the right for Albion River North Side Road, which leads down to the tidal flats beside the river

The Mystery of Sir Francis Drake

Was Francis Drake the first tourist to "discover" the Mendocino Coast, only to have history lose the record?

In 1579 Captain Drake and crew, midway through their piratical circumnavigation of the globe, steered their Golden Hind *into a foggy North Pacific cove surrounded by buff cliffs that reminded them of the White Cliffs of Dover. They stayed five weeks at the place they dubbed Nova Albion, repairing and supplying the ship and getting along famously with the natives.*

Speculation on where Drake put ashore hinges on four known factors: his reading the latitude as 38 degrees, 30 minutes, the white cliffs, a rough wooden fort they built, and the native people they described.

The stated latitude lies on the Sonoma Coast where Russians built Fort Ross 250 years later. The light cliffs and natives there fit the descriptions, but extensive archaeological digs have found no sixteenth century structure. By allowing Drake an error of 1½ degrees in his latitude calculations, his harbor could be anywhere from Santa Cruz to the northern Mendocino Coast.

Theories that the landing was at Drake's Bay near Point Reyes hinged on a brass plate found there in 1933 bearing Drake's name, but the relic eventually

where you will find a small harbor, **ALBION RIVER CAMPGROUND** and **SCHOONER'S LANDING**.

Just north along the Shoreline Highway, try not to be distracted by the llamas grazing on the right lest you miss **ALBION RIVER INN**, lodging, restaurant and bar.

History

In 1835 English sea captain William Richardson erected the first building at San Francisco (then known as Yerba Buena). He later climbed the social ladder by marrying the daughter of the Mexican Commandant of Yerba Buena. In 1845 the Mexicans awarded Richardson a land grant covering the vast territory between the Mal Paso Creek and Big River.

Richardson called the place Albion after his English homeland, having a house and sawmill built by 1853. His first mill, on the river's estuary, was powered by a tide-driven water wheel. This clever design allowed the mill to operate whenever the tide was changing. Immense waves destroyed the mill in the winter of 1853. Richardson rebuilt the mill as a steam operation, then lost the land in 1854 because his grant was never recognized by the U.S. Land Commission.

New owners modernized the sawmill in 1854. By 1861 the growing town had a hotel, livery stable and mercantile near the mill. Workers lived in cabins on the crowded river flats. When the second mill burned in 1867, it was promptly replaced with a larger, better equipped mill. As the town outgrew the crowded river flats, neighborhoods marched up Michigan Hill to the north and Snob Hill to the south, vying for dominance. In 1879 the worst fire of all consumed the sawmill and ten other buildings. Once again the mill and town were rebuilt.

In 1889 a 1200-foot wharf reached out to deep water in the rocky harbor. Miles Standish (a direct descendent of the pilgrim of the same name) and Henry Hickey bought the lumber company in 1891. When another fire razed the fourth mill and most of the town in 1900, Albion rebuilt yet again. Southern Pacific Railroad bought the Albion operation in 1907 to provide wood for railroads they were building in Mexico. They expanded the small logging railway around Albion,

proved false. Another find at Bolinas supported Drake's landing in that spot. Light cliffs occur throughout the north coast, keeping the potential sites numerous.

While anthropologist Alfred Kroeber identified the natives Drake met as Coast Miwok, the presumed Marin site in Kroeber's day was Miwok turf. Kroeber further analyzed the people described as being like the Pomo.

At least one amateur archaeologist argues that Drake's "fit harbour" was at Albion, that remnants of the fort lie beneath a mound atop the high cliffs north of the Albion River's mouth. The native people fit the reports perfectly. The "stinking fogges" described by Drake could fit all the locations at low tide in summer and certainly don't exclude Albion. Is it possible that Englishman William Richardson, who received a land grant at Albion, was privy to some secret record of Drake's landing point?

The controversy rages on.

extending lines to Wendling and Christine in Anderson Valley, and up the Albion River to Keen's Summit, not far from Comptche.

When Smeaton Chase came through in 1911, he hoped to see a microcosm of his own English homeland. He found

> . . . *a fine little town, all buzzing and humming with life, steam whizzing, saws shrieking, locomotive bustling about with cars of lumber, trim schooner at wharf, men wiping perspiring brows, and everything thriving. Down at the river's mouth was a little purple bay, all a-glitter with wind and surf.*

The mill closed in 1928, the railroad shut down in 1930, and Albion's heyday passed into history. Albion survived as a farming and ranching community, with most residents living up on the ridges.

During the 1960s cheap land and the isolated location brought many urban refugees to the area. They coined the term Albion Nation to describe their independent and divergent lifestyles. Marijuana farming brought a new kind of prosperity briefly, but it soon collapsed in theft and violence, then heavy police surveillance. Feminist separatists and other communes revived some of the old farms and ranches, and many of their originators still live here today. In the '70s wildly successful (and successfully wild) Albion People's Fairs celebrated the cultural renaissance and *Country Women* magazine spread the gospel. Today these manifestations of Albion's cultural diversity have become history, but a healthy independent spirit endures.

Albion Lodging

Listings are organized from the most expensive to the least expensive

☆ ALBION RIVER INN $200–310
3790 N. Hwy One/Box 100
Albion 95410
937-1919/800-479-7944
www.albionriverinn.com

A small romantic inn on ten magnificent headland acres with unbeatable views. The gracioulsy appointed guest rooms and cottages have garden entrances, fireplaces, decks and private baths—many with whirlpool tubs. Amenities include full breakfast, newspaper, wine, coffee, robes and binoculars. The inn is private and welcoming, with adjacent, acclaimed restaurant and bar, and a staff dedicated to guests' comfort.

20 rooms; full breakfast in dining room; res. advisable; all major CCs/checks; coffee in room; some rooms private jacuzzi/hot tub; fireplace, refrig bathtub, binoculars, robes, phone in rooms; ocean views, gardens; &

☆ FENSALDEN INN $125–225
33810 Navarro Ridge Rd/Box 99
Albion
937-4042/800-959-3850
www.fensalden.com

Overlooking the Pacific Ocean from twenty pastoral acres, the inn offers a quiet getaway in an 1850s Wells Fargo stagecoach stop. Eight guest quarters include fireplace, queen beds, private baths, evening wine & hors d'oeuvres. Two units with kitchens, bungalow has Jacuzzi tub.

8 rooms; full breakfast; min. stay 2 nights wknds, 3 nights holidays; MC/V/checks; winter rates; fireplace, bathtub in room; 2 suites, 1 bungalow; kitchens in suite and bungalow; evening wine & hors d'ouevres; ocean views, gardens; adj. to hiking; &

Eateries

☆ALBION RIVER INN
3790 N. Hwy One/Box 100
Albion
937-1919
$16–26

Chef Stephen's cuisine features fresh seafood and sparkles with bright Asian and Mediterranean flavors. The setting is understated and romantic, with ocean views, fireplace and bar. Award-winning wine and spirits lists.

Daily 5:30–9, from 5 on Sat, Sun; res. advisable; all major CCs/checks; full bar; seats 85; &

☆ LEDFORD HOUSE
3000 N. Hwy One/Box 688
Albion
937-0282
$8–28

The restaurant reflects the Provençal style of southern France in a warm and welcoming atmosphere with a casual elegance, both comfortable and sophisticated. Expansive windows allow panoramic views of the Pacific to become part of the elegant decor of the two dining rooms. Exquisitely prepared dishes have a strong Mediterranean influence with subtle drawings on Asian and Latin flavors grounded by a California style. *Wed–Sun 5–9 pm; closed mid-February to mid-March; res. advisable; MC/V/AE/Disc/Diner's/ checks; full bar; seats 90; take-out;* ⅋

Campgrounds

SCHOONER'S LANDING
937-5707, Albion River and Hwy One, has 41 sites with hookups and hot showers. $24–29.

ALBION RIVER CAMPGROUND
937-0606, Albion River & Hwy One, has 100 sites with hookups, hot showers and boat launching. $20–28. ⅋

Indoor Activities

Massage

Christine Berchen 937-4835, by appointment.

5. ALBION TO MENDOCINO
8 MILES

THE ROUTE

RAFFIC INCREASES AS THE SHORELINE Highway plies the residential section of coast north of Albion. The relatively short distance passes quickly despite the traffic and restricted speeds. If you stop and take time to look you will find a coastline of enthralling beauty, more populated but every bit as beautiful as Smeaton Chase described it in 1911:

> *The piece of coast between Albion and the next place, Little River, seemed to me almost the finest I had seen. Such headlands, black and wooded, such purple seas, such vivid blaze of spray, such fiords and islets — a painter would be ravished with it.*

THE DRIVE

As you head north from Albion, Highway One traverses a grassy marine terrace offering brief glimpses of the headlands around Albion Head to the west. The coast road veers right and winds through Dark Gulch, where the pavement may be slippery or icy in winter. As you climb out of the gulch, watch on the left for the historic **HERITAGE HOUSE INN AND RESTAURANT** (see Little River Listings). Even if you are not staying there, consider stopping for a meal or a drink just to see the marvelous 37-acre grounds, with cottages cascading down lushly vegetated slopes to the purple sea. Heritage House also offers their **INN STORE.**

James Pullen settled his family here in 1877, building his first home with a sod roof on this spectacular site beside tiny Smith Creek. He operated a mill eight miles upstream from Whitesboro. His family could be found in logging operations from Mendocino to Greenwood. After Prohibition brought rum runners to the Mendocino Coast, the notorious Chicago gangster "Baby Face" Nelson hid from Eliot Ness's G-Men at this location. When World War II broke out, a colony of Japanese abalone divers lived in shanties at Dark Gulch until a couple of Albion rowdies came and shot up the camp. The Japanese divers were gone the next morning.

Heritage House became an inn in 1949, when Lauren Dennen, whose grandfather had helped build James Pullen's house, acquired the property and began to improve it. In 1978 Hollywood filmed Alan Alda and Ellen Burstyn here in *Same Time Next Year.* They returned in 1994 to film the sequel.

Highway One winds through tall Bishop pine forest above the ragged cliffs of Stillwell Point, which tower 200 feet above the crashing breakers. As you descend to cross Buckhorn and Schoolhouse creeks, a string of inns and bed-and-breakfasts lines the east side of the road.

At Buckhorn Creek, known as Stillwell Creek at the time, Silas Coombs operated a sawmill around 1880. A railway carried the cut lumber north to a loading chute at Little River Bay.

Shoreline Highway roughly follows the rail route, climbing a hill into the tiny historic village called Little River. At the top of the hill the old Little River Cemetery is on the left.

On the right is Little River-Airport Road. It climbs east two miles to

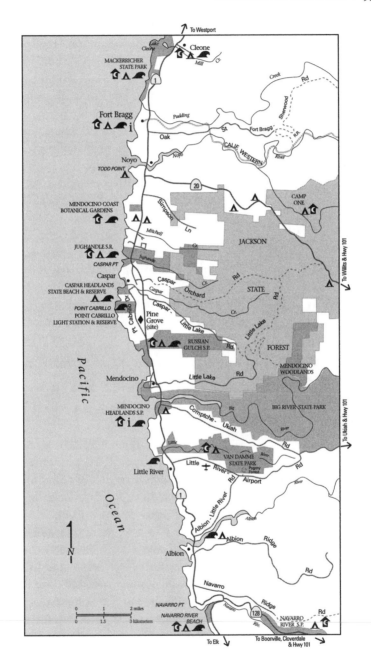

"Thar She Blows!"

No place in California provides better whale watching than the Mendocino Coast. If you visit between December and May, you'll have excellent chances to see some of the 18,000 California gray whales that swim the entire west coast each year. In summer or autumn, you might get lucky and spot humpback whales or harbor porpoises swimming or breeding offshore.

Unlike other whales, grays migrate in sight of land, giving you a great chance to observe their 12,000-mile round trip between Alaska's Bering Sea and Baja California. The gray whales, led by pregnant mothers, first appear off Mendocino in mid-December, continuing their trek south into February. They travel about five miles an hour up to twenty hours a day, cruising a mile or two offshore.

Grays return north in March. Mothers with young calves (1500 pounds at birth!) dawdle along as late as July. The northern trekkers minimize current drag by swimming just beyond the forming breakers.

California's official marine mammals usually travel in pods of three to eight, although some prefer to cruise solo. An average gray weighs 30 tons and is 40 feet long, with a life span similar to ours. They've been making their annual trek for around five million years. Their ancestors once lived on land, turning to the

MENDOCINO COUNTY AIRPORT 937-5129, where charter flights and car rentals are available. Also at the airport, **COAST FLYERS** 937-1224, provide commercial flight services from 30-minute tours to whale watching, photo tours, custom tours, charter services and flight instruction. Price based on number of people and type of plane. Car rentals and lodging too.

Also up Little River-Airport Road is the wheelchair-accessible **PYGMY FOREST TRAIL** of Van Damme State Park. Go 2.85 miles to the signed trailhead on the left. The ¼-mile boardwalk loop tours a prime example of this enchanting forest, dwarfed by nutrient-depleted, acidic hardpan soils. A longer, moderately steep trail descends into Fern Canyon in the eastern heart of the state park.

LITTLE RIVER
(POP. 412, EL. 90)

*B*EYOND THE INTERSECTION WITH Little River-Airport Road you come into the center of Little River. In 1911 Smeaton Chase found Little River "a pretty, straggling village of high gabled houses with quaint dormers and windows, and red roses clambering all about." Today's town is much the same, though probably sleepier than in its heyday. The town's commercial establishments still straggle along about two miles of the coast road, from Heritage House on the south to Stevenswood Lodge on the north. Today's town is mostly inns, B & B's and restaurants.

In the commercial center look left for the tiny, well stocked **LITTLE RIVER MARKET**, groceries, deli, wine, gas. The post office next door hides a tiny treasure behind it, **EDGE OF THE EARTH RESTAURANT**.

LITTLE RIVER INN, across the street, built 1864 as the home of early settler Silas Coombs, offers a busy bar and restaurant along with lodging on its historic grounds. The Inn has seen many famous faces since opening its doors to travelers in 1939. Jane Wyman tended bar here one evening while filming *Johnny Belinda*. Ronald Reagan, her husband at the time, sat quietly at the bar. The Inn also offers **LITTLE RIVER GOLF & TENNIS CLUB** 937-5667, open to the public.

The Shoreline Highway drops nearly to sea level to cross the truly tiny Little River for which the town is named. If Little River has another center it is lovely **VAN DAMME STATE PARK**, named for Charles Van Damme, a lumberman born here in 1880. He bought 40 acres along the river from Silas Coombs, then willed the site, the nucleus of today's park, to the state in 1930.

sea around 30 million years ago.

Humpback whales also migrate off California's coast, but mostly stay far from shore. While spotting humpbacks from land is unpredictable, they come closest to local shores during summer or autumn feeding. Sometimes humpbacks breed along the north coast, a rare sight to see from land. Harbor porpoises, much smaller cetaceans, sometimes visit Mendocino Bay in summer.

You're most likely to spot the whale by its spout or blow, the misty exhalation from the blowhole atop its head. Grays and humpbacks blow steam six to 15 feet high. You might hear the "whoosh" of exhalation from a half mile away.

Whales typically blow three to eight times at 10- to 30-second intervals, then take a deep dive, or sound, flipping the fluke (tail) on the way down. A normal dive lasts about four minutes, reaching depths of 120 feet.

Your best whale watching occurs when the ocean is calm before winds and waves pick up, often in the morning. Binoculars enhance viewing, but when whales are there you can see them with the naked eye. To watch from shore, find a point jutting out to sea. If you are visiting during prime whale season, consider taking a whale watching boat from Fort Bragg's Noyo Harbor.

History

Prosperity came to Little River with the first sawmill in 1864. Even before then the little bay was known and used as one of the safest harbors on the Mendocino Coast. When a ship anchored offshore, its cargo was unloaded by lighters, small rowboats that landed right on the beach. Soon split redwood products (railroad ties, fence posts and shakes) were loaded by a roughly constructed apron chute that descended from the headland at the south end of the beach.

Silas Coombs and his brother-in-law, Ruel Stickney, came from Maine, arriving in Albion in 1856. Their families followed in 1864 and 1859, respectively. With a third partner, Coombs and Stickney built Little River's first sawmill on the river near the group campground of today's park. By 1866 the mill sat on the bank of a large mill pond which occupied most of today's campground area. A rickety wharf built before 1870 was removed by a few seasons of winter surf. It was replaced by a sturdy, longer wharf just north of the river's mouth.

Little River — First dam and bridge c. 1866

The new wharf allowed ships to dock alongside, expediting the loading and unloading of goods. This proved to be a boon to the town's prosperity. The wharf offered such reliable loading that goods were transported

Peterson's ship building yard c.1870s

from as far away as Point Arena and Westport, where ships were loaded by far more primitive means at the time. Ranchers near Westport drove their cattle down the rugged trail to Little River where the stock could be loaded directly on board schooners to be shipped to market. Competitors built other chutes on the north point west of the wharf and at the south end of the bay, but these loaded mostly ties.

Another link in the town's prosperity was forged when Danish ship builder Thomas Peterson opened a yard in 1869. Peterson's boat works were located on the north shore of the cove, between the wharf and the north chute. Peterson built 14 schooners at Little River between 1869 and 1879, and more than 20 others at different locations.

Coombs and company built a larger and better mill in 1874, located on the mill pond's north shore, directly north of today's park entrance kiosk. This mill operated sporadically due to fluctuations in the timber market, and finally closed for lack of logs. Coombs bought out his partners in 1883. By the mid-1880s Coombs prosperity grew more from shipping than lumber. By 1893 local timber supplies were depleted. Coombs closed and dismantled the sawmill, then removed the dam and drained the mill pond. He died the next year.

According to one report the Little River Wharf remained until 1916, but the last ship loaded with freight sailed from port in 1902.

Little River Lodging

Listings are organized from the most expensive to the least expensive

STEVENSWOOD LODGE $150–250
8211 Hwy One, Little River 95456
Mail: Box 170, Mendocino 95460
937-2810/800-421-2810

www.stevenswood.com

A contemporary lodge, built in 1988, nestled in virgin forest adjacent to 2100-acre Van Damme State Park. Private and quiet, well off Highway One, with hiking directly off the grounds. Sculpture garden and art gallery.
10 rooms; full breakfast; closed 2 weeks in Dec; min. stay holidays; all major CCs/checks; AAA 4-diamond suites; winter discounts; ocean views; fireplaces; bathtubs; gardens; hot tub; phone/tv in room; refrigerators, wet bars, computer ports; adj restaurant;concierge services; ⅃

☆ HERITAGE HOUSE $135–500
5200 N. Hwy One
Little River
937-5885/800-235-5885

www.heritagehouseinn.com

Located high on the bluffs overlooking the spectacular Pacific Ocean, with guest cottages scattered over 37 acres, this is truly a place to unwind. Rooms overlook a whitewater cove or have panoramic ocean views from private decks.
66 rooms; closed Dec & Jan; 2 night min. summer & fall wknds; V/MC/AE/checks; winter discounts; suites; some in-room jacuzzis; fireplaces; bathtubs; gardens; wet bars; adj to hiking; adj restaurant; concierge services; retail shop; ⅃

☆ RACHEL'S INN $135–285
8200 N. Hwy One, Little River
Mail: Box 134, Mendocino

937-0088/800-342-9252

www.rachelsinn.com

Surrounded by informal gardens, meadows and trees a few hundred yards from the ocean, the inn offers comfort with style in an 1860s main house and contemporary "barn." Surrounded on two sides by Van Damme State Park, where trails lead to the beach or to bluffs overlooking the ocean.
9 rooms, 2 cottages; full breakfast; res. advisable; min stay wknds, holidays; winter disc; V/MC/checks; suites; coffee maker/refrigerator in suites; children ok some rms; ocean views; fireplaces; bathtubs; computer port; gardens; adj. to hiking; ⅃

☆ BLANCHARD HOUSE $159–189
8141 Pacific Coast Hwy/Box 521
Little River
937-1627
www.blanchardhouse.com

This country Victorian nestles on a hillside overlooking the ocean. Spacious accommodations include king-size bed, private bath with clawfoot tub/tiled shower, and refrigerator. Ultimate privacy with outside entrance and ocean view balcony; fragrant flower gardens. Bordering Van Damme State Park, walk to beach.
1 suite; full country breakfast; res. essential; min. stay 2 nights wknds, 3 nights holidays; V/MC/checks; winter & midweek rates; babies ok; gardens; phone/cable tv/refrig/bathtub/computer port in suite

☆ GLENDEVEN INN $135–235
8205 N. Hwy One, Little River
Mail: Box 914, Mendocino
937-0083/800-822-4536

www.glendeven.com

This 1867 farm complex houses an intimate bed & breakfast inn surrounded by lovely gardens, fields, forests, bay views and nature reserves. The inn offers fireplaces, private baths and a wonderful staff.

10 rooms; full breakfast; res. advisable; min. stay 2 nights wknds; V/MC/AE/Disc/checks; off-season rates; ocean views; fireplaces; art gallery; adj to hiking &

DENNEN'S VICTORIAN FARMHOUSE B & B $125–200
7001 N. Hwy One,
Little River 95456
Mail: Box 357, Mendocino 95460
937-0697/800-264-4723
www.victorianfarmhouse.com

Victorian home, built 1877 and painted by Thomas Kinkade, furnished in period antiques, feather beds, luxury linens. Located on 2 acres with gardens and a year-round creek, across highway from the ocean.

9 rooms, 2 suites, 1 cottage; full gourmet breakfast; res. advisable; min. stay wknds, holidays; V/MC/ AE/checks; winter disc; fireplaces, computer port; kitchen in 1 suite; some ocean views, bathtubs, hot tubs, refrig, tv; gardens; walk to beach; &

☆ LITTLE RIVER INN $110–310
7901 N. Hwy One/Drawer B
Little River
937-5942/888-INN LOVE
www.littleriverinn.com

This historic inn is a coast landmark overlooking a panoramic seascape. The classic country inn offers spectacular Pacific views, scrumptious meals, golf and tennis facilities, salon and day spa, and four generations of family hospitality. A memorable place to stay since 1939.

65 rooms; res. advisable; min. stay 2 nights wknds; V/MC/AE/checks; off-season disc; adj. restaurant/ lounge; some private jacuzzi; phone/tv/vcr, fireplace, refrig, bathtub in room; gardens; adj. to hiking; pro shop; &

☆ THE INN AT SCHOOLHOUSE CREEK $80–235
7051 N. Hwy One, Little River
937-5525

Ocean view rooms and cottages on ten acres, with forest, meadows, and spectacular gardens. Lovely lounge and game room in main house. The inn is quiet, comfortable and clean, with country-style decor. Walk to creek, ocean, and lush forest.

15 rooms; min. stay 2 nights wknds, 3 nights major holidays; V/MC/Disc/AE/checks; winter midweek disc.; pets, families welcome; 2-bdrm suites; cottages w/living rooms; kitchens in 4 cottages; fireplaces; bathtubs; &

SEAFOAM LODGE $110–225
6751 N. Hwy One, Little River
Mail: Box 68, Mendocino
937-1827/800-606-1827
www.seafoamlodge.com

Panoramic ocean views await from every private room. With a forested hillside providing the backdrop, the lodge perches on seven acres of coastal gardens and pines above picturesque Buckhorn Cove.

24 rooms; continental breakfast; V/MC/AE/checks; winter rates; 1 suite w/kitchen; some rooms w/ cooking facilities, fireplaces; children, pets welcome; phone/tv/vcr, refrig, computer port in room; beach access; Crow's Nest Conference Center; hot tub in enclosed gazebo

PACIFIC MIST BUNGALOWS $90–180
6051 N. Hwy One/Box 486
Little River
937-1543/800-955-MIST
www.pacificmistbungalows.com

Cottages are very private, each on an acre, and will sleep up to four, with queen beds in 2 BR, 2 bath units. Secluded spa tub in forest. Weekly discounts available. *5 cottages, 2 rooms; res. advisable; min. stay wknds; lower winter rates; families welcome; MC/V/checks; cottages w/kitchenettes; bathtubs; fireplaces; decks; gardens; phone/tv in room; hot tub*

FOOLS RUSH INN $59–89
7533 N. Hwy One/Box 387
Little River 95456
937-5339

www.foolsrushinn.com

Good value family-style accommodations include full kitchens. *9 cottages; res.advisable; families welcome; checks; ocean views; fireplaces; bathtubs; adj. to hiking; tv in room; ᕃ*

Eateries

STEVENSWOOD RESTAURANT
8211 Hwy One
Little River
937-2810
D $25-38

Award-Winning continental cuisine in a contemporary setting, served by a friendly professional staff. *Fri-Tues from 5:30pm, Thurs-Tues in Summer; closed 1st weeks/Dec; res. advisable; V/MC/AE/Disc/Diner's /checks; beer/wine; seats 40; ᕃ*

HERITAGE HOUSE
5200 N. Hwy One
Little River
937-5885/800-235-5885
WB:$7–15, B: $6–10, D: $18–30, Bar: $7–18

Three separate dining areas enable guests to gaze at the Pacific from nearly every table. Emphasis on fresh country cuisine using mostly local ingredients. Award-winning wine selection. Bar fare too. *Daily breakfast 8–11 am, dinner 6–8 pm, weekend brunch 8 am–1 pm; families welcome; closed Dec and Jan; res. advisable; V/MCAE; full bar; seats 100; ᕃ*

EDGE OF THE EARTH
7750 N. Hwy One (next to Little River Market), Little River
937-1970
D: $18-24

Organic vegetarian and seafood cuisine in an intimate restaurant offering a relaxed dining experience with oceanfront views. *Thur–Sun, 5-9 pm, res. advisable; V/MC/AE/Disc/checks; beer/wine; seats 24; take-out; ᕃ*

LITTLE RIVER INN RESTAURANT
7901 N. Hwy One
Little River
937-5942/888-INN-LOVE
WB: $8–12, B: $4–12, D: $18–22, Bar: $8–12

Enticing, freshly prepared fare in the warm friendly dining room surrounded by beautiful gardens. Ole's Whale Watch Bar serves cocktails and a bar menu worthy of its panoramic ocean view. *Breakfast daily from 7:30–10:30 am, 'til 12 on Sat, Sun; dinner from 6 pm, 'til 8:30 Sun-Thur, 'til 9 on Fri, Sat, ½ hour later during daylight savings; res. advisable; families welcome; MC/V/AE/checks; full bar; seats 75; ᕃ*

LITTLE RIVER MARKET
7746 N. Hwy One, Little River
937-5133
B: $2–5, L, D: $3–6

Their take-out delicatessen also has seating in the back with a great ocean view. Pre-made or custom made sandwiches, plus burritos, enchiladas, and much more.

Mon–Fri 7:30–7, Sat 8:30–7, Sun 8:30–6; MC/ V/AE; food/beer/wine to take out; seats 16; ⅋

Outdoor Activities

LITTLE RIVER GOLF & TENNIS CLUB 937-5667, a challenging and beautiful nine-hole golf course and two championship tennis courts.

VAN DAMME STATE PARK 937-5804, straddles Highway One where Little River empties into a protected, rocky bay popular with divers and kayakers. The surf here is usually calm enough to allow launching small boats and sea kayaks from the beach. Daytime parking and picnicking at the beach is free. At night it becomes overflow camping for the park. Most of the park's 2069 acres lie east of the highway, up verdant Fern Canyon. The park's 74 campsites offer mostly shady sites. A paved trail follows the Little River 2½ miles up the lovely canyon, connecting with a dirt path climbing to the pygmy forest. Among the park's best kept secrets are ten Environmental Camps beside the trail in the upper canyon, offering remote camping away from the roar of highway noise.

SEA KAYAKING from Little River Beach can be easy when the ocean is calm and the surf is low enough to launch. **LOST COAST KAYAKING** 937-2434, www.lostcoastkayaking.com rents kayaks and guides two-hour sea cave tours here in season.

Indoor Activities

Galleries and Shops

Partners Gallery at Glendeven 937-3525, 8221 Hwy One. Fine furniture, ceramics, paintings, handcrafted jewelry and fine prints.

Stevenswood Fine Arts 937-2810, 8211 Hwy One. A living gallery and sculpture garden, plus fine furniture and paintings.

Horsefeathers 962-2253, at Little River Inn. Antiques, turquoise jewelry, garden art and vintage button jewelry.

CONTINUING ON . . .

Coast Highway One climbs from the Little River by tight turns, then straightens out to pass another cluster of lodgings on its way to Mendocino. You ascend over a 200-foot rise in the coastal marine terrace on the short hop to Mendocino. Along the way you pass through the historic Spring Ranch where lettuce is still grown for local consumption. The ranch's large Victorian, built about 1869 by William Kent, sits on your right. The ranch's historic, beautiful barns and pastures on your left now belong to state parks, part of a 300-acre holding west of the highway.

To take a walk on pastoral park lands, turn left into the unmarked grass and dirt parking area opposite Gordon Lane at the top of the hill. A half-mile trail descends to the rocky ocean bluffs near Chapman Point. The short hike offers spectacular long-focus views of Mendocino across Mendocino Bay.

Highway One descends across Brewery Gulch where the elegant new **BREWERY GULCH INN** to sits on your right. Look for a **VISTA POINT** on the left. It offers a postcard look at Mendocino beyond the bay. Your highway rounds a bend and comes to a treacherous intersection. On the right is **COMPTCHE-UKIAH ROAD** (see CHAPTER 11. BACK ROADS), an early stage route between the county seat, Ukiah, and Mendocino. You turn here to reach several near destinations: **BIG RIVER LODGE/STANFORD INN BY THE SEA, CATCH-A-CANOE & BICYCLES TOO, MENDOCINO CAMPGROUND** and **MENDOCINO FARMHOUSE**, an inn (see Mendocino Listings).

Back on Highway One, as the romantic road crosses Big River on a gracefully curved bridge, the lovely spire of Mendocino's historic Presbyterian Church rises above the ever-shifting sands of Big River Beach. On the right you immediately pass Big River Beach Road, a short access way to the public beach along the lower river and the gated old haul road just beyond that explores the wild new 7334-acre Big River State Park. You can launch your own canoe or kayak here or walk or bike east almost eight miles along the tidal river. For the beach, head west along the river's edge and underneath the highway bridge to Big River Beach, popular for beachcombing, surfing, boogie-boarding or picnicking. The beach also boasts one of the few public volleyball spots on the north coast, but you might need to bring your own net and ball.

To enter the town of Mendocino, ascend the four-lane stretch of highway to the top of the hill, where Little Lake Road offers the safest of the three entrances to town thanks to the traffic light and controlled left turn lane there. Turn left and descend Little Lake to the stop sign at Lansing Street.

When you look left on Lansing, you'll see Mendocino's landmark Masonic Hall, with its graceful spired statue of Father Time and the Maiden towering above the breakers surging on Mendocino Bay. Welcome to Mendocino, Jewel of the North Coast!

MENDOCINO
(POP. 1008, EL. 90)

Jewel of the North Coast

*M*ENDOCINO'S APPEAL FOR THE CONTEMPORARY TRAVELER results from a serendipitous blend of its contemporary arts and culture with its natural scenic splendor and historic lumber town roots. The town perches atop a high bluff, surrounded on three sides by the wild Pacific Ocean punctuated by rugged offshore rocks, tiny coves and abundant sea tunnels. The east or fourth side offers a ragged forest skyline, a verdant backdrop bisected by the deep canyon of placid Big River. Add to this an ever-changing climate of swirling foggy mists, crystalline blue skies and raging winter storms that coax both natural flora and cultivated gardens into wondrous profusion of growth and colors, and the result is one of the most soul-stirring landscapes on earth.

E. L. Packard

Mendocino's dramatic natural setting was not what earned it the "Jewel of the North Coast" designation. After its founding in 1852, Mendocino City served for 30 years as the primary supplier of redwood lumber to booming California and as one of several main lumber sources through boom and bust times into the 1920s. Mendocino redwood built much of San Francisco, then rebuilt it after numerous fires and the Great Earthquake of 1906. Other Mendocino lumber became timbers for Sierra gold mines, ties for the burgeoning railroads of the west, and even went around the world, building new cities in Australia and railroads in South America.

Most remarkable today is that so much of this little city survived intact through the 30-year period of neglect following the closing of its sawmill in the 1930s. Mendocino endured thanks to a surplus of community pride and the sheer persistence of the few residents who refused to move on. Still, by the 1950s, the jewel was tarnished and tattered — many buildings sagged from neglect, and weathered and warped boards were far more prevalent than the bright paint you see today.

By 1960 a new generation had begun to discover Mendocino's charms. Urban exiles, many of them artists and writers, trickled into town. The newcomers formed an uneasy alliance with the proud old-timers and began building a new life for the town and for themselves.

Today Mendocino has regained its early prosperity because it draws visitors from around the world who come to marvel at the town's magnificent setting and its historic buildings that so poignantly recall another era. People come to browse in the eclectic mix of shops and galleries, many within view of the sparkling Pacific Ocean, or take a class at the Mendocino Art Center. And they come to enjoy some of the finest, most relaxing inns to be found anywhere in the world.

So many people visit in summer and on holiday weekends that convenient parking is at a premium and solitude sometimes seems scarce. But one can always find solitude by wandering out along the glorious headlands to contemplate the wild ocean and rugged coast, or strolling a back street to admire gardens and houses. Some discover solitude during the sleepy winter or the quiet weekdays of spring and autumn, when Mendocino still feels like an undiscovered jewel and quiet can be found in a saunter along Main Street.

History

Pomo woman weaving a basket, Big River Rancheria

Buldam, the Northern Pomo community near the mouth of Big River, thrived for millennia before the European settlers arrived. Various bands of inland Pomo visited each year to harvest abundant ocean resources and to trade and socialize with their coastal neighbors. The people of Buldam lived in peace, prospering in this bountiful land.

The Pomo must have wondered and worried when big alien ships began sailing along their coast in the sixteenth century. But foreigners attempted no permanent settlement in Pomo territory until the Russians settled Fort Ross in 1812. European contact with the people of Buldam proceeded slowly until Englishman William Richardson settled his Mexican Land Grant at Albion around 1850. While the grant stretched from Big River to Mal Paso Creek, building occurred solely at Albion.

Hotels on Main Street c.1862

The Mendocino Outlaws

In 1879 the dentist of Mendocino City suddenly threw off the garments of his trade . . . and flamed forth in his second dress as a captain of banditti. After a long chase and much gunfighting, the errant toothpuller bit the dust.

— *Robert Louis Stevenson*

On October 15, 1879 two prominent Mendocinans were shot dead while pursuing four men who had rustled a steer. Towns-folk were in an uproar; two large posses rode out to scour the countryside for the murderers.

At the outlaw camp, the searchers found utensils bought by John Wheeler, a local dentist of supposedly good repute. He was arrested as an accomplice to murder. Then one posse caught Samuel Carr, an outlaw who had split from the rest.

Carr revealed that Wheeler served time in San Quentin for stage robbery, where he met John Billings. Three months before the murders, Wheeler enlisted Billings in a plot to rob the tax collector on tax day and make an easy $15,000.

The posses chased the three remaining outlaws over 600 hard-riding miles. After a fortnight one posse exchanged shots with the renegades only to have them escape and the trail go cold.

Rumors bombarded the sheriff about what had become the greatest chase in California

Only after the California Gold Rush took off in 1849 did rapid change and persistent conflict begin to alter this remote corner of the coast. A black man named Nathaniel Smith was apparently the first non-Indian to settle at Mendocino. A story of indeterminate origin says Nathaniel Smith's sailboat was shipwrecked at Big River in 1849 or 1850. Nathaniel Smith built a cabin on the bluff facing the bay at the river's mouth, then filed a land claim with the new state of California, naming the place Port of Good Hope.

A party of German men, possibly sailors shipwrecked or put ashore, settled shortly after Smith, first at Russian Gulch, then around Big River. History never recorded how these Germans arrived or what their intentions were. They may have been gathering hides or making split-wood products, or they might simply have been seeking refuge from a despotic sea captain. Another early settler was Peter Thompson, one of Kit Carson's trappers, who may have arrived as early as April 1851, settling at Pine Grove, about three miles north of Mendocino.

Meanwhile, on July 25, 1850, a two-masted clipper ship named *Frolic* ran onto the rocks and sank off Point Cabrillo north of Mendocino. En route from Canton to San Francisco with a load of Chinese trade goods valued at $150,000, the *Frolic's* officers rowed a lifeboat to San Francisco where newspapers reported their story, precipitating a chain reaction.

Henry Meiggs, a San Francisco lumber merchant and entrepreneur, heard of the wreck and sent employee Jerome Ford overland to Mendocino to search for salvage in 1851. Ford found no Chinese goods but met German William Kasten, who took him up Big River to see the vast stands of immense redwoods. Ford returned to San Francisco and reported the timber to Meiggs, who immediately ordered a steam sawmill sent from the east coast.

In the spring of 1852, Jerome Ford came overland up the coast to Big River with oxen and livestock for the new enterprise. He purchased Nathaniel Smith's land for $100 and searched for a site for the sawmill, which was now being shipped from San Francisco on the brig *Ontario* with 40 workmen and supplies. The leaky craft took a month to complete its stormy voyage, arriving at Big River on July 19, 1852.

Napolean Bever at incline, second mill

history. One rumor bore fruit — one fugitive had a brother-in-law in the Sierra near where the trail disappeared. On a frosty December morn, deputies surrounded the suspect cabin. When one outlaw came out and was told to "stick 'em up," he dove inside instead, but was shot in the shoulder. The two other fugitives ran in opposite directions along a brushy creek. When the injured desperado came out firing, a deputy shot him dead.

The next morning the posse captured one of the remaining fugitives at a nearby cabin. The sheriff took the exhausted hombre back to Ukiah with his dead confederate. The other lawmen tracked the last outlaw into the mountains, then down the Yuba River where, after five more days of hunting, he was nabbed.

Carr testified at the trials and the three fugitives were sentenced to hang; their sentences were reduced to life in prison. Wheeler apparently killed himself in his cell, ingesting chloral hydrate hidden in his coat lining. Carr went free after the trials.

Years later, an odd rumor spread through Ukiah — John Wheeler was seen in San Francisco with his wife. She had taken his body home after he was pronounced dead, then revived him from a deep sleep induced not by chloral hydrate, but by some mystery drug.

E. L. Packard

All hands went to work building the sawmill on the point at the northwest edge of Mendocino Bay, but delays were numerous in this wild setting. The mill finally started up in spring 1853, producing 50,000 board feet a day. That same year the Mendocino Lumber Company began a second mill one mile east beside Big River, a location less exposed to winter storms and closer to the timber. By 1854 the second mill was cutting most of the lumber. When the mill on the point shut for good in 1858, the spot remained the loading point for lumber ships, with an oxen- or horse-drawn railway hauling the cargo from the second mill.

The town beside these mills, first known as Big River or sometimes Meiggsville, grew slowly at first. Few women and children had arrived. The men worked long hours in the woods, at the mill, and on the loading chute.

The entire enterprise nearly collapsed in autumn 1854 when Henry Meiggs fell $800,000 in debt and fled San Francisco under warrant of arrest. The lumber company's creditors shut down the mill while Jerome Ford and E.C. Williams scrambled to save the company. The population dipped to 28 before Mendocino's growth resumed after spring 1855, when the reorganized company reopened the mill.

Henry Meiggs amassed a new fortune building railroads across the Andes using redwood bought from the Mendocino

Three schooners loading by chutes c.1868

mill, becoming a hero in South America. Only in 1993, after 140 years, did the city of San Francisco cancel the warrant for his arrest.

The little town at Big River grew fast after the financial logjam was cleared. Several large new hotels on the west end of Main Street vied for the visitors arriving by schooner. Mendocino won its first post office in 1858. It was often called Mendocino City to distinguish it from the county and cape of the same name. When Mendocino County broke off from Sonoma County in 1859, Mendocino City residents were upset by the choice of tiny Ukiah as county seat. Over the next 20 years several movements attempted to establish a separate coastal county. A whole block in the center of Mendocino, now preserved as Heider field on Little Lake Street between Ford and Kasten, was left vacant in the hope it would one day hold a county courthouse.

The second mill burned in 1863. The third mill began operations at the same site within a year. A bridge

Passengers disembarking

Mendocino in Literature

by Anthony Miksak, owner,
Gallery Bookshop, Mendocino

Mendocino is a hell of a long way from anywhere and it always was that way. The old Pomo paths have become roads, and roads become highways. Despite the asphalt the curves and the distance still keep many people away.

On his 1858 visit here, J. Ross Browne wrote of a wild coast of "rugged peaks and dismal fortresses of slimy rocks." Walt Whitman found "a thought impalpable to breathe as air" when he ventured into the Northern California wilderness. He heard the sound of "dryads, fading, departing" and "choppers . . . quick-ear'd teamsters and chain and jackscrew men." Whitman sang his Song of the Redwood Tree *to "the new society . . . genius of the modern . . . clearing the ground . . . to build a grander future."*

By the time Smeaton Chase rode by Mendocino in 1911, he found rivers "blocked with great logs, and agile lumbermen with 'peavies' extricating them one by one." The great rush to turn the forests into marketable timber had resulted in numerous small communities, bridges and roads. Still, Mendocino remained an exotic, unknown world to outsiders.

It is still that way. The transformation from wild, largely replaced the ferry across Big River, but a toll was still charged.

By 1865 the population had grown to 700, with schools and churches established. These helped counteract the "evil" influences of the many saloons and bawdy houses in the east end of town, called Fury Town for its typical mood on a Saturday night. Fury Town catered to the desires of the working men after their long hard work week. Stacked on gaming tables there were Big River Bits, the local name for $20 gold pieces. One of the bars boasted the only piano in the county at that time.

In 1868 the street grid still in use today was imposed on Mendocino's unruly youthful growth. Most early buildings were utilitarian in design, clustering along Main Street and west of Kasten Street. Most mill hands lived in rustic shacks down on Big River Flat.

When a fire destroyed 26 buildings in October 1870, the town rebuilt rapidly. In the process, the center of town moved east of Kasten Street. Most of Mendocino's landmark buildings were constructed in the 12 years following the fire. The grand and refined nature of those buildings reflect the prosperity of those years, as well as the New England roots of the majority of the prominent citizens.

By 1880 Mendocino City was considerably larger and more prosperous than before the fire — the largest, richest town in the county by far. While a few more landmark buildings were constructed over the next 20 years, the town already looked much as it does today.

Visitors came more frequently to Mendocino as transportation improved. Wells Fargo had established stagecoach service by 1860, but the trip from San Francisco via Anderson Valley took two or three bumpy days of mud, dust, flies and cramped quarters. By 1874, when Charles Nordhoff visited by stage and called this "one of the most remarkable coasts in the world," overland passengers could choose from three routes: via Anderson Valley, up the coast from the Russian River, or over the new stage road from Ukiah via Comptche. Whichever route you chose, the trip was still no picnic.

By 1878 weekly steamship service connected Mendocino with San Francisco, providing a quicker trip than the stage and a far more regular schedule than lumber ships. But passengers arriving at Mendocino still had no wharf upon which to disembark. Women rode a chair hoisted up the cable of the wire chute, but men had to climb the rigging.

In 1892 Ninetta Eames, aunt and foster mother of Jack London's future wife, wrote about her arrival in Mendocino by stage in the popular magazine *Overland Monthly.*

From a distance . . . the city seems to have an imposing array of cupolas,

uninhabited land to zip code in the global village has been immensely quick. Mendocino is linked to the rest of the world but remains darned hard to find. It's difficult to get here, difficult to stay, and near impossible to make a living.

Savor what untamed spirit and untrampled wildness you can discover. Stand on the rocky surf line at sunset and gaze into the dying light. Listen carefully. Observe closely. Not all the dryads have gone.

Mendocino still entices the imaginations of writers. Today's voices are expressed by people who hold the place in their hearts rather than by intrepid travelers.

Thomas Pynchon's Vineland *fingered the serpentine scene of the north coast woods, "the alder and Sitka spruce still dancing in the wind, and the stars thickening overhead." James Blaylock depicts a fantastically strange, familiar coast peopled with fanatic followers of John Ruskin in* The Paper Grail.

In the Northwest anthology Edge Walking on the Western Rim *(Sasquatch Books), Sharon Doubiago tells of finding her "voice here, in the fog and dark and layers of bluffs and ridges and redwoods, the soft golden light so erotic on the skin, and the ocean everywhere . . . the only place I have ever been where the dominant paradigm is, To thine own self be true."*

which are in reality water tanks with windmills of every known pattern, water works not found in any other place of its size. When the wind blows . . . these divers windmills set up a medley of discordant creaks and groans, each pitched in a different key and whether heard singly or collectively, all equally nerve-rending. One could get used to the constant slapping, straining and screeching, for nowhere are people more serene, healthy and home-loving than in this breezy town of Mendocino.

The little town at Big River had definitely established its own distinctive character. It continued to grow and prosper, though more fitfully than in the early years. By this time Mendocino had established neighborhoods of Chinese (perhaps as many as 700 by 1880), Portuguese, Scandinavians and Finns who added to its colorful nature.

It was a hard-working town in an era of long workdays, can-do attitudes and community spirit. The latter quality shined forth on the holidays, when everyone played with the same gusto normally reserved for work. Every Fourth of July started with a big parade (a tradition revived in 1976) and continued with ice cream socials, ball games, races and dancing into the night.

Fort Bragg's Union Lumber Company bought out the Mendocino Lumber Company in 1905, but the mill continued operating much as before. The powerful 1906 earthquake toyed with town landmarks. The high school slid off its foundation. The Occidental Hotel moved five feet. On Big River Flat a span of the bridge came down, the mill twisted out of true and its tall chimney of a million bricks collapsed. Miraculously no one was killed or even seriously injured.

When the mill shut down in 1934, Mendocino suddenly became a town without a focus. Families made do during the Great Depression, expanding their vegetable gardens and raising chickens. Many harvested huckleberries to sell outside the area. Fortunately the New Deal came to the Mendocino Coast, providing federal jobs building new highway bridges and developing Russian Gulch State Park and the Mendocino Woodlands.

Then World War II sent many local boys around the world, and some of the men returned home to start anew. The Mendocino mill never reopened, but the timber industry enjoyed a tremendous boom after the war, Fort Bragg becoming the center of the lumber trade.

It took artists fleeing the cities to give the town of Mendocino its new life. When Jennie and Bill Zacha moved to Mendocino in 1957, weathered, unpainted storefronts and houses reminiscent of a ghost town greeted them. To keep food on the table, Bill became the art teacher at Mendocino High School. Two years later the Zachas bought a block on Little Lake Street for $5500 and started organizing the Mendocino Art Center, which soon became the cornerstone of the local cultural revolution.

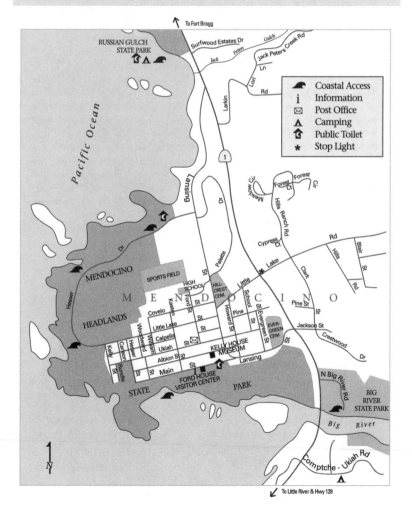

To Fort Bragg

RUSSIAN GULCH
STATE PARK

Surfwood Estates Dr

Gulch

Jack Peters Creek Rd

Jack

Peters

Ln

Loli

Larkin

Rd

Pacific Ocean

	Coastal Access
i	Information
⊠	Post Office
Λ	Camping
🚻	Public Toilet
*	Stop Light

Lansing

Dr

Meadow Cir

Forest Ct

Forest

Cir

Hills Ranch Rd

Cypress Ct

Lake

Rd

Hills

Blair St

Rd

MENDOCINO

SPORTS FIELD

HIGH SCHOOL

HILLCREST CEM.

St

Palette

School St

Little

Clark

Pine St

St

M E N D O C I N O

HEADLANDS

Hesser Dr

Covelo

Kasten

Ford St

Howard St

Pine

St

Evergreen St

EVERGREEN CEM.

Jackson St

Crestwood

Little Lake

St

Woodward

William

Calpella

St

Ukiah St

⊠

KELLY HOUSE MUSEUM

Dr

Kelly

Carlson

Hesser

Albion St

St

St

Main

St

Rundle St

FORD HOUSE VISITOR CENTER

Lansing

N Big River Rd

BIG RIVER STATE PARK

STATE

PARK

Big River

Comptche - Ukiah Rd

1
N

Λ

To Little River & Hwy 128

Mendocino in the Movies — Hollywood North?

If you recognize a scene as you're touring the Mendocino Coast, it isn't necessarily deja-vu — you probably saw it in a movie! More than 50 feature films have been shot here, including six Academy Award winners and some TV movies. Starting in 1916, movie-makers used the Mendocino Coast at least twice in every decade but the thirties.

Seven silent films used Mendocino scenery before 1924, but Hollywood hit its stride here with Frenchman's Creek, a pirate tale filmed in 1943 at Albion Harbor, Big River Beach and Little River, for which Joan Fontaine got the Best Actress Oscar.

Oscars boosted the next two local films. Jane Wyman won Best Actress for her young deaf-mute in moody Johnny Belinda (1948), with the coast vividly portraying a rustic fishing community. Watch for scenes at Crown Hall, the Presbyterian Church, High School Hill and the mouth of Mitchell Creek in Fort Bragg. In 1955, Jo Van Fleet won for her supporting role as James Dean's errant mother in East of Eden. While Mendocino only plays in the first 15 minutes of the epic, the dirt streets, old buildings and fog set the right tone.

In 1965 Hollywood visited Anchor Bay to shoot Island of the Blue Dolphins. Alan Arkin copped a gold statue that year for my favorite Mendocino flick, The Russians Are Coming, The Russians Are Coming. Its humor remains fresh and poignant, and the local scenes evoke Mendocino's sleepy '60s atmosphere, with shots of the Presbyterian Church, headlands and Ten Mile Beach.

The headlands starred again in 1971's Summer of '42, which won Best Actress for Jennifer O'Neill's lonely war bride and another Oscar for score. Director Mulligan returned to make Same Time Next

Year in 1978. Scenes of Mendocino and Fort Bragg played prominently in 1979's Strangers. Bette Davis won an Emmy for that TV drama.

Gold statues have eluded Hollywood's local films since then, but star vehicles continue shooting here: 1984 Racing with the Moon — Sean Penn, Nicolas Cage, Elizabeth McGovern. Great scenes of Fort Bragg's Eagle's Hall and Super Skunk. 1987 Killing Time — Beau Bridges, Kiefer Sutherland. 1988 Overboard — Goldie Hawn, Kurt Russell. Shot mostly at Noyo Harbor and sailing along the coast. 1989 Karate Kid, Part 3 — Ralph Macchio, Pat Morita. 1991 Dying Young — Julia Roberts, Campbell Scott, Colleen Dewhurst, Ellen Burstyn. Many Mendocino scenes, including shots of a mansion, really just a shell, built on Main Street. 1992 Forever Young — Mel Gibson. Filmed around Point Arena. 1994 Pontiac Moon — Ted Danson, Mary Steenburgen. Shot on Little Lake Street. 1994 Same Time Next Year, Part 2 — Alan Alda, Ellen Burstyn return to Heritage House. (TV movie)

Ironically Mendocino's use in location scenes for TV's popular Murder, She Wrote series has probably brought more fame than all the films made over 80 years. The Blair House, Little Lake at Ford streets, plays Jessica Fletcher's house, the Masonic Hall is her library, and if you know the show, you'll surely spot other Cabot Cove scenery. The episode that most features Mendocino portrays a tinseltown version of the fight to save the headlands from subdivision.

With special thanks to Bruce Levene for information from his fascinating book, Mendocino & the Movies.

Mansions on Little Lake Street c.1900s

E. L. Packard

Mendocino Headlands State Park officially opened in 1960, thanks to a large donation of land by the pioneer Heeser family. The town's south headlands, facing Main Street, remained in timber company ownership until 1972. The threat of development there spurred resident artist Emmy Lou Packard to start a movement in 1969 which led to inclusion of the south headlands in the state park. An outgrowth of this effort was the listing of Mendocino on the National Register of Historic Places in 1971, an essential step toward protecting Mendocino's nineteenth-century flavor.

Exploring Town

Everyone who visits takes a walk along picturesque Main Street, with its eclectic mix of shops on the north side contrasting with the dramatic headlands of Mendocino Bay on the south. Stop by the historic 1854 Ford House there. This state park visitor center and museum offers interpretive exhibits of natural and human history, including a detailed model of the town as it appeared in 1890. Make note that next door to the Ford House are Mendocino's only official public rest rooms. Across the street, Kelley House Museum has revolving exhibits in another historic home.

When you find Main Street too crowded for comfort, you can escape the throngs by strolling south and west along the interweaving pathways of Mendocino Headlands State Park to gaze at the ocean or descend to little Portuguese Beach or expansive Big River Beach.

After Main Street the second most important commercial street is Lansing, the original coast road through town. There you'll find the largest grocery, **MENDOSA'S** (8 am to 9 pm daily, established 1909) and its companion hardware store; the only ATM (automated teller machine) at the **SAVINGS BANK** in the historic Masonic Building at the corner of Ukiah Street; the only liquor store, barber, an English-style pub and more. The post office is on Ukiah Street. Other commercial enterprises are on Ukiah Street, Little Lake Street and Albion Street, the sleepy alley between Ukiah and Main. Quiet Kasten Street and little Ford Street nearly round out the commercial side of town. Peaceful Evergreen Street, in what was once Fury Town, shelters a pet supply shop and, on the corner of Ukiah Street, the town's most famous restaurant, **CAFE BEAUJOLAIS**.

Most visitors take a slow spin around Heeser Drive north and west of town, where the marvelous headlands continue, meeting the brute force of Pacific waves head on in an enthralling scramble of offshore sea stacks and islands, coves and inlets, arches and tunnels, cliffs and beaches. To enjoy this mystical coast most fully, park your car, don your hat and windbreaker and walk the windswept headlands, being careful not to topple over a cliff or trample the wildflowers underfoot.

Other visitors plan ahead to enroll in some of the varied classes and workshops offered by the **MENDOCINO ART CENTER** 937-5818, which draws its faculty from the talented, diverse artists and crafts people of the coast and Northern California. The Art Center, located on Little Lake Street between Kasten and William streets, also has galleries open to the public on its lovely grounds.

Fans of television's *Murder, She Wrote* will want to walk east along Little Lake to Ford Street, where the Blair House will be recognized as Jessica Fletcher's home.

If you're still in a walking mood, explore the quiet back streets where more of Mendocino's nineteenth-century redwood homes cluster amidst gingerbread fences and gates and old-fashioned gardens. Remember that people live here, so respect their privacy: don't stare in windows, enter gardens, pick flowers or approach the residents with questions better answered by your innkeeper or people at the visitor center.

Among the gardens, you'll see many exotic plants thriving in the mild climate: dracaena palms, fuchsias, antique roses, melianthus, and the bizarre *Echium* or Tower of Jewels that grows to 25 feet and attracts zinging hummingbirds. Those who especially love the old-fashioned roses can call **MENDOCINO HEIRLOOM ROSES** 937-0963, for a brochure detailing the most significant specimens.

Today about 35 of Mendocino's water towers still stand, many functional, although electric pumps long ago replaced the creaking windmills. They help to alleviate the perennial water shortages that plague the town during the dry season. You can help by conserving water during your visit.

Mendocino Lodging

Listings are organized from the most expensive to the least expensive

☆ STANFORD INN BY THE SEA—
BIG RIVER LODGE $215–450
Hwy One & Comptche-Ukiah Rd
Box 487, Mendocino 95460
937-5615/800-331-8884

www.stanfordinn.com

Elegantly rustic lodge atop a meadow sloping to the sea. Rooms have woodburning fireplaces, down comforters and the amenities expected at the finest hotels. Home of Big River Nurseries and Big River Llamas. The finest canoes, kayaks and bicycles available for exploring.
41 rooms; full breakfast; 2 night min. wknds; all CC/checks; 1- & 2-bdrm suites, some w/kitchens; pets ok; group jacuzzi/sauna; heated indoor swimming pool; ocean views; bathtubs; adj. to hiking; *phone/tv/vcr/stereo/refrig. in room; afternoon hors d'ouevres; adj restaurant; ঙ*

REED MANOR $175–450
10751 Palette Dr/Box 127
Mendocino
937-5446/www.reedmanor.com

There is room to stretch out in this contemporary manor house. Elegantly furnished, each room offers oversized whirlpool tub, fireplace, and sitting nook. Telescopes are available to guests for whale watching.
5 rooms; continental breakfast; min. stay wknds, holidays; V/MC/AE/checks; suites; well-supervised, quiet children over 12 ok; ocean views; gardens; phone/ tv/vcr in room

☆ CYPRESS COVE $215–265
Box 303, Mendocino 95460
937-1456/800-942-6300

www.cypresscove.com

Oceanfront suites for two overlooking Mendocino Bay, fully equipped kitchens. Wrap up in thick robes after a jacuzzi bath for two, and enjoy privacy, comfort and romance with down comforter, fireplace, flowers, brandy, and chocolates.

2 suites; min. stay 2 nights; res advisable; comp coffee & tea; V/MC/checks; mid-week winter disc; fully equipped kitchens; jacuzzis; fireplaces; gardens; adj. to hiking; phone/tv/vcr/stereo

☆ BREWERY GULCH INN $150–295
9401 N. Hwy One Mendocino
937-4752/800-578-4454

www.brewerygulchinn.com

On a wooded hillside overlooking Smuggler's Cove and the ocean, the inn's distinctive craftsman architecture utilizes virgin redwood timbers, eco-salvaged from Big River. Comfortable, well-appointed rooms with arts and crafts decor have ocean views, fireplaces, Jacuzzi tubs for two, private decks, tvs, dataport phones. Wine bar, concierge services and gourmet breakfast presented by professional staff.

10 rooms; full brkfast; wine & hors d'oeuvres; min. stay 2 nights wknds, 3-4 nights some holidays; V/ MC/AE/checks; winter rates Nov-Mar; Jacuzzi tubs, private decks, ocean views; gardens; adj. to hiking; phone/tv in room; &

☆ WHITEGATE INN $159–289
499 Howard St/Box 150
Mendocino
937-4892/800-531-7282

www.whitegateinn.com

Elegant and romantic 1883 Victorian inn filled with French and Victorian antiques.

In the heart of the village, the inn is surrounded by award-winning gardens and views of the rugged coast. All rooms have European feather beds, fireplaces, tvs, and private baths. Full breakfast in dining room and evening wine and hors d'oeuvres hour in the parlor.

7 rooms; 4 bedrm house avail for families, pets; full breakfast; min. stay 2 nights wknds; MC/V/ AE/; midweek off-season disc.; some rms ocean views, refrig, Jacuzzi, bathtubs; adj. to hiking; phone/tvcomputerport in room; afternoon wine & hors d'ouevres in parlor

☆ ALEGRIA OCEAN FRONT INN $149–274
44781 Main St/Box 803
Mendocino
937-5150/800-780-7905

www.oceanfrontmagic.com

Ocean front B & B located in the villge features ocean views from all rooms and cottages, fireplaces, decks, a hot tub and a path to the beach. Great restaurants and shops as well as the ocean, Mendocino Headlands State Park, and the new Big River State Park are just a stroll away.

6 rooms; full breakfast; 2 night min. stay wknds, 3 nights some holidays; V/MC/AE/Disc/checks; res. advisable; winter midweek disc; fireplaces; bathtubs; tv/refrig/coffee in rm; 1 cottage w/ kitchen; ocean views; gardens; hot tub; adj. to hiking

MENDOCINO SEASIDE COTTAGES $131–391
10940 Lansing St, Mendocino
485-0239/800-94-HEART

www.romancebythesea.com

Secluded and private lodging overlooks Mendocino Headlands, with dramatic views of the Pacific Ocean and Cabrillo Lighthouse and a short stroll to the heart of the village. Newly built in 1997, cottage suites and vacation home are luxurious and romantic, feature fireplaces and champagne for your romantic getaway or celebration.

4 cottages & vacation home; checks; res. advisable; smoking rms; suites have phone/refrig/microwave/ wet bar/tv/dvd/stereo, robes; kitchen in home; pets welcome–luxury pet accom.; compl. coffee & champagne breakfast; jacuzzi; spatubs; fireplace/ wood stoves; gardens; decks; adj. to hiking

☆ AGATE COVE INN $129–299
11201 Lansing Street/Box 1150
Mendocino 95460
937-0551/800-527-3111

www.agatecove.com

Perched on a bluff above the Pacific, the 1860 farmhouse and cottages have grand ocean views and spectacular gardens. Oversized rooms have king or queen beds, fireplaces, private baths and private deck. Full country breakfast is served in the farmhouse dining room with its breathtaking whitewater ocean view.

10 cottages; full breakfast; min. stay some wknds, holidays; V/MC/checks; mid-week winter disc; catv/ vcr/cd player in room; bathtubs; ocean views; gardens; adj. to hiking; families welcome

SEA ROCK BED & BREAKFAST INN $149–279
11101 Lansing Street/Box 906
Mendocino
937-0926/800-906-0926

www.searock.com

Individual cottages have dramatic views of the sea and the rocky cliffs of Mendocino Headlands. Cozy cottages and newly built suites, all with private baths and decks, offer an informal, relaxed atmosphere surrounded by gardens and century-old cypress trees.

14 cottages & suites; breakfast; res. advisable; min. stay 2 nights wknds; mid-week winter disc; MC/V/ Disc/AE/checks; ocean views; fireplaces; phone/catv/ vcr in rm; bathtubs; some refrig, kitchens; hot tub; gardens; adj to hiking; children 12+ ok

MACCALLUM HOUSE INN $120–265
45020 Albion St/Box 206
Mendocino
937-0289/www.maccallumhouse.com

The main house, a beautiful 1882 Victorian built by William Kelley as a wedding gift for his daughter, is surrounded by gardens and endowed with ocean views. It sits in the heart of Mendocino village. The outbuildings are renovated into lodging units with private baths, wood stoves or fireplaces, all comfortable and distinct.

19 rooms w/private bath; full gourmet breakfast; res. advisable; min. stay 2 nights wknds; MC/V/ AE; winter discounts; 2 units w/ kitchens, some ocean views, Jacuzzis, fireplaces, refrig; adj. restaurant/ lounge; hot tub; bathtubs; adj. to hiking; phone/tv/computer port in room; families, pets welcome; &

MENDOCINO HOTEL & GARDEN SUITES $95–295
45080 Main St/Box 587
Mendocino
937-0511/800-548-0513

Established in 1878, the hotel is in the heart of Mendocino Village overlooking the bay. Rooms and suites feature fireplaces, ocean views, balconies, four-poster beds and antiques.

51 rooms; min. stay holidays & wknds; V/MC/AE/ checks; midweek winter disc; suites; 37 private baths/14 shared; compl. coffee in lobby; adj. restaurant; wood stoves; bathtubs; gardens; adj. to hiking; phone/tv in room; room service; &

HILL HOUSE INN $117–250
10701 Palette Drive/Box 625
Mendocino
937-0554/800-422-0554

www.hillhouseinn.com

The inn captures the past in the present

with style and elegance. Guest rooms feature brass beds with comforters, elegant furnishings and the convenience of private baths, tvs and phones.
44 rooms; res. advisable; min. stay 2 nights wknds; smoking rms; V/MC/Disc/AE/checks; winter midweek rates; coffeemakers in room; adj. restaurant; ocean views; fireplaces; bathtubs; gardens; &

JOHN DOUGHERTY HOUSE
$110–240
571 Ukiah St/Box 817,
Mendocino 95460
937-5266/800-486-2104
www.jdhouse.com

This historic house, built in 1867, has some of the best ocean views in the village, plus rooms with new jet tubs. Enjoy quiet peaceful nights seldom experienced in today's fast urban lifestyle. Park your car for several days and visit California as it was 140 years ago.
8 rooms; full breakfast; min. stay 2 nights wknds; V/MC/Disc/checks; mid-week disc; 2-rm suites w/ jet tubs; fireplaces; verandahs; ocean views; bathtubs; gardens; adj. to hiking; tv/computer port/ refrig in room

☆ HEADLANDS INN $100–215
Howard & Albion Streets/Box 132
Mendocino
937-4431/800-354-4431
www.headlandsinn.com

Charming and cozy, this beautiful 1868 salt box Victorian inn offers whitewater ocean views, English-style garden, guest parlor and lovely antiques. The innkeepers will pamper you with a full, gourmet breakfast delivered to your room. Woodburning fireplaces, private baths, and queen or king-size feather beds in rooms.
6 rooms, 1 cottage; full breakfast, afternoon tea; res. essential; min. stay 2 nights wknds; V/MC/ checks; bathtubs; adj. to hiking; limited &

☆ JOSHUA GRINDLE INN $99–240
44800 Little Lake Rd/Box 647
Mendocino
937-4143/800-GRINDLE
www.joshgrin.com

A prominent, architecturally significant home in the National Register Historic District situated on two beautifully landscaped acres overlooking Mendocino village and rugged coastal headlands. Experience quiet solitude, savor gourmet breakfasts, and chat with fellow guests over evening sherry while you relax and refresh. The only 4-diamond B&B in the village.
10 rooms; full breakfast; res. essential; min. stay 2 nights wknds, 3 nights holiday wknds; MC/V/ checks; off-season midweek rates; ocean views; fireplaces/wood stoves; bathtubs; gardens; adj. to hiking; limited &

C. O. PACKARD HOUSE $95–249
45170 Little Lake St, Mendocino
937-2677/800-578-2677
www.packardhouse.com

Beautiful 1878 carpenter's gothic Victorian with ocean views and surrounded by gardens. Elegant blend of antiques, modern furnishings, and museum quality art. Amenities include fireplaces, jet tubs and gourmet breakfast. Centrally located in a residential part of the village — short walks to shops, restaurants and the romantic coastline.
5 rooms; full breakfast; min. stay 2 nights wknds, 3 nights most holidays; V/MC/checks; winter disc.; some fireplaces, jet tubs, ocean views; phones/tv/vcr in room; gardens; adj. to hiking

BLAIR HOUSE $100–210
45110 Little Lake St/Box 1608
Mendocino
937-1800/www.blairhouse.com

This 1888 Victorian has become famous as the television residence of Jessica Fletcher of "Murder, She Wrote." Located two blocks from Main Street, this is one of the few historic homes in Mendocino whose exterior has been kept intact since it was built.

4 rooms, 2 w/shared baths; full breakfast; res. advisable; min. stay 2 nights wknds; V/MC/checks; lower midweek rates; pets ok; ocean views; adj. to hiking

SWEETWATER SPA & INN $70–295
44840 Main St/Box 337,
Mendocino 95460
937-4076/800-300-4140

www.sweetwaterspa.com

A unique array of choices right in the village for renewal and restoration of your spirit. Water towers, cottages with hot tubs, fireplaces and kitchens, luxury ocean-view spa suites, even private homes with hot tubs. All rooms come with free hot tub and sauna privileges.

19 rooms, 1 w/ shared bath; res. advisable; min. stay 2 nights wknds, 3 nights holidays; V/MC; winter discounts; some phones, tvs, kitchens, bathtubs, hot tubs, ocean views, computer ports; families welcome, pets ok; bathtubs

MENDOCINO VILLAGE INN
$85–195
44860 Main Street/Box 626
Mendocino
937-0246/800-882-7029

www.mendocinoinn.com

An 1882 Queen Anne Victorian in the village and across Main Street from the headlands and beach. Inn features several opulent parlor rooms, water tower suites, and some rooms with spa tubs for two. Most rooms have fireplaces, some have ocean and river views. Hearty breakfasts, free spa privileges at Sweetwater Spa, afternoon wine, tea and snacks.

12 rooms; full breakfast; min. stay 2 nights wkends;

V/MC; winter mid-week disc; 2-story watertower suite; 2 rooms w/ shared bath; ocean views; fireplaces/wood stoves; bathtubs; tea parlor; gardens; adj. to hiking; private & common decks; ⅃

☆ MENDOCINO FARMHOUSE
$105–145
43410 Comptche-Ukiah Rd
Box 247, Mendocino
937-0241/800-475-1536

www.mendocinofarmhouse.com

A secret place hidden in a redwood forest. Close to town but away from the crowds. Lovely English gardens and lots of room to walk and picnic make this a quiet and secluded retreat. Stop by for a visit!

6 rooms; full breakfast; min. stay 2 nights wknds, 3 nights most holidays; V/MC/checks; midweek winter disc; fireplaces; bathtubs; gardens; adj. to hiking

BLACKBERRY INN $80–205
44951 Larkin Rd, Mendocino
937-5281/800-798-8826

www.blackberryinn.biz

Located on a quiet hill a half mile from the village, the inn is comfortable and serene, with a touch of old west atmosphere. Western theme rooms offer a stay in the bank, the sheriff's office, the general store, the schoolhouse, or in the saloon and more.

17 rooms; continental breakfast; res. advisable; min. stay 2 nights wknds, 3 nights holidays; MC/V; winter disc.; some kitchenettes, fireplaces, ocean views; forest cottage sleeps 5; decks; jacuzzi tubs; phone/tv/ computer port in room; families, pets ok; ⅃

LARKIN COTTAGE $135–150
44950 Larkin Rd, Mendocino
937-2567/www.larkincottage.com

This private, one-bedroom garden cottage a mile from the village has a fireplace, tv/vcr, music system and a fully equipped kitchen. Guests are greeted with fresh flowers, cheese, crackers, wine and other goodies.

1 cottage; res. advisable; 2 nights min. wknds; V/ MC/checks; 1-bdrm suite w/kitchen, bathtub, fireplace, gardens; ng; phone/ans mach//tv/vcr

NICHOLSON HOUSE INN $90–189
951, Ukiah St, Mendocino 95460
937-0934/800-9620934

7 rooms;guest kitchen; some ocean views, tubs; families welcome, 2 night min in high season; all CC's, checks; gardens; tv/vcr in room; adj to restaurant, hiking

BLUE HERON INN $95-125
390 Kasten Street/Box 1142
Mendocino
937-4323

The intimate inn has 3 rooms, 2 with ocean views, offering European country charm and simple elegance in the heart of Mendocino village. A short stroll across the headlands brings you to the Pacific Ocean.

3 rooms, 1 w/private bath, 2 shared; continental breakfast; min stay 2 nights wkends; V/MCchecks; bathtub; gardens; ocean views; adj to hiking

BEGGS-BISHOP GARDEN COTTAGE $110
Box 393, Mendocino
937-2353/www.beggs-bishop.com

Private and cozy garden-view cottage with a complete kitchen, wood stove/ fireplace, antiques and queen bed. Located in Mendocino's historic residential neighborhood, offering an easy walk to restaurants, theater, shops and headlands.

Cottage w/kitchen; refrigerator stocked w/ snacks; checks; phone/radio/tape player; gardens; adj. to hiking

MCELROY'S COTTAGE INN
$85–125
998 Main Street/Box 1881
Mendocino
937-1734/www.mcelroysinn.com

Comfortable, colorful rooms and suites at affordable prices are surrounded by gardens and facing Mendocino Bay. The inn is within easy walking distance of shops and restaurants. Trails to beach and headlands are right across the street.

4 rooms; continental brkfst;min. stay 2 nights wknds; MC/V/checks; midweek winter disc.; suites w/sitting rooms; families welcome, pets ok; ocean views; fireplaces; gardens; refrigs; adj to hiking

SALLIE & EILEEN'S PLACE FOR WOMEN ONLY $80-100
Box 409, Mendocino
937-2028/www.seplace.com

Now in their sixteenth year of providing a private, safe, comfortable lodging for women. Located in the woods three miles east of town, their dog Libby will greet you with a smile and much tail wagging.

2 cabins w/kitchens, private baths; res. essential; min. stay 2 nights, 3 on holiday wkends; checks; comp. coffee; fireplace/wood stove; bathtubs; hot tub; gardens; families, pets ok

SEA GULL INN $55–165
44960 Albion St/Box 317
Mendocino
937-5204/www.seagullbb.com

Built in the 1870s, this is one of Mendocino's first bed and breakfast inns. Flourishing gardens surround the inn, giant fuchsias shade the walks. Meticulously maintained, the inn and its grounds create a charming and memorable atmosphere.

9 rooms; continental breakfast; min. stay 2 nights some wknds; MC/V/checks; suites; 1 rm w/half bath; bathtubs; adj. to hiking; some rooms w/tv; &

MENDOCINO VILLAGE COTTAGES $60–125
45320 Little Lake St/Box 1295
Mendocino 95460
937-0866/www.mendocinocottages.com

Charming cottages facing Headlands State Park and near Mendocino Art Center. Ocean views, gardens, fireplaces, kitchens and quiet.

3 cottages; 2 night min. unless 1 fits in; V/MC/ checks; $385–650/weekly rate; full kitchens; families welcome; bathtubs; gardens; adj. to hiking

REEVE'S GARDEN COTTAGE $85
511 Ukiah Street, Box 345
Mendocino
937-5686/www.mendocottage.com

The cottage in the residential part of town sleeps two and has a kitchenette, wood stove and electric heat. An outdoor spa on a large deck is fenced for privacy.

1 cottage w/kitchenette, bath; res. advisable; min. stay 2 nights; checks; wood stove; hot tub; gardens; deck

Eateries

☆ MACCALLUM HOUSE RESTAURANT/GREY WHALE BAR & CAFE
45020 Albion St/Box 500
Mendocino
937-5763
B: $6–11.50, D: $7–12 cafe, $19–32 dining room

Located in Daisy MacCallum's historic 1882 Victorian, fine North Coast cuisine is served in three distinct dining areas. The Grey Whale Bar serves cafe fare at friendly prices in sun porch and parlor. Or choose white linen service in the original dining room and library, warmed by river stone fireplaces. The menus emphasize fresh local seafoods, organic meats and produce from neighboring farms and ranches, including foraged wild mushrooms and huckleberries from surrounding woods. Excellent food is beautifully presented, served by friendly and knowledgeable staff.

Daily, breakfast 8-10:30, 'til 11 weekends, dinner: bar from 4:30, dining room from 5:30 ; V/MC/ checks; full bar; seats 65; mature children welcome; take-out; &

☆ MENDOCINO HOTEL RESTAURANT
45080 Main St/Box 587
Mendocino
937-0511
B: $6–11, L: $6–13; D: $18–32

Breakfast, lunch and dinner are served in the Garden Room Cafe and the Victorian main dining room. California Cuisine is the specialty, complemented by an exceptional wine list. Winner of Wine Spectator Award for Excellence in 2001 and 2002.

Daily from 8 am–10 pm, 'til 9 pm in winter; res. advisable; V/MC/AE/checks; full bar; seats 60; &

☆ CAFE BEAUJOLAIS
961 Ukiah St/Box 1236, Mendocino
937-5614
D: $20–26

Eclectic cuisine, influenced by France, Italy, Asia & Mexico featuring organic produce and free-range meat and poultry as much as possible. Extensive wine list. Bread is baked daily in a wood-fired brick oven and is available for sale.

Daily 5:45–9:45; closed 3 weeks in early Dec; res. advisable; all CC/checks; beer/wine; seats 55; well-behaved mature children only; limited &

955 UKIAH STREET RESTAURANT
955 Ukiah St/Box 34
Mendocino 95460
937-1955
D: $18–24

Located in Emmy Lou Packard's old studio, this restaurant uses local products whenever possible. Wide ranging menu with an accent on freshness includes large assortment of seafood, steaks, roast duck, lamb, pasta dishes and more.
Wed to Sun from 6 pm; res. advisable; MC/VI checks; beer/wine; seats 50; take-out; ᘐ

☆ THE MOOSSE CAFE
390 Kasten Street, Mendocino
937-4323
L: $5.50–14, D: $16–22

California eclectic cuisine using fresh organic regional ingredients served in a warm and casual setting with ocean and garden views, plus outdoor dining when the weather allows. They offer an select wine list featuring Northern California wines, many available by the glass.
Daily, lunch 11:30–3:30, dinner 5:30–9, 'til 9:30 in summer; closed early December; res. welcome; V/MC/checks; beer/wine; seats 50; take-out; ᘐ

☆ RAVENS VEGETARIAN RESTAURANT
44850 Comptche-Ukiah Rd
at Stanford Inn, Mendocino
937-5615/800-331-8884
WB: $10–14, B: $8–14, D: $13–23

Nationally acclaimed organic cuisine inspired by the freshest organic ingredients for breakfast and dinner. Dinner features gourmet vegan/vegetarian dishes including Sea Palm Strudel, pizzas and more, plus chocolate torte. Breakfast features organic

omelets, waffles, burritos and more.
Daily from 7:30 am, breakfast 'til 11 weekdays, 12 weekends, dinner from 5:30 'til 8 or 9, 'til 9 or 9:30 in summer; all CCs/checks; families welcome; beer/wine; take-out ᘐ

MENDOCINO CAFE
10451 Lansing/Box 1054
Mendocino
937-6141
L: $6–13, D: $7–22

A casual, convivial atmosphere and health conscious food. Serving Pacific Rim cuisine using organic ingredients when available. Glad to satisfy special requirements whenever possible. Desserts made on the premises. Featuring imported beers and Mendocino County wines.
Weekdays 11:30–4, 5–9, weekends 11–4, 5–9, 1 hour later in summer; res. advisable for parties of 5+; V/MC/checks; beer/wine; seats 50; take-out; ᘐ

BAY VIEW CAFE
45040 Main/Box 991, Mendocino
937-4197
B: $6–8, L: $6–14, D: $7–20

Overlooking Mendocino Bay and Mendocino Headlands State Park, the cafe provides affordable food in a friendly family-style, casual setting.
Daily from 8 am; closed Dec 1–21; dinners on weekends only in winter; checks; full bar; seats 94 inside, 32 outside; take-out

RICK'S OF MENDOCINO
10701 Palette Dr/Box 625
at Stanford Inn, Mendocino
937-0577
SB: $5–10, D: $8–18

Located at the Hill House Inn, Rick's serves comfort food at reasonable prices. Rick's Lounge downstairs has a full bar and serves dinner in the relaxing atmosphere of a Scottish pub. Sunday champagne brunch is served upstairs in

the Ocean View Room.
Dinner Thur-Mon 5–9; Sun brunch 9-2; V/MC/ checks; full bar; seats 50; &

PATTERSON'S PUB
10485 Lansing/Box 1095
Mendocino 95460
937-4782/www.pattersonspub.com
L: $4–9, D: $7–10

This Irish-style pub is a gathering place. Enjoy the quiet pub atmosphere during the day, or party at night. Excellent clam chowder.

Daily 10 am–12 pm, Fri–Sat till 1 am; checks; full bar; seats 40; take-out; &

MENDOCINO BAKERY & CAFE
10483 Lansing St/Box 1501
Mendocino
937-0836
B: $3–6, L: $3.50–7, D: $6-10

Casual dining with counter service. Homemade bagels, bialys, pastries baked daily. Menu includes soups, salads, pizza, burritos, empanadas and other entrees for sit down or take-out. New York style pizza after 4 pm on Thur-Mon. Full espresso bar featuring 100% organic coffee and espresso drinks.

Daily 7:30 am–7, 'til 8 in summer; checks; seats 22 inside plus 30 on outside deck; take-out; &

☆ LU'S KITCHEN
45013 Ukiah St, Mendocino
937-4939
$5–10

Specializing in an eclectic and original blend of organic, garden fresh vegetarian food made to order. Vegan choices too. Cross-cultural cuisine with south of the border and across the ocean inspirations. Espresso drinks. Vibrant food!

Daily from 11:30, flexible winter hours; checks; garden seating for 22; children & animal friendly; take-out; &

☆ TOTE FETE CARRY-OUT & BAKERY
10450 Lansing/Box 685
Mendocino
937-3383/937-3140 (bakery)
B: $1.75–5, L: $2.50–9, D: $4–10

Gourmet take-out and bakery with everything made from scratch featuring freshly baked country breads, desserts, salads, soups and entrees.

Carry-Out: Mon–Sat 10:30–7, Sun till 4 pm; seats 10 plus garden seating; Bakery: Daily 7:30–4; checks. &

MENDOCINO MARKET
45051 Ukiah/Box 380
Mendocino
937-3474
L: $3–9, D: $4–10

Full service deli featuring soups, salads, hot & cold sandwiches, lemon oregano chicken and other delights. Fish and meat market, gourmet goods, local products including smoked salmon. Great tiramisu and other desserts.

Daily 10–6:30; seats 10 inside, 18 outside; MC/ V/checks; beer/wine; take-out

MENDO BURGERS
10483 Lansing/Box 1146
Mendocino
937-1111
$4–8

Burgers of all types (veggie too!), fresh fish & chips,real ice cream shakes, and the only ice cream in town. On Lansing Street behind Mendo Bakery.

Daily 11–5, 'til 6 in summer; checks; seats 19 plus outside tables; take-out; &

CULTURED AFFAIR
45104 Albion St, Mendocino 95460
937-1430
$5–7

Simply fresh, wholesome homemade food. A clean and friendly environment with wonderful outdoor garden seating, this is a favorite spot with locals for lunch and frozen yogurt.
Mon–Sat 10–4:30; local checks; seats 30; take-out; ♿

MENDOSA'S DELI
10501 Lansing/Box 85
Mendocino
937-5879
L: $4–5, D: $4–8

Deli sandwiches, rotisserie chicken, roasts and ribs to take out.
Daily 8 am–9 pm; beer/wine; ♿

LIPINSKI'S MENDO JUICE JOINT
Ukiah Street west of Lansing
Mendocino
937-4033
$2–6

Serving fresh organic fruit and vegetable juices and the tastiest, healthiest smoothies on the coast, plus nutritious meals like sandwiches, falaffels and soups. Breakfast, middle eastern and southern style specialties. Espresso drinks and chai too. Free internet access.
Daily from 6:30 am. Mon-Thur 'til 7 pm, Fri, Sat 'til 10:30 pm, Sun 'til 8:30 pm; V/MC/ checks; seats 30; ♿

COMMUNITY COFFEE & COOKIE
10450 Lansing St/Box 630
Mendocino
937-4843
$1–4

Daily fresh baked muffins, scones, cookies and more. Organic coffee and espresso drinks, blended coffee drinks and smoothies. Family owned for 19 years. Internet access.
Daily 7–5, 6-6 in summer; checks; bar-style seating, take-out; ♿

Outdoor Activities

CATCH-A-CANOE & BICYCLES TOO 937-0273. Rentals and sales of canoes, kayaks, mountain bikes and street bikes. Located on the estuary of Big River State Park, this outfitter offers a prime location for trips up the gentle tidal waters of the Mendocino Coast's biggest stream. They'll help plan your boat trip to mesh with the tides and suggest biking routes appropriate for any level.

MENDOCINO AUDIO TOURS 937-5397 at the Ford House. Rent a tape and Walkman to take you on a historical walking tour.

MENDOCINO CARRIAGE CO. 895-2546, 800-399-1454. Horse-drawn carriage tours and narrated historical tours from Mendocino Hotel, plus hire for special events.

DISCOVERY WALKS OF MENDOCINO 937-3128. Trained naturalist Helene Maddock tailors a guided walk to fit the interests of your party, by appointment.

FARMERS MARKET, Fridays 12–2. Howard St. between Main and Ukiah streets, May through October. Fresh produce and homestead products.

MENDOCINO TENNIS CLUB
937-0007, 43250 Little Lake Rd.
Open to guests by appointment.

BIG RIVER NURSERIES
937-5027. Nursery at Big River Lodge.
California Cerfitied Organic Grower.
By appointment.

MENDOCINO CAMPGROUND
937-5322. Rustic tent camping in a
forest setting a mile from town. Open
Apr–Oct, 60 sites, hot showers, $19/
vehicle.

Parks

MENDOCINO HEADLANDS
STATE PARK 347 acres. The spirit of
the town hides out here, whether
glistening in sunlight or shrouded in
fog. Don't miss it.

RUSSIAN GULCH STATE PARK
937-5804. Fee. This 1305-acre park
occupies a deep canyon and the
wondrously convoluted headlands and
shoreline at its mouth. Though logged
around 1900, the lovely park shows
little evidence of this today. More than
ten miles of trails explore headlands, a
delightful waterfall, and steep, lush
canyon walls. A beautiful picnic area
perches atop the cliff overlooking the
dramatic cove. Park open daily, 30
campsites open Apr–Oct; &.

BIG RIVER STATE PARK 937 5804.
This amazing new park offers 7334
wild acres acquired in 2002. It included
the largest coastal estuary north of San
Francisco, 1500 acres of wetlands, and
a network of trails following old
logging roads. Find it immediately
south of town and east of the highway

bridge. Great for canoeing, kayaking,
hiking or mountain biking.

Indoor Activities

FORD HOUSE MUSEUM &
STATE PARKS VISITOR CENTER
937-5397, 735 Main Street, Daily 11–
4. This 1854 house has exhibits and
programs about natural and
human history, plus wonderful scale
models of the town in 1890, a doghole
schooner and loading chutes.

KELLEY HOUSE MUSEUM
937-5791, 45007 Albion St.
Daily except Wed. in summer, 1–4,
Fri–Mon in winter. This private
nonprofit museum in an 1861 house
has revolving exhibits, plus extensive
archives of local artifacts, books and
photos.

Mendocino Theatre Company
937-4477, www.1mtc.org . Helen
Schoeni Theatre at the Mendocino Art
Center, Little Lake St. Excellent plays
year round, drama and comedy, from
traditional to avant garde.

Mendocino Music Festival
937-2044. Box 1808. mid-July. Every
summer a big tent goes up beside the
Ford House on the Mendocino
Headlands, providing a venue for
symphony and chamber concerts,
opera and jazz. Get your tickets early
and dress warmly.

Galleries

You probably won't visit them all, but take a look at some of these collections. You'll find that Mendocino has a diverse, vital arts community. Without picking favorites, we list Main Street galleries east to west, then explore the back streets. On the **SECOND SATURDAY** of each month many Mendocino galleries stay open until 8 p.m. with openings and/or artist's receptions.

Art That Makes You Laugh/Leedy Gallery 937-1354, 45000 Main. Enjoy the art of nationally known humorist, Jeff Leedy. Original oil pastels, fine limited editions,gifts for deserving friends and family. Fun! Daily.

Just up the walkway before the Big River Trading Company . . .

Mendocino Jewelry Studio 937-0181 Local artists exhibit their work in a colorful, well designed space. Jewelry by Nancy Gardner and Ellen Athens, Judith Beam and Conni Mainne, pottery by Leslie Campbell, plus Jan Hinson's tile furniture and stained glass lighting

Highlight Gallery 937-3132, 45052 Main. Quality handmade furniture, sculpture, art, pottery, textiles, glass, jewelry and more fine craft work in Mendocino's largest gallery. Daily.

Two Visions Gallery 937 3898, 45104 Main. Striking fine art photography by Lisa Kristine and Chris Honeysett.

Panache Gallery on Main 937-0947, 45110 Main. Important fine art and crafts. All disciplines represented. Daily.

Jim Bertram Studio 937-5182, 45170 Main.

Artists Co-op of Mendocino 937-2217, 45270 Main. Fine art by local artists, featuring the Mendocino scene. Artists staff this upstairs gallery with a great view of Mendocino Bay.

Panache 937-1234, Kasten at Albion. Sculpture, paintings, art glass, estate and designer jewelry.

Wilkes Gallery 937-1357, Lansing at Ukiah. The pleasant space of the upstairs gallery features several local artists in revolving shows.

William Zimmer Gallery 937-5121, Ukiah Street at Lansing. Fine painting, jewelry, woodworking and contemporary craft, furniture commissions a specialty. Daily 10:30–4:30.

Clinton Smith Gallery 937-2261, Kasten at Albion St. Fine Art American landscape photography in vibrant, true colors. Come in and meet the artist, whose work has been praised by the likes of Ansel Adams and the New York Times.

Color & Light 937-1003, 10525 Ford. Custom designed art glass, baskets and jewelry in a working studio/gallery.

Coastside Gallery 937-4960, Calpella Street near Lansing. Gorgeous and evocative Mendocino landscape paintings, plus other California scenes. Meet the artist and see his fine book, *Mendocino: A Painted Pictorial.*

Mendocino Art Center 937-5818, 45200 Little Lake. Three galleries, retail art shop, library, gardens, classes, events. A place of life enrichment. Daily.

Shops

Here's a representative sampling. Some are community institutions, some just fun shopping. Again we start on east Main and head west, then work around town.

Moore Used Books 937-1537, 990 Main. A broad selection of quality recycled books in a tiny space.

Kelley building (long known as the Ex Lax Building)...

Whistlestop Antiques 961-0902, Main at Lansing. This long-time Fort Bragg institution now has a Mendocino location as well. Antique glassware, contemporary collectibles and home decor.

Upstairs you'll find...

Gallery of the Senses 937-2021, Main at Lansing. Sip a sample of their exclusive selection of fine teas while you explore their collection of fragrances from around the world, They also sell fine custom, handcrafted speakers.

Walk past the Kelley House and duck pond. Just before the Big River Trading Company, up the walkway beneath the water tower...

Hidden Treasures & T-Shirt Company 937-3800. Gifts, jewelry, apparel.

Big River Trading Company 937-2514. Clothing and gifts.

Stones 937-0397. A gallery of art on earth's canvas plus self-contained water sculptures.

Fittings for Home and Garden 937-0160. Housewares and garden goods in a craftsman cottage.

The Irish Shop 937-3133. Walk the garden path, duck under the giant datura to find quality imports from Ireland, Scotland and Wales.

Fetzer Tasting Room 937-6191. Wine tasting and sales, plus gifts for wine lovers.

MacGeraty's Estate Jewelry 937-2993. Quite a switch from the old ice-cream store.

Southern Exposure 937-4436. Hairstyling, manicuring and massage with a heavenly view.

Golden Goose 937-4655. Fine Austrian and French linens and housewares artfully presented.

The Courtyard 937-0917. Country kitchen atmosphere showcases culinary gifts and specialty items.

Gallery Bookshop & Bookwinkle's Children's Books 937-2665. This community institution since 1962 is in the historic Jarvis-Nichols Building. Staff will recommend literature beyond bestseller lists from their extensive stock, computer search for special needs, and ship for reasonable fees. Add cards, music, magazines, rubber stamps and stickers and you've got one of Northern California's great book stores. (Author admits bias, having worked here 13 years.)

Right around the corner on Kasten Street . . .

Mendocino Gift Company 937-5298. Cards, pottery, stained glass, photography of the area, jewelry and other fine gifts.

Lark in the Morning 937-5275. A store for traditional music including acoustic instruments and recordings from around the world.

Back on Main . . .

Out of This World 937-3335. Science and astronomy fun for all ages. Robots, holograms, games and brain-teaser puzzles. Sample state of the art binoculars and telescopes to watch birds soar and waves break across the bay.

Indulgence 937-3510. Bed, bath and nightware.

Zacha Travel 937-5205, 1-800-994-TRAV. Tour the world with Lucia!

Red Rooster Records 937-1165, 1-800-422-6553, 45156 Main. A great selection of CD's, tapes and collectibles.

Papa Bear's Chocolate Haus 937-4406. Candy made on the premises.

Safari 937-1900, 45160 Main. Apparel, artifacts, accessories, jewelry.

Creative Hands of Mendocino 937-2914. Gifts and clothing handmade by local artisans. Clothing in fascinating fabrics from far-away places.

Ocean Quilts of Mendocino 937-4201, 45270 Main. Antique and comtemporary quilts, folk art and reproduction Bauer pottery.

Visual Feast 937-0124. Cameras, film, processing, batteries, digital supplies, blank casette tapes, all with a Mendocino Bay view.

Mendocino Jams & Preserves 937-1037. At the west end of Main, sample the locally made natural preserves, an ideal gift.

Round the corner onto sleepy Osborne Street, then go right again up Albion past the red and green Temple of Kwan Tai, a Taoist temple dating from 1854. At Kasten Street the shops resume.

ARTicles 937-1284. Worth a visit just to tour one of town's landmark water towers, this shop has an eclectic selection of adventurous art, antiques, collectibles and jewelry.

Compass Rose Leather 937-5170. Come smell the fine leather, with custom work and many goods made on the premises.

Sticks 937-2621. A fun and eclectic collection of rustic furniture and other rough-hewn wood objects for home and garden.

Amerind Bay Clothing Co. 937-3434. Native apparel, jewelry and more.

Tote Fete Bakery 937-3140. The town's gourmet bakery. Scones, donuts, danish for breakfast to focaccia and toothsome breads for a special lunch or dinner. Daily 7:30–4.

The Great Put On 937-5161. Boutique of wearable art for women plus fine men's wear, featuring natural fiber designs.

Old Gold 937-5005/800-992-5335. Antique and contemporary jewelry, gold specialists.

You're back to Lansing Street, just a half block north of your starting point. If you turn right, descend to . . .

Rainsong 937-4165. Men's and women's contemporary clothing, featuring Patagonia.

To the north, up Lansing Street past

Community Coffee & Cookie to . . .

Village Toy Store 937-4633. Quality toys and kites from around the world for kids of all ages.

WilkesSport 937-1357. Fashionable San Francisco clothier Wilkes Bashford opened his sport line here in 1994. Despite the casual slant, they're still some of the fanciest men's and women's clothes in town.

West along the wooden walkway . . .

Deja-Vu, the Mendocino Hat Company 937-4120. Thousands of hats including Stetson, Akubra and Borsalino, hats for kids, plus accessories.

Around the corner . . .

Silver and Stone Jewelry 937-0257. Imports in a creatively designed space.

Twist 937-1717. Groovy gear for the conscious consumer.

Corners of the Mouth, The Natural Food Store 937-5345. In addition to a full line of whole foods, produce, herbs and vitamins, Corners offers a good selection of sweets without sugar.

Beyond the Mendocino Market, the shops thin out for a bit. On the right side of the street in the old Mendocino Beacon Building . . .

Mendocino Yarn Shop 937-0921, everything for the knitter, spinner and fiber artist.

Beyond Kasten Street on the left . . .

Bebe Lapin 937-0261. Children's gifts, apparel and toys especially for the youngest.

Mendo Video 937-1720.

Saunter back to Lansing for the last but not least of our shop-til-you-drop tour. On the corner in the Seagull Building is . . .

Mendocino Village Pharmacy 937-4800.

Wild Thing 937-0937. Clothing for the imagination.

Just west of Lansing on Ukiah . . .

Tickle Your Fancy 937-0747. Clothing and accessories.

Fancy That 937-0448. Natural fiber clothing and accessories.

Interiors 937-0709. Cool and creative items for your home.

North on Lansing you'll find . . .

Mendocino Chocolate Company 937-1107. Delicious handmade truffles and chocolates.

Rainsong Shoes 937-1710. Men's and women's shoes and socks. Specializing in comfort, quality fashion and the unusual.

Across the street . . .

Sallie Mac 937-5357. Gifts and accessories from the European countryside.

Village Spirits 937-5873. The town's full service liquor store.

Rubaiyat Beads 937-1217. Beads, jewelry, fragrances and tarot from around the world, plus tarot and palm readings.

Back on the east side of the street . . .

Mendosa's Hardware 937-5879, is the non-food mirror of the grocery store next door, everything mundane and essential that you can't get in Mendocino's other shops. If it ain't here, you've gotta go to Fort Bragg, or beyond.

Left around the corner on Little Lake Street . . .

Village Florist 937-0907. Flowers for all occasions, wreaths, delivery.

Natural Herb Gardens Boutique and Mendocino Village Gallery 937-4999. Art, aromatherapy, flower essences, ayurvedic oils and more. Check out their lovely and evolving herb garden in front, then step inside to sample their broad selection.

Massage, Hot Tubs, Sauna

Sweetwater Gardens 937-4140. 955 Ukiah St. Hot tubs and sauna for rent, massage by appointment.

Orr Hot Springs Resort 462-6277. Developed hot springs 30 miles east of Mendocino. Reservations required (see CHAPTER 11. BACK ROADS).

Barefoot Mendocino 937-2636. Reflexology (foot massage) based therapies in numerous flavours.

Massage at Southern Exposure 937-4436.

Mendocino Massage 937-0111. Massage, facials, body wraps.

Massage at Visage Salon & Day Spa 937-2602.

Events

Contact the Chamber of Commerce, 961-6300, www.mendocinocoast.com, or local publications for exact dates.

JANUARY: Mendocino Crab & Wine Days

MARCH: Mendocino Whale Festival
Mendocino Art Center Bead Bazaar

APRIL: Spring garden tour

MAY: Historic House Tour
Mendocino Heritage Days
Mendocino Art Center Heritage Crafts Fair
Mother of All Garage Sales

JUNE: Mendocino Coast Garden Tour

JULY: Fourth of July Parade & Ice Cream Social
Mendocino Music Festival
Mendocino Crafts Fair, Heider Field (Last weekend in July)
Herb Fair

AUGUST: Mendocino Rotary Art Auction
Mendocino Art Center Summer Arts Fair

OCTOBER: Kelley House Silent Auction & Yard Sale
Amnesty International Benefit

NOVEMBER:
Mushroom Festival, Ford House
Wine and Mushroom Festival
Mendocino Country Christmas
Mendocino Art Center Thanksgiving Fair

DECEMBER: Celebrity Cooks & Kitchens Tour
Mendocino Christmas Festival
Sing-Along Messiah
Bed & Breakfast Candlelight Tour

THE FOG COMES
on little cat feet.
It sits looking
over the harbor and city
on silent haunches
and then moves on.

— Carl Sandburg,
Fog (excerpt)

6. Mendocino to Fort Bragg
10 miles

THE ROUTE

HIS LEG OF THE SHORELINE HIGHWAY OFFERS
the road's straightest stretch north of San
Francisco, forging a solid link between the
Mendocino Coast's two largest towns. Here
you will also find two of the biggest changes
since this book was first published nearly ten
years ago: the renaissance of the sleepy town
of Caspar, and the construction of the new
Noyo Bridge, scheduled for completion in
2005. The modern highway traverses coastal
terraces high enough to offer glimpses out to
sea, but drivers had best keep eyes on the
road to cope with relatively heavy, fast-
moving traffic. The original road here was
far different than today's straightaways,
winding through the communities of Pine
Grove and Caspar and dipping nearly to sea
level to contend with mud bogs and cross

Wreck of the Frolic

On the foggy night of July 25, 1850, the two masted schooner Frolic, built in Baltimore by the company that held the slave papers on Abolitionist Frederick Douglass, ran aground on the rocks north of Point Cabrillo. The Frolic, which normally ran opium from India to China, was taking oriental trade goods to booming San Francisco, where top dollar would be paid for the silks, porcelain, preserved ginger, and Canton-bottled Edinburgh ale on board.

The ship's captain and his mates took the leaky lifeboat to San Francisco, while the crew — all people of color — probably walked straight to the Sierra gold fields. When the shipwrecked officers reached the City, entrepreneur Henry Meiggs dispatched a salvage crew to the wild coast of Mendocino.

When salvage boss Jerome Ford found the wreck's location, the Pomo women camped nearby wore shawls of Chinese silk — the local natives had already scavenged the goods from the wreck, eating the ginger and making beads from the china. Ford went back to San Francisco empty handed, but told Meiggs of the vast redwood forests so close to the little bay at the mouth of Big River.

Meiggs soon sent Ford back up the coast, shipping a sawmill to meet him. By 1853 the little

several creeks on floating bridges. The contemporary route propels you between Mendocino and Fort Bragg in a scant 15 minutes.

THE DRIVE

Beyond the traffic signal at Little Lake Road, Highway One quickly reverts to two lanes, descending to cross the deep canyons of Jack Peters Creek and Russian Gulch on concrete spans built by the federal Works Progress Administration in 1939 and 1940.

Shoreline Highway climbs briefly to an intersection with Point Cabrillo Drive, the old highway. A left turn leads to the entrance to **RUSSIAN GULCH STATE PARK** (see Mendocino Listings) and, farther north, the Point Cabrillo headlands, now held in the public trust by California State Parks. **POINT CABRILLO LIGHT STATION AND PRESERVE** 937-0816 offers 300 acres of blufftop hiking (bicycles and leashed dogs OK on paved road only) and a 1909 lighthouse, now fully restored to its original style with a working Fresnel lens. A right turn leads to the headquarters for **MENDOCINO AREA STATE PARKS** 937-5804, where information on local parks is available.

Highway One continues north over a gentle hill. At the top you may glimpse the coastal headlands rolling west to Point Cabrillo and the Pacific. The Coast Highway descends to meet the north end of Point Cabrillo Drive, where a left turn winds down to tiny **CASPAR STATE BEACH**, sandwiched between the mouths of Doyle Creek and Caspar Creek. Across the road from the beach is **CASPAR BEACH R.V. CAMPGROUND** 964-3306, 14441 Pt. Cabrillo Dr. It has 89 sites, hookups, hot showers, laundry, cable tv, propane and store, $16–23, &.

Immediately after the state highway crosses a large span over Caspar Creek, a **VISTA POINT** on the left overlooks the site of the Caspar Lumber Company mill on alder-choked Caspar Creek where it empties into Caspar Bay. At the next intersection, a left turn detours into the once prominent town of Caspar.

CASPAR
(POP. 20, EL. 80)

*T*HE SLEEPY CASPAR YOU SEE TODAY makes it difficult to imagine it as having been one of the most prosperous towns on the Mendocino Coast. Nonetheless, Caspar thrived as a mill town slightly longer than Mendocino, shipping lumber from 1862 until 1955. In terms of celebrity, Caspar's shining moment came in 1925, when local beauty Fay Lanphier became Miss America.

Caspar took its name from another German settler, Siegfried Caspar, the first to settle in this locale. In 1861 he sold land to Mendocino pioneer William Kelley, who teamed up with Captain Richard Rundle to build a sawmill near the mouth of Caspar Creek. Jacob Green Jackson soon arrived and bought into the enterprise. By 1864 he purchased the company from Kelley and Rundle,

lumber town at Mendocino Bay was booming and the wreck of the Frolic was forgotten.

Roughly 80 years later some Pomo people camped at Point Cabrillo told a settler named Freitas about the old shipwreck. Local divers found the wreck, salvaging remaining goods and exploring the ruins. Some thought the wreck was a Chinese sampan, others had their own theories, but the wreck's true identity had been lost.

*Only after 1984, when archaeologists found arrow points of green glass and beads made of Chinese ceramics in excavations of a Pomo village site between Fort Bragg and Willits, did Dr. Thomas Layton fit the puzzle pieces together and reveal the wreck's historic identity. The remains of the Frolic are now on the National Register of Historic Places, and another big piece of Mendocino Coast history has been saved. Dr. Layton tells the whole enthralling story in his book,*Voyage of the Frolic, *published in 1997 by Stanford University Press.*

Caspar with mill and pond in foreground, 1910s.

expanding operations and building an apron chute on the north bluff.

When timber became scarce along Caspar Creek, Jackson built a standard-gauge railway from the mill north to his property along Jughandle Creek in 1874, allowing the timber harvest to continue. Animals pulled the first cars, but in 1875 Jackson brought a locomotive from San Francisco, establishing the first steam railroad in the county. By 1880 the railroad was 3½ miles long and a second loading chute had been built on the point.

The town of Caspar grew up on the bluff north of the mill. In 1880 Caspar had two stores, two hotels, a livery stable, three saloons, a church, a blacksmith shop, a shoe shop and an express and telegraph office. By 1885 the town's population grew to 500, and two years later Caspar got the first electric lights on the coast. Disaster struck in 1889 when the mill burned to the ground. But in the short span of five months, a better,

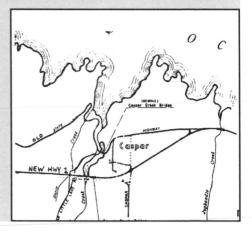

larger mill was in full swing.

Meanwhile, in 1884 the railroad crossed Jughandle Creek on the world's largest railroad trestle, 1000 feet long and 146 feet high. Caspar Lumber Company expanded its holdings north and east. By 1912 it owned more than 80,000 acres of prime redwood land reached by 18 miles of track. The railway peaked at 30 miles in 1924, then declined in fits and starts until it was closed down in favor of truck hauling in 1946. The Caspar sawmill closed in 1955. It had been owned by the same family for 93 years, with two men and two women presidents.

Recently Caspar has been awakening from a relative slumber of the last 50 years. Residents have been organizing since 1998 to revive and improve the town after its existence was threatened by the potential sale of much of the town's land. They have established the new **CASPAR COMMUNITY CENTER AND VILLAGE GREEN**, helped acquire 142 acres for state parks, and have an effective community organization for the first time since the sawmill shut down. More improvements are in the works, but you will already find a wealth of community events centered around the community center, like the new **CASPAR WORLD FOLK FESTIVAL** held in August. Stop by and see what's happening.

Today Caspar also offers **CASPAR INN** 964-5565, Caspar Road. The coast's roadhouse is open Tuesday through Saturday, from 4 pm to midnight on Tuesday through Thursday, from noon to 2 am on Friday and Saturday and features live entertainment most weekend nights, plus a full bar, pool, darts and sports TV. Next door, **LA PLAYA RESTAURANTE MEXICANA** 964-3989, is a tiny eatery serving tasty Jalisco-style Mexican food with an ocean view. Eat in or take out. Mon-Fri from 11am until 8 or 9pm, 'til 10pm on Fridays, Sat 4-10pm; $3–9. **WHAT'S AFOOT GALLERY**, downtown, hosts individual and group shows. **MASSAGE BY DEBRIN COX** 937-4024, at the Healing Room in Caspar.

CONTINUING ON . . .

The Shoreline Highway descends to cross Jughandle Creek, where two nature-oriented attractions sit beside the road. On the right **JUGHANDLE CREEK FARM & NATURE CENTER** 964-4630, Hwy One/Box 17, Caspar 95420, offers hostel-style accommodations in seven rooms of the 110-

Jughandle trestle with work train 1884

year-old farmhouse and programs for nature interpretation. The 39-acre farm features trails and meadows adjacent to Jughandle State Reserve, and provides a relaxing retreat site for groups or individuals. A left turn before the bridge enters the parking lot for **JUGHANDLE STATE RESERVE**. This lovely and important park preserves 778 acres of the Ecological Staircase, the prime example of the tectonic uplift of five successive marine terraces over the past half million years, and the resulting diverse plant communities that form the coastal landscape we enjoy today. These range from marvelous, wildflower-spattered coastal headlands on the first (newest) terrace, through stunted pygmy forest on the third terrace, to tall pine, cypress and redwood forests mixed with ancient dunes on the fifth terrace. The main trail is five miles long, with an interpretive brochure available at the parking area. Many other trails also explore the public lands.

Highway One crosses the 1938-vintage WPA bridge over Jughandle Creek and aims north toward Fort Bragg. Along the way you pass two more out-of-town lodgings. At Gibney Lane on the right is **ANNIE'S JUGHANDLE BEACH BED AND BREAKFAST INN**. In a half mile on the left is **PINE BEACH INN** (see Fort Bragg Listings).

Shoreline Highway ascends through forest over a small hill, then makes a gentle descent into the outskirts of Fort Bragg, where you encounter more commercial enterprises like the new **HENRY'S MEADOW** 964-7444, home and garden store, and **ANANSE VILAGE** 964-3534,

African import shop, than you have seen since entering Mendocino County. Traffic increases substantially and reduced speed is quickly required, although it is another ½ mile to the important junction with Highway 20, where there's a full service shopping center. Continue across the Noyo Bridge – being rebuilt into a wide four-lane concrete span, due for completion in 2005 as this book goes to press – and in 1½ miles you'll find the true heart of Fort Bragg, where many shops, specialty stores and galleries invite a stroll through the historic downtown.

In your impatience to arrive in town don't overlook one of the area's finest attractions, the **MENDOCINO COAST BOTANICAL GARDENS**, on the west side of the highway north of Ocean Drive.

FORT BRAGG
(POP. 6275, EL. 80)
Commercial Center & Former Mill Town

*T*HE LARGEST TOWN ON THE COAST BETWEEN SAN FRANCISCO and Eureka, Fort Bragg offers a full range of services for visitors and residents, including four banks and three car rental agencies. While lumber was king throughout most of the town's 115-year existence, today tourism keeps Fort Bragg a growing, prosperous community.

Compared to Mendocino's picturesque nineteenth century flavor, the city of Fort Bragg, established 1889, has always been proud of being a modern town. In addition to economical motels and shopping centers, you will find charming bed and breakfast inns, art galleries and shops.

Fortunately, Fort Bragg has retained pride in its historical buildings even as it continues to modernize. The downtown area is a Main Street Project City, receiving state and federal funding to retain and enhance its memorable buildings and flavor. Be sure to take a walk around the old town, along Main and Franklin streets between Redwood and Pine streets, sampling its historic buildings and browsing in the antique stores, shops and galleries they house. Nearby is the depot for the Skunk Train, offering daily excursions on an old rail line into the forests and canyons of the interior, a journey well worth taking.

Hiding in a deep canyon on the south edge of Fort Bragg is the rustic fishing village of Noyo. The large commercial fleet here has been struggling with reduced seasons in the last few years, but Noyo still retains its salty flavor. It offers a chance to eat fine fresh seafood while looking out at the harbor. You can also drive out to the jetty at the harbor's mouth or visit the sea lions that sometimes hang out near the dock at **SHARON'S BY THE SEA.** If you are slightly more adventuresome, sign up for a sport fishing, whale watching or sailboat charter and head out on the open ocean to see what this beautiful coast looks like from sea.

For the landlubber Fort Bragg's prime location at the heart of the coast's natural treasures offers many opportunities. Adjacent to the north end of town, 2299-acre **MACKERRICHER STATE PARK** offers miles of ocean front, forest and dune with choices for walks, fishing and beachcombing. Even closer to town is the pleasant stroll to **GLASS BEACH** and the Pudding Creek headlands. If you like your natural beauty more cultivated, head for the **MENDOCINO COAST BOTANICAL GARDENS** south of town, where native plants mingle with excellent collections of rhododendrons, azaleas, fuchsias, heritage roses, heathers and much more.

History

In 1852 George Hegenmeyer built a small sawmill three miles up the Noyo River. The local Pomo drove the settlers off during the first winter and took all they could, except for the guns the natives feared.

Military post at Fort Bragg, c.1860

In 1855 the home of Captain Rundle, who had a fishing station on the Noyo, was raided. Fifty-one coast residents cited these incidents in 1855 when they petitioned the

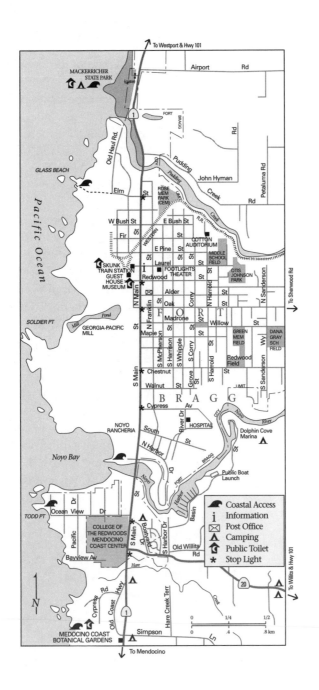

To Westport & Hwy 101

MACKERRICHER STATE PARK

Airport Rd

FORT BRAGG

GLASS BEACH

Old Haul Rd.

Pudding Creek

John Hyman

Petaluma Rd

Rd

Elm St

ROSE MEM PARK (CEM)

Rd

Pacific Ocean

W Bush St

E Bush St

Fir St

E Pine St

COTTON AUDITORIUM

WESTERN

MIDDLE SCHOOL FIELD

SKUNK TRAIN STATION GUEST HOUSE MUSEUM

Laurel St

FOOTLIGHTS THEATER

OTIS JOHNSON PARK

Redwood St

N Main

Alder St

N Sanderson

SOLDIER PT

Oak St

N Harrold

Corry

To Sherwood Rd

Pond

N Franklin St

F O R T

Madrone St

GEORGIA-PACIFIC MILL

Maple St

Willow St

GREEN MEM FIELD

DANA GRAY SCH FIELD

S McPherson

S Harrison

S Corry

S Whipple

S Harrold

Redwood Field

S Sanderson

Chestnut St

Grove St

Walnut St

LIMIT

B R A G G

Cypress Av

NOYO RANCHERIA

South St

River Dr

HOSPITAL

Noyo River

Dolphin Cove Marina

Noyo Bay

N Harbor St

Noyo St

FORT BRAGG

Public Boat Launch

Basin

Ocean View Dr

Dr

Harbor Dr

Coastal Access

Information

TODD PT

Pacific

COLLEGE OF THE REDWOODS MENDOCINO COAST CENTER

S Main

Harbor Dr

Old Willits Rd

Post Office

Camping

Public Toilet

Stop Light

Bayview Av

Hare

To Willits & Hwy 101

Cypress Rd

Old Coast Hwy

Hare Creek Terr

20

N

0   1/4   1/2
0   .4   .8 km

MEDOCINO COAST BOTANICAL GARDENS

Simpson

Ln

To Mendocino

The Man with the Wooden Dolls

Every North Coast mill town and logging camp teemed with colorful and strange characters. Fort Bragg's William Bennett was one of the strangest. In 1910 this handsome but lonely bachelor, tired of living alone in his large home, built himself a family of life-sized wooden dolls — father, mother and five daughters. As Frank Hyman tells it,

This family he could live with and be pleased — no backbiting women or squealing children for him. Bennett talked to them about the follies of womankind and found great comfort in their companionship. He always had the family at dinner with him and took pleasure in conversation with them. They were a very polite family.

When a neighbor's daughter got married, Bennett dressed the male doll in a wedding suit and one of the girl dolls in a bridal gown and put them on his front porch while the wedding went on across the street.

Bennett would bring the whole family to weekly dances, dressing the marble-eyed mannequins up real pretty. He put roller skates on one of his girls and danced the night away along with the rest of the crowd.

As Hyman relates, "When it became impossible for him to care

federal government, "that the Indians be provided for, and looked after, in such a manner, as will prevent their stealing our crops . . . and property." Within a year the U. S. Government established the Mendocino Indian Reservation, the fourth reservation in the nation. The reservation's 25,000 acres were bounded on the north by Ten Mile River, on the south by Noyo River, and on the east by the first line of hills.

In 1857 U. S. Army Lieutenant Horatio Gibson arrived with 20 soldiers to establish a post to keep peace on the reservation. They built the fort where the town of Fort Bragg is today. Lt. Gibson named the fort in honor of his friend and West Point classmate, Braxton Bragg, who would soon side with the Confederacy in the Civil War, eventually becoming a general in Robert E. Lee's army.

The reservation probably never held more than 1700 native people. Most of them had lived on or within 50 miles of the reservation lands, though the original purpose was to bring natives from all over northwestern California. By 1858

Noyo 1863, ferry at lower right

the reservation administrators were charged with graft and corruption. White workers were paid from reservation funds while native residents verged on starvation. Alexander Macpherson was lent native laborers to build a sawmill on reservation lands at the Noyo station, which brought many white settlers and ensuing conflicts. So many young native women were kidnapped at gunpoint by white men that the reservation was derided as "the U.S. Brothel" in 1859.

The fort closed in 1864 and the reservation was officially discontinued in 1866. Slowly the native people were forced to move east to the Round Valley Reservation at Covelo. In 1869 the lands of the Mendocino Indian Reservation were sold for $1.25 per acre.

Many settlers came to purchase the reservation lands. Macpherson continued to operate his mill while living in a grand eighteen-room house on the bluff, where Harbor Lite Lodge is today. His company suffered financial losses in 1877, and when he died in 1880, his heirs were left with very little except the house and mill.

As the town's population grew, so did the violence. When one immigrant arrived at Noyo in 1884, he stepped off the boat to hear a gunshot ring from a

for them in the style to which they had become accustomed, he decided to part with them rather than have them neglected." Bennett took them out in the yard, lit a big funeral pyre and cremated each one.

"Let's Go Get Some Seafood, Papa!"

Endangered Fisheries

Almost since time began, people have journeyed to the coast to enjoy a seafood meal. Just as ancient Pomo and other native peoples from far inland made seasonal trips to the shore to gather the ocean's bounty, families come today to fish for, dive for and even just dine on marine delicacies at coastal campgrounds and cafes.

The north coast's abundance of delectable marine goodies often amazes people on their first trip here, but if you've been visiting for years, you know today's bounty is but a pale shadow of past catches.

Supplies of salmon, shark, halibut, Dungeness crab, shrimp and even surf fish have dwindled greatly in recent decades, while steelhead fishing has all but disappeared as a north coast pastime. It's not that we eat too much. What is happening here?

Overfishing has contributed to the waning seafood wealth, but other factors most imperil our marine meal tradition. Rampant clearcutting of forests has

saloon. When the bar's back door opened, a dead body was thrown into the street. "I've come to a tough place!" the greenhorn remarked.

In 1885 the Fort Bragg Lumber Company was born when Charles R. Johnson moved down from Kibesillah and opened a sawmill near the old military post in Fort Bragg. Johnson installed a new band saw, the first of many innovations he made that modernized the redwood lumber industry. A pier was built at Soldier's Harbor, beside the mill at the foot of Oak Street. Fort Bragg Lumber Company laid its first standard gauge railroad tracks up Pudding Creek to extensive virgin redwood forests. The following year, the first locomotive arrived and Fort Bragg Lumber purchased most of the Noyo mill holdings.

C.R. Johnson also worked on developing a new city at the site of the old military post beside the mill. The Fort Bragg post office opened in 1886. When Fort Bragg incorporated in 1889, voters chose Johnson as the first mayor.

In 1893 the Union Lumber Company was created when Fort Bragg Lumber acquired White and Plummer's extensive Noyo holdings. The railroad reached the Noyo River forests after a tunnel extended the Pudding Creek line into the Noyo watershed.

Both the new town and the new company

Watching ships, Noyo Landing

grew rapidly. By 1904 the Union Lumber Company railroad reached 18 miles east to Alpine. Regular daily passenger service began on what had been strictly a logging railway until then. At Alpine one could make a stagecoach connection for Sherwood, north of Willits, where one could catch a train to Sausalito, with ferry connections across the bay to San Francisco. In 1905 the rail line was renamed California Western Railroad, the same name the Skunk Train operates under today. In that same year Union Lumber acquired the Mendocino Lumber Company and half of the Glen Blair Lumber Company.

The 1906 earthquake gave a big jolt to young Fort Bragg. Although the town sustained nearly one million dollars in damage, it could have been far worse. Most of the many fires started by the pre-dawn temblor were extinguished quickly despite the failure of Fort

dislodged tons of gravel and mud over the years, clogging north coast rivers and creeks and threatening salmon and steelhead runs. These fish begin their lives in freshwater streams, migrate to the ocean to grow big and strong, then return to their birthplace to spawn. While forestry regulations protecting rivers and creeks have been tightened in recent years, the changes may be too late for the prized local fish.

The other force most endangering north coast fisheries is recent treaties allowing giant factory ships from Asia to fish within a few miles of our shore. These immense floating factories indiscriminately scoop everything from the sea, discarding vast amounts of marine life as waste and processing gargantuan amounts of seafood compared to the mom 'n' pop nature of northern California's commercial fishing fleets.

Be sure to have a seafood feast during your visit. And when you get home tell your elected representatives to work for preserving natural marine resources.

If you visit around the Fourth of July, attend Noyo's **World's Largest Salmon Barbecue,** *a great party where everyone feasts on fresh salmon and dances to local bands. All the proceeds work toward restoring damaged salmon habitat.*

Barrel Race, Main Street c.1900

Bragg's water system. A company locomotive pumped water to extinguish the mill fire and an offshore steamship supplied town fire crews.

By 1910 Fort Bragg had surpassed Mendocino as "the liveliest, busiest town in the county," with the census counting 2300 residents. The railroad company struggled to push the tracks over to the main line at Willits. The effort was set back by the hard winter of 1906 and the depression of 1907. CWRR finally reached the main line at the end of 1911. The entire city of Fort Bragg seemed to turn out to celebrate the first run to Willits. Regular passenger trips began in summer 1912, giving Fort Bragg the first rail link between the Mendocino Coast and the outside world.

Fort Bragg was already doing well, but with the new rail link it thrived. Though the city streets remained unpaved, cement sidewalks wrapped around several blocks in the center of town. In addition to the usual numerous stores, banks, churches, schools, hotels and restaurants, Fort Bragg boasted two movie theaters, a newspaper, bottling works and hospital. By 1913 Fort Bragg promoted itself as the town "where Prosperity reigns, and where it rains Prosperity." Fort Bragg remained the largest town in the county until Ukiah surpassed it after the end of World War II.

Fort Bragg Lodging

Listings are organized from the most expensive to the least expensive

OCEAN VIEW LODGING $125–255
1141 N. Main, Fort Bragg 95437
964-1951/800-643-5482
www.oceanviewlodging.com

With Grecian-columned steps, pedestalled king or queen beds, and patios or balconies, these rooms with 180-degree whitewater ocean views are charming, spacious and comfortable.
30 rooms; min. stay summer & major holidays; V/ MC/AE/Disc; ocean views; phone/tv/refrig/bathtub/ computer port/coffee/hair dryer in rms; some rms w/spatubs/gas firplaces; adj. to hiking; ⛄

☆ ANNIE'S JUGHANDLE BEACH B&B INN $119–229
32980 Gibney Lane at Hwy One
Fort Bragg
964-1415/800-964-9957
www.ajinn.com

Whale watch from the front porch of this B&B, built in 1883 and furnished with family antiques, or hike to the ocean and Ecological Staircase Trail at Jughandle State Reserve. The owners/ innkeepers go out of their way to make guests comfortable in a farmhouse atmosphere.
4 rooms, 2 suites; full gourmet breakfast; MC/V/ checks; midweek rates; coffee in room; ocean views; wood stoves, spa tubs; some fireplaces

NORTH CLIFF HOTEL $99–225
1005 S Main St, Fort Bragg
962-2500/866-962-2550

New luxury hotel perched above the mouth of the Noyo River overlooking the Pacific. Rooms are quiet and spacious, with ocean views and balconies.

39 rooms; in-room continental breakfast; res. essential; all CCs; winter rates; phone/tv/refrig// computer port in room; some jacuzzis, fireplaces; ocean views; families welcome; ⛄

☆ GREY WHALE INN $90–220
615 N. Main St, Fort Bragg
964-0640/800-382-7244
www.greywhaleinn.com

A Mendocino Coast landmark since 1915, built in the classic Revival style. The inn offers spacious comfort, romantic decor, and the utmost in privacy. Enjoy a lavish buffet breakfast, then stroll to ocean, restaurants, shops, galleries, theatre, or Skunk train. AAA 3 diamond and Mobil 3 star approved.
14 rooms; full buffet breakfast; min. stay 2 nights wknds, 3 nights holiday wknds; MC/V/AE/checks; midweek winter disc.; 3 rooms w/mini-kitchens; private jacuzzi 1 rm; some ocean views, fireplaces, bathtubs; gardens; phone/tv in room; fireplace lounge w/ pool table, vcr; meeting facilities; facilities for children are limited; ⛄

ATRIUM B &B $99–175
700 N. Main St, Fort Bragg
964-9440/www.atriumbnb.com

Experience Victorian charm and uniquely decorated rooms. Centrally located inn provides ideal setting for a relaxed, romantic getaway. The lush indoor garden offers a comfortable place to reflect at day's end, cozy up with a book, or savor a glass of wine at sunset.
10 rooms; full gourmet breakfast; res advisable; V / MC/checks; off-season discounts;children over 12 welcome; some ocean views, bathtubs; tv/dvd/cd players in rm; gardens; adj to hiking

THE LODGE AT NOYO RIVER

$95–175
500 Casa Del Noyo Dr
Fort Bragg 95437
964-8045/800-826-1126
www.noyolodge.com

A quiet 125-year old country inn on beautifully landscaped grounds overlooking Noyo Harbor has old-fashioned spacious rooms and luxurious view suites with fireplaces, double bathtubs and private decks. Breakfast is served in the dining room or on sunny decks while sea lions, seals and pelicans cavort below.

17 rooms; continental breakfast; min. stay 2 nights wknds; reservations essential; V/M/AE; winter rates; river/harbor views, bathtubs; some rooms w/tv, fireplaces, soaking tubs; ♿

☆ WELLER HOUSE $95–170

524 Stewart St, Fort Bragg
964-4415/877-893-5537
www.wellerhouse.com

Ten luxurious guest rooms in an elegant 1886 residence listed on the National Register of Historic Places. Each room, impeccably decorated in high Victorian style, has its own theme, including two in a 40-foot high water tower, the tallest building in town, topped by an ocean-view hot tub. Relax on the gracious porch, saunter in English gardens, snuggle by the fireplace, and enjoy a bountiful breakfast in the upstairs ballroom. Featured in Sunset and the New York Times.

10 rooms w/ private bath; res. advisable; 2 night min. stay wkends in high season; all major CCs/ checks; midweek discounts; coffee & tea, refrig, microwave in commom area; some private spa tubs, ocean views, fireplaces, refrig; adj. to hiking; phone/ computer port, bathtub in rooms

COLONIAL INN $80–180

533 E. Fir St, Fort Bragg
964-1384/877-964-1384
www.colonialinnfortbragg.com

A 1912 Craftsman-style timber mansion houses Fort Bragg's oldest inn. It sits on beautiful grounds in the town's quiet, premier residential neighborhood, four blocks from downtown. Has the privacy, scale and services of a hotel with the warmth and charm of a B&B.

8-10 rooms (varies seasonally); full buffet brkfast; closed 2 wks early Jan; res. advisable; min. stay 2 nights major holidays; checks; some fireplaces, bathtubs; tv in rooms; concierge services; pets on approval; phone/computerport/refrig/admission to Botanical Gardens & full-service health club avail for guests; gardens

PINE BEACH INN $69–175

Hwy One, 3 miles S. of Fort Bragg
Box 1173, Fort Bragg
964-5603/888-987-8388

Walk to beach and cove through 12 acres of landscaped grounds in a majestic setting of redwoods by the sea.

51 rooms; min. stay 2 nights holiday wknds; V/ MC/AE; off-season reduced rates; smoking rm; 9 two-room family & deluxe suites; adj. restaurant; some ocean views, bathtubs; tennis; phone/tv in room; ♿

OLD STEWART HOUSE INN

$100–145
511 Stewart St, Fort Bragg
961-0775/800-287-8392
www.oldstewarthouseinn.com

Fort Bragg's oldest house, built 1876.

5 rooms; full breakfast; res. advisable; min. stay 2 nights summer wkends; V/MC/AE; tv in room; some fireplaces, bathtubs; gardens, families, pets welcome; ♿

☆ AVALON HOUSE $68-155
561 Stewart St, Fort Bragg 95437
964-5555/800-964-5556

www.theavalonhouse.com

A 1905 Craftsman house in a quiet, residential neighborhood close to attractions. Rooms with private baths, fireplaces, whirlpool tubs, down comforters, and ocean views. Enjoy all the romance of the Mendocino Coast, even if you never leave your room.
6 rooms; full breakfast; res. advisable; min. stay most wknds, holidays; MC/V/AE/Disc/checks; midweek disc. except holidays; some rms spa tub; gardens; adj. to hiking; private decks

HARBOR LITE LODGE $74-142
120 N. Harbor Dr, Fort Bragg
964-0221/800-643-2700

www.harborlitelodge.com

Most rooms at the lodge have private balconies overlooking Noyo River and fishing village. A cordial staff will assist you with meeting or vacation needs and information.
79 rooms; continental brkfast; res. essential; min. stay 2 nights wknds; V/MC/AE/Diners/checks; smoking rms; winter midweek non-holiday disc.; 2-bdrm unit; compl. coffee/tea/cocoa in office; sauna; 6 rooms w/wood stoves; bathtubs; phone/ tv/computer port/refrig in room; some ocean views, woodstoves; trail to fishing harbor; meeting facilities; ﹩

RENDEZVOUS INN $79-109
647 N. Main St, Fort Bragg
964-8142/800-491-8142

A charming B&B in a Craftsman-style house built in 1897 by the town apothecary. Four comfortable rooms upstairs and two pet-friendly rooms in the cottage all offer queen beds and private baths. The cottage is also available as a suite for families or couples traveling together.
6 rooms; full breakfast; 2 night min. stay some holiday wknds; MC/V/Disc/checks; tv in rooms; winter rates; 2 family suites; adj. restaurant; 1 rm w/wood stove; some ocean views;gardens; families, pets welcome

WISHING WELL COTTAGES $75-85
1.5 miles inland on Hwy 20
Fort Bragg
961-5450/800-362-9305

www.wishingwellcottages.com

Cottages with queen or king bed located in an older, rural neighborhood with flowers, trees and four acres of forest to walk, enjoy deer, quail and doves. BBQ and outside table for guests to use on sunny days.
2 cottages; min. stay 2 days, 3 on holidays; res. essential; V/MC/AE/Disc/checks; $10 each addt'l. person (up to 4); $375-425/week; complete kitchens; pets ok w/dep; phone/tv/vcr/microwave/ coffee/tea in cottages; piney woods

COUNTRY INN $65-145
632 N. Main St, Fort Bragg
964-3737/www.beourguests.com

This 1890s redwood residence offers charming and cozy rooms, all with private baths. Sit in the cozy parlor, enjoy the flower garden, munch in the vegetable garden, or soak in the hot tub.
8 rooms; continental buffet breakfast; 2 night min. stay wknds, 3 nights major holidays; res. advisable;MC/V/AE/Disc/checks; some ocean views, fireplace/woodstove, bathtubs; adj. to hiking; ﹩

GLASS BEACH INN $60-195
726 N. Main St, Fort Bragg
964-6774/www.glassbeachinn.com

A gracious inn that offers warm hospitality, relaxation, and breakfast cooked to order each morning. Located within walking distance to train, beaches, shops, restaurants, tennis,

swimming pool, and more.
8 rooms; full breakfast; MC/V/Disc/AE; off-season rates; ocean views; fireplaces; jacuzzi; bathtubs; adj. to hiking; phone/tv/computer port in room; children welcome, pets considered

EMERALD DOLPHIN INN $59-195
1211 S. Main St, Fort Bragg 95437
964-6699/866-964-6699
www.emeralddolphin.com

One of the newest inns on the coast, located on Highway One at Ocean View Drive, only ¼ mile from the Pacific and majestic coastal cliffs. Large adjacent field is ideal for kite-flying, dog walking, ball playing.
43 rooms; continental brkfast; coffee in rm; 2-3 night min. holidays; V/MC/AE/Disc/checks; winter rates; smoking rms; some ocean views, spa tubs; adj. to hiking; phone/catv/refrig/hairdryer/iron/safe in room; families, pets welcome; &

SURF & SAND LODGE $59-175
1131 N. Main St, Fort Bragg
964-9383/800-964-0184

Well-appointed new rooms, from singles to family units, on the waterfront at MacKerricher State Park. Sunsets and whale watching from your room or close at hand.
30 rooms; res. advisable; compl. coffee, tea; all CC; winter rates; fireplace, hot tub in deluxe rms; phone/tv/vcr/refrig/hair drier in room; ocean view; private decks; adj. to hiking; &

TRADEWINDS LODGE $59-150
400 S. Main St, Fort Bragg
964-4761/800-524-2244
www.fortbragg.org

Comfortable rooms in the heart of Fort Bragg at the largest full service motel in town. Family oriented, with many packages available.
92 rooms; min. stay holidays & special events; all CC; smoking rms; suites; apt. units w/kitchen; adj.

restaurant; group jacuzzi, heated indoor pool, exercise room, bathtubs; phone/tv/bathtubs in rm; guest laundry; pets OK; convention center; &*

BEACH HOUSE INN $59-150
100 Pudding Creek Rd., Fort Bragg
961-1700/888-559-9992
30 rooms; min. stay holidays; all major CCs; winter & midweek discounts;estuary views; phone/tv/refrig/microwave/coffee/bathtub in room; some fireplaces, ocean views; &

OLD COAST HOTEL $55-155
101 N Franklin St, Fort Bragg
961-4488/888-468-3550
www.oldcoasthotel.com

Recently renovated and restored 1892 Victorian hotel has pressed tin walls and shares plenty of history with the town. Each room has unique styling and a brass bed. Friendly staff provides helpful suggestions and can make reservations for local actiivities.
15 rooms; continental brkfast; all major CCs; phone/tv/bathtub in room; some fireplaces, filtered ocean views, balconies; gardens; adj. restaurant; families welcome; &

SEA BIRD LODGE $60-112
191 South St, Fort Bragg
964-4731/800-345-0022

Centrally located motel with restaurant adjacent. Swim in the indoor pool and revitalize in the whirlpool spa.
65 rooms; special package rates;V/MC/AE; adj. restaurant; jacuzzi/hot tub; heated indoor pool; bathtubs; phone/tv/refrig/coffeemaker in room; &

BEST WESTERN VISTA MANOR LODGE $49-299
1100 N. Main St, Fort Bragg
964-4776/800-821-9498

Refurbished rooms facing the ocean offer pleasant family-style lodging in a park-like setting. Close to beach and other attractions.

55 rooms, 3 suites, 2 cottages; continental brkfast; all CC; 2 suites w/bdrm, LR, fireplace; kitchens in cottages; heated indoor pool; ocean views; fireplaces in suites; bathtubs; gardens; phone/tv/hairdryer/iron in room; beach access tunnel

ANCHOR LODGE MOTEL $40–175
780 N. Harbor Drive/Box 1429
Fort Bragg 95437
964-4283/www.wharf-restaurant.com

Modern waterfront and economy rooms allow the visitor to become part of the river life of this quaint fishing village. Close to beach and fishing.

19 rooms; closed 2 weeks early January; MC/V/Disc/ checks; winter rates; smoking rms; penthouse apt. w/kitchen; adj. restaurant; ocean/river views; phone/ tv in rm; beach access; 1 rm க

SURF MOTEL $45–135
1220 S. Main St/Box 488
Fort Bragg
964-5361/800-339-5361

Very clean motel rooms with a beautiful center garden area with patio seating. Located at the south end of town away from town traffic, the motel provides a secluded area where fisherman guests can clean their fish.

54 rooms; light continental brkfst; all CC; seasonal rates; smoking rms; 2 1-bdrm efficiency apts; in-room coffee, tea, cocoa; bathtubs; gardens; phone/ tv in rm; BBQ/picnic area, horseshoe pit

EBB TIDE LODGE $45–129
250 S. Main St, Fort Bragg
964-5321/800-974-6730

In the heart of Fort Bragg, the lodge offers a landscaped garden and quiet, inviting rooms newly redecorated. Within walking distance of the famous Skunk Train and restaurants.

31 rooms; V/MC/AE/Diners; winter rates; smoking rms; some 2-room units; 5-rm suite w/kitchen (sleeps 8); bathtubs; gardens; phone/catv/coffee in room

COAST MOTEL $45–105
18661 N. Hwy One, Fort Bragg
964-2852

Located on five quiet, wooded acres with landscaped picnic and BBQ areas and pleasant poolside lounging. Clean rooms at reasonable rates, close to fishing, beaches, restaurants, and botanical gardens, without the bustle of downtown.

28 rooms; V/MC/checks; smoking rms; 2-bdrm unit; 3 rms w/kitchen; families, pets welcome; heated pool May-Oct; bathtubs; phone/catv/coffee in rm; க

SHORELINE COTTAGES $50–75
18725 N. Hwy One, Fort Bragg
964-2977

Newly remodeled, this basic economy motel is close to town and attractions.

11 rooms; res. advisable summer & holidays; V/MC; winter rates; catv in room; BBQ

SUPER 8 MOTEL $39–110
888 S. Main, Fort Bragg
964-4003

Affordable newly renovated rooms in a convenient location.

53 rooms, incl. 2 smoking rms; V/MC/AE/Disc; seasonal rates; adj. restaurant; some ocean views, refrig, microwave; bathtub/phone/catv in room; க

CHELSEA INN & SUITES $38–65
763 N. Main St, Fort Bragg
964-4787/800-253-9972

Located just three blocks from Glass Beach, three blocks from Skunk Train and close to North Coast Brewing Company, the inn offers clean rooms, friendly managers, and great value. Cafe One, featuring delicious vegetarian food, adjoins the motel.

49 rooms; V/MC/AE/Disc; off-season rates; adj. restaurant; bathtubs; smoking rms; adj. to hiking; phone/tv in room; க

Eateries

☆ THE RESTAURANT

418 N. Main St, Fort Bragg 95437

964-9800

www.therestaurantfortbragg.com

SB:$6–12, D: $18–26

Over 30 years in the same location with owner/chefs Jim Larsen and Susan Larsen. Enjoy fine dining in a charming art-filled dining room. Fresh seasonal fish, great steaks, house-made desserts, local wines and much more. Everything except bread made on premises. Three Stars Mobil Guide 29 years running.

Thur–Mon from 5 pm, Sun brunch 10–1; closed March; res. advisable; MC/V/Disc/checks; beer/ wine; seats 80; well behaved children welcome; &

THE RENDEZVOUS

647 N. Main St, Fort Bragg

964-8142/800-491-8142

D: $16–25

Focusing on superb service and French Country cuisine served in cozy, comfortable surroundings, one of the Mendocino Coast's fine dining experiences. Winner of Wine Spectator's Award of Excellence.

Wed–Sun from 5:30-8:30 pm, Fri, Sat 'til 9, ½ hour later each night from July 4-Labor Day; closed Wed in Jan, Feb; res. advisable; MC/V/Disc/checks; beer/wine; seats 40; &

WHARF RESTAURANT

32260 N. Harbor Drive/Box 1429

Fort Bragg

964-4283

L: $5–12, D: $7.50–25

A favorite spot of locals and coastal visitors for over 40 years. Panoramic views of the Noyo River and the Pacific Ocean create a unique atmosphere while guests relax, enjoying a cocktail or specialty of the house, featuring fresh fish, steak, or prime rib.

Daily; 11am-10 pm, bar open later; closed early January; res. advisable; MC/V/Disc/checks; full bar; seats 200; take-out; families welcome; &

☆ SHARON'S BY THE SEA

32096 N. Harbor Dr, Fort Bragg

962-0680/www.sharonsbythesea.com

L: $5–16 D: $10–24

Casual dining on the wharf with warm and personal service. Cozy tables by the fire or open air on the dock look out to Noyo Harbor. All food made to order, featuring fresh seafood and salads with a southern Italian touch.

Daily 11:30–3, 5–9; closed early December; res. advisable for dinner; AE/V/MC/Diners/local checks; beer/wine; seats 30 inside, 40 outside; take-out

CLIFF HOUSE OF FORT BRAGG

1011 S. Main St, Fort Bragg

961-0255

D: $14–25

Continental cuisine with emphasis on fresh fish and steak. Every table has a great view of ocean, bay or dock.

Daily 4–9, 'til 9:30 in summer; res. advisable; V/ MC/Disc; full bar; seats 200; take-out (x Sat); families welcome; &

CARINE'S FISH GROTTO

Noyo, Fort Bragg

964-2429

L/D: $9–25

Casual harbor view dining in a friendly family atmosphere since 1947. Italian seafood dishes made from scratch. Ciopinno, clam chowder, and great burgers. Dine inside or on the riverfront dock.

Daily 12–9; closed periodically in winter, call ahead; beer/wine; seats 80; take-out; &

OLD COAST HOTEL BAR & GRILL

101 N. Franklin, Fort Bragg 95437
961-4488/888-468-3550
L: $7–12, D: $8–22

The newly renovated hotel restaurant features Italian and California cuisines, specializing in seafood, pastas, steak and prime rib. Extensive wine list and full bar too.

Lunch Fri-Sun from 12, dinner Thurs-Tues from 4 pm; res. advisable; all major CC; full bar; seats 100, plus patio; take-out; families welcome; ♿

☆PIACI PUB & PIZZERIA

120 W Redwood Ave, Fort Bragg
961-1133
D: $9–20

A delicious blend of European and American style pizza — home of the adult pizza. Plus good salads, calzones and focaccias and the largest selection of micro-brew beers on the North Coast. Good wine selection too.

Daily from 4–9 pm, 'til 10 on Fri, Sat; V/MC/checks; beer/wine; seats 38; take-out; ♿

☆ MENDO BISTR0

301 N. Main St, Fort Bragg
964-4974
D: $8–20

Creative American and northern Mediterranean cuisine, featuring fresh house-made pastas, seafood, steaks and vegetarian choices. Over 30 Mendocino County wines, all available by the glass, plus ten draft beers including Guinness and local micro breweries.

Daily 5–9 pm; reservations only for parties of 7 or more; closed Thanksgiving, Christmas;V/MC/Disc/AE/Diner's/checks; beer/wine; seats 200; take-out; families welcome; ♿

NORTH COAST BREWING CO. TAPROOM & GRILL

444 N. Main St, Fort Bragg
964-3400
L: $5–11, D: $8–19, Bar: $5-15

Featuring their own national award-winning beers — recently named "One of the ten best breweries in the world" at the World Beer Championships in Chicago — the restaurant serves fresh salmon, pastas, Cajun specialties, fish and chips. Chosen '93–'94 Mendocino County "Restaurant of the Year" by the Great Chefs of Mendocino County.

Daily 11:30 am–11 pm; ; V/MC/Disc/AE/checks; beer/wine; seats 150; take-out; families welcome; ♿

CAFE ONE

753 N. Main, Fort Bragg
964–3309
SB: $6–12, B: $6–10, L: $7–14, D: $8–18

Find this popular organic restaurant at the north end of town. The spacious atmosphere is family-oriented and casual with a friendly staff. They serve vegetarian and vegan dishes plus organic chicken, turkey and seafood.

Mon–Sat 7–2:30, Sunday brunch 8–2, dinner Thur–Sat 5–8:30 pm; V/MC/local checks; beer/wine seats 63; take-out;families welcome; ♿

OSCAR'S RESTAURANT & PHANTOM CAFE

Hwy One, south of Fort Bragg
Box 1404, Fort Bragg
964-0203
B: $6–8, D: $10–15

Casual family dining featuring Italian cuisine dinners and hearty breakfasts; lounge with full bar facility. Live jazz every night.

May–Sept only; B: 7–11:30 am, Sun 'til 2 pm, 6–9:30 for dinner; checks; full bar; seats 115; take-out; ♿

TW'S GRILLE & BAR
400 S. Main, Fort Bragg 95437
964-4761
B: $3–7, L: $4–10, D: $7–19
Casual family-style restaurant serves large portions at reasonable prices.
Daily 5 am–11 pm; all major CC's; full bar; seats 200; families welcome; take-out; ♿

SAMRAAT CUISINE OF INDIA
546 S. Main St, Fort Bragg
964-0386
L: $6–8, D: $8.50–15.50
Serving a toothsome selection of Indian foods, with tandoori, curry and vegetarian specialties plus samosas, pakoras, mulligatawny soup, masalas and nan breads.
Daily, lunch 11:30–2:30 (no lunch Sunday), dinner 5–9:30; res. advisable; V/MC/Diner's/AE/ local checks; beer/wine; seats 85; take-out; ♿

CHAPTER & MOON
780 N. Harbor Dr, Fort Bragg
962-1643
L: $5.25–10, D: $8-15.50
New restaurant on the waterfront serves fresh fish and meat sandwiches, plus fish & chips, meatloaf, chicken, steaks, salads.
Tues–Sun 11–8; V/MC; beer/wine; seats 30; families welcome; ♿

☆ D'AURELIO'S & SONS
438 S. Franklin, Fort Bragg
964-4227
D: $8–15
A family owned and operated restaurant serving homemade pizza and traditional Italian dinners from pasta to meat to seafood in a casual family atmosphere. Daily specials available.
Daily 5–9 pm; V/MC/Disc/checks; beer/wine; seats 62; families welcome; take-out; ♿

NORTH COAST SPORTS CAFE
118 E. Redwood, Fort Bragg
964-1517
L/D: $7–21
Enjoy multiple large tv screens as you eat. Specialties include steaks, seafood, pastas, chicken and salads plus several kids meals and ten beers on tap.
Thur–Fri, Mon from 3 pm, Sat–Sun from 11 am; V/MC/local checks; beer/wine; seats 114; take-out; ♿

☆ VIRAPORN'S THAI CAFE
Chestnut & Main (across from Rite-Aid), Fort Bragg
964-7931
L/D: $6.50–19
Everything is prepared to order by owner/chef Viraporn Napan Lobell using authentic and fresh ingredients in her family style Northern Thai cuisine, with vegetarian, seafood and meat choices.
Wed–Mon 11:30–2:30, 5–9; large parties call ahead; checks; beer/wine; seats 22; take-out

EL SOMBRERO
221 N. Franklin St,
Fort Bragg
964-5780
L: $6–8, D: $7–14
Traditional Mexican food made fresh daily. Specialties include crab enchiladas, seafood burritos, camerones, fajitas and carne adobada. Live music on Friday, Saturday and Sunday nights.
Tues–Sat 11:30–9:30, Sun 4–8; all CCs/checks; full bar; seats 120; families welcome; take-out; ♿

RESTAURANT EL MEXICANO
701 N. Harbor Dr, Fort Bragg
964-7164
B/L/D: $7–12
Home style Mexican food at Noyo Harbor. Large portions or a la carte.

Mon–Sat 10:30–8:30; V/MC/checks; beer/wine; take-out; seats 50; ⟲

MAIN STREET DINER
322 N. Main, Fort Bragg 95437
964-7910
WB/L/D: $8–11

Hearty traditional American food. Nobody leaves hungry. Weekend brunch too.

Mon–Wed, Fri 11 am–7 pm; brunch on wkend 8:30–1; V/MC/ local checks; seats 15

☆BERNILLO'S PIZZERIA & SUBS
220 E. Redwood, Fort Bragg
964-9314
$6–22

Classic hand tossed pizza with fresh ingredients and dough made daily. Hot subs, salads and beer on tap. Pizza by the slice for lunch.

Mon–Sat 11–9, closed 3 weeks in January; checks; beer/wine; families welcome; take-out; seats 35

ROUND TABLE PIZZA
740 S. Main/Box 740, Fort Bragg
964-4987
$5–22

Pizza plus salad bar, fresh made sandwiches, family atmosphere. All you can eat lunch buffet Mon–Fri 11:30–2.

Daily 11–9 pm, later in summer; V/MC/checks; beer/wine; seats 120; take-out; delivery in town; ⟲

PAPA MURPHY'S PIZZA
Boatyard Center, Fort Bragg
961-0777
$7–16

Take and Bake pizza and calzones. Pizzas made to order using the freshest ingredients and dough made daily in-store.

Daily 10–8; local checks; ⟲

PIZZA FACTORY
111-C Boatyard Center
Fort Bragg
961-0580
$7–14

If you're on the road without a tv, head here for pizza, pasta, hot sandwiches or salad bar and get your sports fix on one of two big-screen tvs, or send the kids to spend their quarters on the game arcade.

Daily 11–9, to 10 pm in summer; V/MC/Disc/checks; beer/wine; seats 100+; take-out; delivery; ⟲

PERKO'S FAMILY DINING
898 S. Main, Fort Bragg
964-6420
B: $3–10, L: $5–7.50, D: $7.50–12

Family-style restaurant with friendly staff serves steak, burgers, seafood, pasta, chicken and more, plus daily specials. Several soup choices daily. Many choices for breakfast too.

Daily 6 am–9 pm; 'til 10 pm in summer; V/MC/ Disc/AE; beer/wine; seats 110; families welcome; take-out; ⟲

EGGHEAD'S RESTAURANT
326 N. Main St/Box 2540
Fort Bragg
964-5005
B/L: $5–13

Homestyle local favorite with Wizard of Oz theme since 1976. Breakfast served all day—prepared-from-scratch omelettes, cinnamon bread, and other egg dishes. Burgers, sandwiches, salads for lunch. Vegetarian treats always available.

Thurs–Tues 7 am–2 pm, may close early Dec.; V/ MC/checks; seats 35; families welcome; take-out; ⟲

LA BAMBA TAQUERIA
124 N. Franklin, Fort Bragg
964-7747

L/D: $4.50–13

Diverse Mexican fare in the back of a Mexican grocery. Menudo on weekends.

Daily 10–8; take-out; seats 20

☆CAP'N FLINTS

32250 N. Harbor Dr,
Fort Bragg 95437
964-9447
L/D: $4–12

Casual, sit-down, full service seafood restaurant with river /harbor views serves fish and chips, shrimp louies, stuffed artichokes and more for the seafood lover. Hamburgers, hot dogs and children's portions.

Daily 11–8:30, 1 hour later in summer; closed Thanksgiving & Christmas; checks; beer/wine; seats 100; families welcome; take-out; &

DAVID'S RESTAURANT & DELICATESSEN

450 S. Franklin, Fort Bragg
964-1946
B/L: $5–10

Full country breakfast with homemade biscuits and gravy, "eggs-taters-n-toast," and creative omelettes. Gourmet sandwiches and hamburgers.

Mon–Sat 6 am–2 pm; V/MC/checks; seats 65; families welcome; take-out; &

THE FISH HOUSE

1064 S. Main, Fort Bragg
964-7075
B: $2–9, L/D: $3–16

Home-cooking, nothing frozen; fresh fish from the harbor.

Daily 8–8; local checks; seats 26; take-out

RESTAURANTE LOS GALLITOS

130 S. Main St, Fort Bragg
964-4519

L/D: $3–12.25

Authentic northern Mexican food made fresh daily, a la carte and combination plates. Specializing in fresh local seafood served Mexican style. Menudo on Sundays.

Mon–Wed, Fri–Sat 11–8, Sun 10–7; checks; beer; seats 36; families welcome; take-out; &

HOME STYLE CAFE

790 S. Main, Fort Bragg
964-6106
B: $4.50–11; L: $4–11

"Where good cooking comes first." A broad selection of freshly made dishes are served in a casual, friendly atmosphere.

Tues–Sun 5 am–2 pm; closed last half Jan.; V/MC; take-out; seats 52; &

TAQUERIA RICARDA

647 Oak St, Fort Bragg
961-8684
B/L/D: $3–8.50

The most authentic taqueria in town, where the owner, Ricarda, is also the head cook. Authentic Mexican food made fresh every day, with traditional meat, bean and chicken choices to fill a la carte burritos and tacos, plus hearty combination plates with beans and rice.

Tues–Fri 11–8:30, Sat–Sun 10–9 ; checks; beer/wine; seats 39; families welcome; take-out; &

CAFE VIENNA

120 S. Main St, Fort Bragg
964-8674
B: $4–7, L: $4.50–6.50

This European-style coffeehouse serves good espresso drinks and breakfast daily. Thier lunches include great salads and hot entrees: homemade soups, veggie dishes, sausages, wienerschnitzel and more.

Daily, Mon–Fri 7–5,Sat 8–5, Sun 8–3; checks; seats 30; families welcome; take-out; &

NOYO BOWL

900 N. Main St, Fort Bragg 95437
964-4051
B/L/D: $3–10

A family-oriented bowling center/diner serving homemade food.

Daily 7 am–11 pm; Fri–Sat 'til 12 am; checks; full bar; seats 65; take-out; ♿

☆ HEADLANDS COFFEEHOUSE

120 E. Laurel, Fort Bragg
964-1987
www.headlandscoffeehouse.com
B/L/D: $2–10

Traditional-style coffeehouse in downtown serves espresso drinks, teas, fresh juices, beer and wine. A wide variety of delicious entrees, sandwiches, salads, snacks and delectable desserts. A lively place with live music nightly and conversation always, plus local art displays.

Daily 7 am–10 pm, 'til 11 on Fri, Sat; MC/V/ Disc/checks; beer/wine; seats 40; families welcome; take-out; ♿

JENNY'S GIANT BURGER

940 N Main, Fort Bragg
964-2235
L/D: $2.50–7

Family owned and operated business serves great burgers, fries and shakes. Old fashioned quality and friendly service.

Daily 10.30–9 pm; checks; seats 20 + outside; take-out; families welcome; ♿

LAUREL DELI & DESSERTS

The Depot, 401 N. Main,
Fort Bragg
964-7812
B/L: $1.25–6

Fresh food made from scratch in a homey atmosphere. Award winning clam chowder. Fresh baked goods.

Daily 7–3, Sat 8–4; V/MC/ local checks; take-out; seats 60; ♿

B&L ESPRESSO

The Depot, 401 N. Main, Fort Bragg
964-7778
B/L: $1.50–5

Full breakfast and lunch specials daily. Homemade soup, fruit smoothies, milkshakes, chai, espresso drinks.

Daily 6am–5pm, 1 hour later in summer; ATM/ checks; beer/wine; seats 60; ♿

HARVEST MARKET DELI & BAKERY & SAN PAN STIR FRY

171 Boatyard Center,
Fort Bragg
964-7000
$1–10

Full service delicatessen serving vegetarian, organic and gourmet entrees. Features include sushi made daily and authentic Chinese food, plus soup, salad, sandwiches and desserts. From-scratch bakery goods, fruit/vegetable platters and cakes to order.

Daily 5 am–11 pm; V/MC/AE/checks; beer/wine/ liquor; some seating (no alcohol at tables); take-out; riding shopping carts, ♿

MENDOCINO COOKIE CO.

301 N. Main, Fort Bragg
964-0282
$1.60–5

Award winning coffee and espresso drinks plus pastries, muffins, scones, bagels, ice-cream, shakes and of course, cookies.

Daily 6:30 am–5 pm, half an hour later in summer; V/MC/AE/checks; take-out; ♿

ESPRESSO DRIVE-THRU
1080 S. Main St, Fort Bragg 95437
964-3350

$1-4

This drive-through espresso bar just south of the Noyo bridge offers quality coffee drinks plus fruit smoothies, Italian ices and baked goods.

Daily, Mon–Sat 6–6, Sun 6–5; take-out

☆ COWLICK'S ICE CREAM CAFE
250B N. Main St, Fort Bragg
962-9271

$1-5

This new fun spot makes and serves yummy handmade ice cream. Lunch items include hot dogs, chili dogs, sausages, etc., but enjoy a cone, sundae or banana split. Watch them make ice cream, throw a birthday party, even treat your dog to free ice cream!

Daily 11 am–9 pm, 'til 10 on Fri, Sat in summer; seats 55; take-out; &

Campgrounds

WOODSIDE RV PARK 964-3684, 17900 Hwy One, has 104 sites with hookups, hot showers, sauna, cable tv and store. $19–27.

POMO CAMPGROUND 964-3373, 17999 Tregoning Lane, has 120 sites, hookups, hot showers, cable tv, laundry, propane and store. $22–29. &

LEISURE TIME CAMPGROUND 964-5994, 2½ miles east on Hwy 20, has 83 sites, hookups, hot showers, laundry and cable tv. $19–27.50. &

DOLPHIN ISLE RV PARK 964-4113, 32399 Basin St, has 83 sites, hookups, hot showers, laundry, propane and deli. $25. &

HARBOR RV PARK 961-1511, 1021 S. Main, has 83 sites, hookups, hot showers, laundry and cable tv. $23–25.

HIDDEN PINES CAMPGROUND 961-5451, 18701 Hwy One, has 50 sites, hookups, hot showers and cable tv. Pets ok. $18–28.

Outdoor Activities

MENDOCINO COAST BOTANICAL GARDENS 964-4352, 18220 Hwy One. This 47-acre showcase garden slopes down to the shoreline. The east end displays wondrous collections of rhododendrons, azaleas, roses, heathers, fuchsias, succulents, ivies and camellias you can explore on winding paths. As you wander west, native plants mingle with gardens until natives dominate in pine-sheltered Fern Canyon and on the grassy headlands. Bloom peaks in May, but something's blooming here every month. The splendid grounds invite a walk any time, and deserve a picnic lunch when the sun shines. A delightful gift shop and excellent retail nursery help support the nonprofit effort. Daily 9–5 March–Oct, 9–4 Nov–Feb.

Fort Bragg boasts several small specialty nurseries gardeners might want to visit. We suggest calling first. Working north from the Botanical Gardens:

Regine's Fuchsia Gardens & Orchid Bench 964-0183
Heritage Roses 964-3748
Simply Succulents 964-0536
Hortus Botanicus 964-4786, Hanson Lane. Orchids, D. Austin English roses, clematis, and much more.
Summers Lane Nursery 964-8912
Sherwood Nursery 964-0800. By appointment.
Iris Gallery 964-3907. May, June, Fri-Mon 10–5.

California Western Railroad THE SKUNK 964-6371, 1-800-77-SKUNK, www.skunktrain.com, foot of Laurel St. Take a train trip through the redwood forest on this historic line. Antique rail cars pulled by diesel or steam locomotives, or self-powered trolley cars, run 25 miles to Northsur, crossing 30 bridges and passing through a long tunnel. A must for rail buffs and one of the coast's biggest attractions.

Fort Bragg Cyclery 964-3509, 221 N. Main. Bike rentals and repairs.

Ricochet Ridge Ranch 964-7669, 24201 Hwy One, Cleone. Lari Shea leads guided horseback rides on the beach or in the redwoods. Western or English tack.

Lost Coast Trail Rides 961-0700, Fort Bragg. Call to reserve for private or group rides on the beach, in the forest, or on a working cattle ranch.

Outdoor Store 964-1407, Main at Redwood. Gear sales and rental. Trail information. Guided hiking trips to the Lost Coast.

Lost Coast Kayaking 937-2434, sea cave kayak tours and rentals.

Farmers Market Wednesdays 3:30–6 on Laurel Street between Franklin and McPherson, May–Oct.

Ocean Fishing & Whale Watching Trips

ANCHOR CHARTER BOATS 964-4550, Box 103. Fishing and whale watching trips on the *Lady*

Irma and *Trek II.*

NOYO FISHING CENTER
964-3000. Coastal cruises, sport fishing and whale watching daily.

PARTY BOAT PATTY-C 964-0669, Box 572. Fast 30-foot boat fishes six people for salmon and bottom fish.

TALLY HO II 964-2079, Old Fish House, N. Harbor Dr. Fishing and whale watching trips.

Diving

SUB-SURFACE PROGRESSION 964-3793, 18600 Hwy One. Dive information, gear sales and rental and classes. Also kayak, boogie board and surfboard rentals and fishing charters.

NOYO PACIFIC OUTFITTERS 961-0559, 32400 N. Harbor Dr. Kayak rental, dive information, gear rental.

Parks & Beaches

GLASS BEACH, Elm St. and Old Haul Rd, northwest corner of Fort Bragg. Site of the town dump into the 1960s, relentless surf has washed and worn it into tiny glittering shards of the past.

MACKERRICHER STATE PARK 937-5804, with 143 campsites, is one of the nicest coastal parks in California. The park's 2299 acres offer picnicking, tidepooling, hiking, biking and equestrian trails, excellent whale-, seal- and bird-watching at Laguna Point, rock and surf fishing along the 8-mile shoreline and freshwater fishing at 15-acre Lake Cleone. ⑃

JUGHANDLE STATE RESERVE

937-5804. See Caspar.

JACKSON STATE FOREST 964-5674. More than 50,000 acres of forests east of Fort Bragg and Mendocino are managed for timber, but also provide free campsites and picnic areas plus trails and old logging roads for hiking and mountain biking. Call for a map and current information about areas closed for logging.

Indoor Activities

GUEST HOUSE MUSEUM 964-4251, 343 N. Main. 10–4 Tues–Sun in summer, Wed–Sun 11–3 rest of year. Built 1892 by the brother of the founder of Union Lumber, this fine old house has historical exhibits about the area.

Fort Bragg Fort Building 430 N. Franklin. Built 1857 as the commissary for the military post. Visit the only remnant of the fort, with historic photos and maps.

Coast Cinemas 964-2019, Franklin and Madrone streets. First-run movies at this fourplex.

Noyo Bowl 964-4051, 900 N. Main.

Redwood Health Club 964-6336, 401 Cypress. Indoor pool, racquetball courts, gymnasium, tennis courts. Daily. Daily passes available.

Fort Bragg Recreation Center 964-9446, 213 E. Laurel. Public indoor pool, roller rink, exercise and other classes.

Second Story Studios 964-3504,

307 E Redwood. Walk-in and on-going dance classes for all ages.

Redwood Coasters Square Dance Club 964-5140. Call for dates of hoedowns or to attend weekly workshops.

Chamber of Commerce 961-6300/ 800-726-2780, 332 N. Main/Box 1141, Fort Bragg 95437.

Performing Arts

Gloriana Opera Company 964-7469 Musical comedy productions of outstanding quality, now in its twenty-seventh year. Energetic company takes on several productions each year. Call for info.

Opera Fresca 937-3646 . This new company has won critical praise for their innovative productions.

Footlighter's 964-3806, Laurel and McPherson. Gay '90s reviews and melodramas for more than 45 years. Lots of silliness and song, Memorial Day through Labor Day, Wed & Sat, 8pm.

Symphony of the Redwoods 964-0898. Excellent local symphony concerts under the musical direction of Alan Pollack, founder of the Mendocino Music Festival. 18 and under admitted free. October through May.

Galleries & Shops

We'll take you on a walking tour of the art venues and fun shops in downtown Fort Bragg. The town has been experiencing a cultural renaissance in recent years, with many new stores opening and artists coming out of the woods to show their work in local galleries and a few of the shops. Our gallery/shop walk starts at the Town Hall on the southwest corner of Main and Laurel, where you'll find clean public rest rooms.

☆ **FIRST FRIDAYS** are the best time to celebrate and experience Fort Bragg's new cultural florescence. Starting about 6 pm on the first Friday of each month, hundreds of locals, both artists and patrons of the arts, take over the normally nighttime-quiet downtown for a gala party with openings, refreshments and special events, sometimes including ballroom dances and live music, all within a two block area. On First Fridays no one knows what might happen, so come down and find out.

Cross Main to the east side and . . .

Tangents 964-3884. This shop, started 17 years ago in Mendocino, is a favorite. It holds fascinating surprises, whether unique crafts, clothing, curiosities, uncommon cards, or artifacts and objects from around the world including Africa and New Mexico, plus unusual magazines. Also the ticket outlet for many area events.

Walk south to . . .

Northcoast Artists Gallery 964-8266. This co-operative gallery of local artists banded together with their neighbors to create First Friday. They display diverse fine arts including painting, photography, jewelry, ceramics, wearables, sculpture and woodwork.

Triangle Tattoo & Museum 964-8814, upstairs, takes the ancient skin art to new places.

For the Shell of It 961-0461. Find pieces of the ocean to take home.

The Spunky Skunk Toy Store 961-5443 features games and puzzles for all ages, plus toys.

Paws for Cats & Dogs 964-3322. Fun things for your pets.

Teamwork 964-9122 does quality, long-lasting T-shirt transfers, so get that favorite photo or art copied at Mendo Litho 964-0062 and bring it here for a souvenir shirt.

Carol Hall's Hot Pepper Jelly Co. 961-1422 sells locally made food products and gifts as well as their flagship line, with daily tasting of many goodies.

Out on a Limb 964-4846. Creative gifts for the garden.

Windsong Books & Records 964-2050 has new and used books, vinyl and CDs, plus cards and gifts.

Walk to the corner. Across Main Street is . . .

The Company Store. Renovated in 1997,the original Union Lumber Co. store now houses a variety of shops, including:

Navarro River Knits 964-9665 has gifts and supplies for knitters, plus great yarns.

Casual Collections 964-1563 stocks women's clothing and accessories.

Station House Cigar Shop 961-0933. Fine cigars plus cool clothes and hats.

House in the Country 962-0110. European-inspired decorative accessories for home and garden.

The Music Merchant 964-6920. CDs and casettes for a wide range of tastes.

Candies By the Sea 964-4716. A cool selection of unusual candies, plus smoothies and shaved ice treats.

Cooking Up Ideas 964-5223. New and used cookbooks, mixes and more.

Kid's Corner 964-9577.Baby and children's clothing up to size 16, plus toys.

Across Redwood Street is:

The Outdoor Store 964-1407, where you'll find camping and hiking gear and topographic maps, plus trail info.

Walk east on Redwood Street a half block to . . .

Mendocino Moulding 964-4932. Shows by regional artists. Original, limited edition, poster art.

Continue up Redwood to the next block. On the south is . . .

Family Hands 961-0236, a gallery of unique furnishings for your home. Gifts from around the globe.

Guatemala for Now 964-6915. Colorful clothing and import goods.

Across the street is . . .

The Bookstore 964-6559. Exhibits by local painters amidst their well chosen selection of used books.

Walk back west across Franklin Street and go right. On the west side are . . .

Well House West 964-2101. Distinctive house and kitchen wares, clothes.

Bragg About Books 964-7634. Broad selection of used books.

Across the street you'll find lingerie and the heart of the antique district . . .

Understuff 964-5013. Intimate apparel from pre-teens to plus sizes.

Wildlife Workshop & Gallery 964-6598. Limited-edition prints and originals of wildlife art, including the owner's fish reproductions. Nature learning center, custom rod building.

Gone Surfing 961-0889 has hip clothes, skateboards and surf gear.

Good Stuff 964-3032, **Por Richard's** 964-4531, **Mendocino Vintage Emporium** 964-5825, **Market Place Antiques** 961-1070 and **Whistlestop Antiques** 961-0902 all offer antiques and collectibles of a wide variety. This block also offers **Racine's** 964-2416, art supplies and stationery.

On the southwest corner of Franklin at Laurel Street is . . .

Cheshire Bookshop 964-5918. Fort Bragg's full service bookstore since 1973.

Across Laurel Street (the Rodeo Drive of Fort Bragg) is . . .

Wind & Weather 964-6598. Everything weather watchers might want, including the latest forecast, plus garden sculpture.

Heading west on Laurel Street . . .

Ballard & Dodge 964-6435, 800-701-SOAP. A bath and shower shop.

North Soles Footwear 962-9111. Unique European styles.

Vie Vie Boutique 962-0687. Clothing and accessories.

Small Treasures 964-7288 has gifts for babies.

Erin Dertner Gallery 964-5300.

Papa Birds 964-5604. Field guides, feeders, nest boxes, baths.

Riley Creek 964-7509. Gifts for home and garden.

Green Door Studio 964-6532. Sculpture by Dan Hemann.

Headlands Coffeehouse 964-1987 has revolving exhibits in their clean, well lit space, plus live music nightly.

Frame Mill Artworks 964-6464. Good selection of art prints, plus gifts and professional framing.

Sacred Beginnings 961-1650. Gifts, beads, incense and alternative books.

Mendocino Hemp Company 962-0557. Broad choice of hemp items from clothes to stuffed anmals and body care products.

Down on the corner at Main Street is . . .

Fiddles & Cameras 964-7370. Monthly photography exhibits, plus a complete camera and music shop.

For the culinary portion of our tour, walk north on Main Street to . . .

Round Man's Smokehouse 964-5954, 800-545-2935. They feature premium smoked salmon and other smoked and fresh meats, fish and cheese. You'll also find picnic and kitchn supplies.

Another block north leads to . . .

Mendocino Chocolate Company 964-8800. They make and sell their delicious truffles here.

Walk back south on the west side of Main to . . .

North Coast Brewing Company Brewery Store 964-2739. Ask about tours of the brewery where they make their award-winning beers, or find glassware, beer books and gift packs.

Continue south on Main to the . . .

Fort Bragg Depot 964-6261. This mall houses a dozen shops in a former auto dealership—some do handcrafts on the premises. A common area displays gallery exhibits and antique rail gear. The south wing has **Pacific Gift Company** 962-0925, housewares, ceramics, lamps and more; **MacNeil Glassworks** 964-2245 hand sculptured glass; **Oh Baby!** 964-1901,clothes and fun things for infants and toddlers; and **The Shirt Shop**. There's a food court in the back of the building, plus **Chernoff's Jewelers** 964-2224, the town's fine jewelers since 1956.

That concludes our little shopping spree. Of course we've only hit some highlights; Fort Bragg has many more shops you can discover on your own.

Massage

Wendy Daniels 964-7764, 18300 Old Coast Hwy, Ste. 9. Swedish massage, aromatherapy, facials, waxing.

Transformative Body Therapy 964-4343. Certified massage therapist Diana Esser provides soothing and restorative massage.

Pamela Tidd 964-8073, 347-C Cypress St. Massage.

Gail Faram 964-6915. Therapeutic massage.

Munshado Massage 962-9396 Therapeutic massage, Swedish Esalen, deep tissue, Thai style, pregnancy massage and couples massage.

Events

Contact the Chamber of Commerce, 961-6300, www.mendocinocoast.com or local publications for exact dates this year.

JANUARY: Crab & Wine Days

MARCH: Kiwanis St. Patrick's Day Celebration

Fort Bragg Whale Festival—chowder contest & beerfest

Gem & Mineral Show

Sports Card & Comics Show

Symphony of the Redwoods

APRIL: Symphony of the Redwoods

Spring Garden Tour

Sunset Run 964-9446

MAY: Cinco de Mayo Festival, downtown 964-6598

Annual Rhododendron Show

Memorial Day Quilt Show

JUNE: Abalone Dinner

Kaleidoscope Fair Arts & Crafts Show

JULY: World's Largest Salmon Barbecue, Noyo 964-6598

Gem & Mineral Show 964-1430
Redwood Coasters Anniversary
  Hoedown 964-5140
AUGUST: Shoreline Riders Rodeo
  Art in the Gardens, Botanical
  Gardens 964-4352
SEPTEMBER: Paul Bunyan Days

Gem & Mineral Show
Ugly Dog Contest
Square Dance Festival 964-5140
Fuchsia Show and Plant Sale,
  Botanical Gardens
Friends of the Library Book Sale
Winesong! 964-5185
Portuguese Festa, Pentecost Hall

OCTOBER: Oktoberfest
Symphony of the Redwoods

Fort Bragg Fireman's Ball

NOVEMBER: American Legion
  Auxiliary Bazaar
Wine & Mushroom Fest
Hospice Inn Lights, Grey Whale Inn

DECEMBER: Fort Bragg Hometown
  Christmas
Lighted Logging Truck Parade
Bed & Breakfast Candlelight Tour

7. FORT BRAGG TO WESTPORT
15 MILES

THE ROUTE

ON THIS BEAUTIFUL SEGMENT OF THE COAST, THE
Shoreline Highway begins as a busy, relatively
straight section of road on its way to Cleone,
then becomes progressively more winding
and less traveled heading north to the
remote, isolated town of Westport. Along the
way you pass plenty of rugged scenery and
the sites of several historic towns, with the
only accommodations clustering around the
tiny towns of Cleone and Westport.

THE DRIVE

Highway One heads north out of Fort Bragg,
crossing Pudding Creek, named by early
settlers, probably when they saw its waters
running thick and muddy after storms.

Around 1870 the coast road north of Fort
Bragg simply followed the tide line along the

beach's wet sand for several miles. A better road was built across the bluffs before 1900. The picturesque trestle crossing the mouth of Pudding Creek was built in 1916 to carry the logging railway that ran north, then east up Ten Mile River. The old bridge will become a link in the California Coastal Trail when the state Coastal Conservancy restores and improves it. East of the highway Pudding Creek forms a series of freshwater lagoons, temporary homes to various migratory birds.

West of the highway Pudding Creek marks the southern limit of sprawling MacKerricher State Park. Pudding Creek Beach is a popular sunning spot with locals. People often sunbathe here when the coastal fog retreats a few feet offshore.

Just north of Pudding Creek, a gravel parking area on the left provides access to the **OLD HAUL ROAD** of MacKerricher State Park, a popular route for walkers and joggers. This is the closest, most convenient access to MacKerricher State Park if you are in Fort Bragg. Highway One provides several other access points to the Haul Road and MacKerricher State Park in the next seven miles north. The Old Haul Road overlays the former logging railway up Ten Mile River. Union Lumber Company built this rail line in 1916 to reach the extensive timber in the canyons of Ten Mile River. The rails were paved over in 1949 when trucks became more efficient than trains for hauling the cut timber. The road was used until 1982, when huge waves driven by high tides and winter storms destroyed a mile of the road about three miles north. The State Parks system has acquired the land from Georgia-Pacific.

The highway north passes a final string of lodgings: **BEST WESTERN VISTA MANOR LODGE, BEACH HOUSE INN, OCEANVIEW LODGING** and **SURF & SAND LODGE** (see Fort Bragg Listings). Highway One veers inland slightly, bisecting an industrial zone interspersed with commercial sprawl.

A bit farther, at milepost 63.7, Virgin Creek Trail on the left heads west to a pretty beach beyond the Haul Road, where surfers like to check out the waves. The highway continues through a primarily residential area. Watch on the right for **FUCHSIARAMA** 964-0429, 23201 N. Hwy One, open daily 9-5, until 6 in summer.

Soon on the left you pass **GREEN ACRES RV PARK** 964-1435, 23600

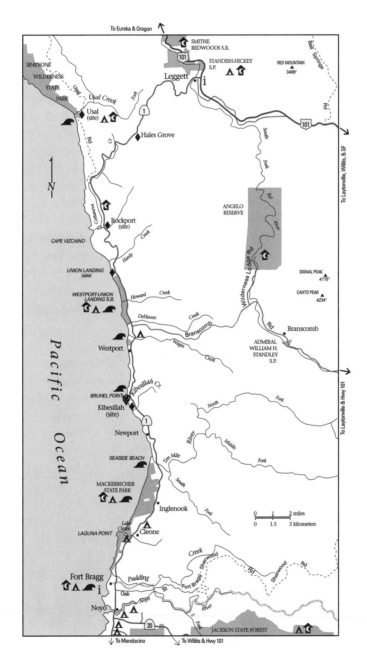

Hwy One, a private campground and RV park with 100 sites, hookups and hot showers, $16–25, ♿.

The Coast Highway has been newly straightened in its next stretch, abolishing a beautiful stand of pioneer cypress trees. Where the road dips down to cross Mill Creek, look left for the main entrance to **MACKERRICHER STATE PARK.** With 143 campsites it is the Mendocino Coast's largest public campground and one of the most pleasant coastal parks in California. The park's 2299 acres offer picnicking, tidepooling, hiking, biking and equestrian trails, excellent whale-, seal- and bird-watching at Laguna Point, rock and surf fishing along the eight-mile shore and freshwater fishing at 15-acre Lake Cleone, a former tidal lagoon now stocked with rainbow trout. ♿.

Canadian immigrant Duncan MacKerricher ran a dairy farm near Kibesillah to provide dairy goods for the Mendocino Indian Reservation. When the reservation was closed in 1868, he purchased surplus lands along Laguna Creek for $1.25 an acre. To register his land claim the homesteader had to go to the State Land Office in Eureka. MacKerricher rode a horse on the newly completed

Chute at Laguna Point (note mussel beds)

Humboldt Trail, which followed the coast, more or less, from Fort Bragg to Eureka. His family deeded what remained of the ranch to the state in 1949, creating the state park. Their grant deed specified that access to the land would be free in perpetuity.

CLEONE
(POP. 570, EL. 80)

*H*IGHWAY ONE ENTERS CLEONE, A LITTLE TOWN OFFERING the last services on the trip north before tinier Westport, 12 miles north. Cleone stems from a Greek word meaning gracious or beautiful.

Horse-drawn railway at Cleone c.1890s

Originally called Laguna, Cleone started as a ranching community. In 1883 two sawmills were built in the area. A gravity powered tramway brought the lumber to a wharf and loading chute at Laguna Point.

When the government opened the post office for the little village, they gave it the name Kanuk. MacKerricher was not pleased with the choice, Kanuk being a derogatory term for a Canadian, so he lobbied to call it Cleone. Cleone soon had two hotels, two saloons, the mills and a store. Timber supplies were exhausted and the mills closed down in 1904 and 1918, but Cleone continued as a farming community. The Laguna Point landing shipped ties, tanbark and posts into the 1930s.

Cleone offers Lari Shea's **RICOCHET RIDGE RANCH** (horse riding—see Fort Bragg Listings), **CLEONE GROCERY** 964-2707, 24400 Hwy One, and . . .

CLEONE GARDENS INN $86-140
24600 N. Hwy One
Fort Bragg 95437
964-2788/800-400-2189

www.cleonegardensinn.com

This park-like inn presents quiet accommodations in gracious and beautiful surroundings. Enjoy being comfortable near beach, lake, and trails. Stables are nearby with guided horseback rides available.

11 rooms & suites, 1 beach house; 2 nights min. wknds, holidays; MC/V/Disc/AE; family suites; cooking facilities in family suites, beach house; pets, families welcome; compl. coffee/tea/baked goods; tv in rm; some ocean views, fireplaces, bathtubs; gardens; hot tub; adj. to hiking; 1 unit fully &

☆ PURPLE ROSE MEXICAN RESTAURANT
24300 N. Hwy One, Cleone
964-6507
D: $5-11

Soups, tamales, chimichangas, chile rellenos and more for dinner, with sopaipillas or flan for dessert served in a friendly, festive atmosphere run by the same crew for 17 years. Great margaritas. *Wed–Sun 5–9 pm; closed 3 weeks before Christmas; checks; full bar; seats 100; families welcome; take-out; &*

CLEONE CAMPGROUND
24400 Hwy One, Fort Bragg
964-4589
D: $15-20

30 sites, hookups, hot showers, laundry and store.

CONTINUING ON . . .

As the Coast Highway winds north from Cleone, the traffic thins considerably. The traditional territory of the Northern Pomo people is behind you now. The remote lands of the Coast Yuki people stretched north from here. After a sharp bend to the right, look left to see the tallest of the Ten Mile Dunes. Steep sand hills tower 80 feet over tiny homes which appear to be in danger of being swallowed by the dunes. It wouldn't be the first time these dunes buried a building. The sand hills drifted over several homes, roads, fences and a barn in the 1920s and 1930s. The sands stretch north nearly four miles from here to the mouth of Ten

Yuki dwellings on reservation, c.1860

Mile River. In places the dunes are nearly a mile across, forming one of the largest dune complexes in California. As you pass the highest sand hills, look northwest for a view across the sands to the Pacific breakers.

Highway One winds along the eastern edge of the dunes, offering sweeping coastal views but no access for several miles. You pass the **INGLENOOK GRANGE HALL** (pancake breakfast first Sunday of each month, 8 am–12 noon) and Inglenook Cemetery, primary evidence of the

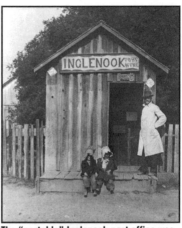

The "portable" Inglenook post office was moved around to various locations

once thriving farming community named for an early settler's Scottish homeland. Inglenook today is primarily a residential community.

Inglenook was settled in 1885 when a lumber mill was built to manufacture wooden pipe for Fort Bragg's new water system. The mill did not last long, but for years Inglenook grew abundant crops of peas, beans and potatoes, providing a primary source of produce for the isolated Mendocino Coast when many other goods had to be brought in by ship. A cannery was here in the early 1900s, and a turkey farm survived into the 1970s.

Narrow Highway One continues winding past pioneer and contemporary homes. After dipping and winding to cross Inglenook Creek, you pass through the heart of the old community, where an immense cypress windbreak borders the right side of the road. You get another glimpse of the dunes on the left, held in check here by a stand of large eucalyptus trees. The road climbs to a terrace overlooking dunes on the left and the vast canyons of Ten Mile River on the right. As you descend to cross the river, you pass one last, undeveloped access point for MacKerricher State Park. A small dirt parking area on the left just before the long bridge offers parking for a few cars and a sandy trail north to meet the Old Haul Road where it turns inland to head upriver. You cannot follow the road upstream (private), but you can walk west to the mouth of the river, or follow the haul road or beach south through a wonderfully remote area.

As you head north across the river on the curving Frank Hyman Memorial Bridge (named for a coast native born at Virgin Creek in 1889), notice the extensive wetlands

Fred LeValley's stage at Ten Mile

upstream, prime habitat for migrating and resident birds. The private timberlands upriver still harbor significant populations of bear, mountain lion and other wildlife. A few elk graze the area as well, but they were reintroduced in the 1970s.

The river now called Ten Mile was called Bidato (mush river) by the Coast Yuki people, the original inhabitants of the coastal strip from Cleone to Rockport.

The river got its new name from the fact that it is ten miles north of the mouth of the Noyo River. Ten Mile River formed the northern boundary of the short-lived Mendocino Indian Reservation. In 1879 Mendocino outlaw Elijah Frost was lynched here for his part in a family feud that took six lives in a 15-second gunfight. Logging first occurred along the river around 1880.

The Coast Highway winds north past a few more homes, then past pretty Seaside Creek Beach beside the road, where just a short walk allows you to dip your feet in the icy Pacific waters. Until the 1980s a small barn east of the highway provided a popular and often photographed landmark. The barn was covered with antique pink roses, under whose fragrant load it finally succumbed.

Your highway now winds up and over Ten Mile River Bluff. As you descend into the canyon of Abalobadiah Creek, a tidy white fence surrounds a pioneer cemetery on a hill beyond the canyon, the graveyard for the old town of Newport. The creek's hybrid name comes from its Pomo name, Belobeda crossed with the abalone so abundant in nearby waters. As the highway winds out of the canyon, you quickly come to **SOUTH KIBESILLAH COASTAL ACCESS**, which offers striking views, a picnic table, but no access to the water. Several large sea stacks stand offshore, slowly eroding from the relentless pounding of the surf. The largest of these, visible south of the access point, was used for a Chevrolet commercial in the 1970s. The production company dropped a car onto the sea stack by helicopter to get a great shot of the lone car surrounded by roaring surf. The Ten Mile Dunes sprawl beyond the rocks offshore.

Two towns graced these rolling headlands during the last third of the nineteenth century. Newport was a shipping point for a variety of enterprises from 1875 to about 1900. It sat on the promontory immediately north of today's coastal access point. A private ranch is there today. (Actor Steve McQueen nearly bought the ranch in 1979 before he died.) Newport had the first Mendocino Coast sawmill north of Noyo, built by the Field brothers in 1875. After that mill burned in 1877, Stewart and Hunter came and built a new mill nearby and a loading chute on the point at Newport.

Kibesillah stood about one mile north of Newport, beside the creek that shares its name. H. Chadbourne started the settlement

Kibesillah in its heyday

with a hotel and blacksmith shop in 1867. In 1870 the town had two hotels, a store, a school and a blacksmith shop. At that time the mail only got delivered when someone took a trip to Noyo, acting as voluntary postman along the road on the way home. The town finally gained a post office in 1874, but really began to boom when the sawmill and loading chute were built at Newport.

Before long the nearby timber sources were depleted and the mill was moved seven miles south to the South Fork of Ten Mile River.

The cut lumber was then hauled six miles to Newport to be shipped. Kibesillah continued to grow, soon boasting four hotels, a church, a justice court and a newspaper. The North Pacific Telegraph Company was headquartered here, with lines running from Petaluma to Crescent City. In Kibesillah's heyday, its saloons had a big reputation for gambling, with several tables running night and day.

In the early 1880s a young man named Charley (C.R.) Johnson moved into town. He bought a share in the mill, and soon acquired the rest of the investor's shares. Johnson made a point of traveling up and down the coast, seeing for himself what it had to offer. He saw great potential at the site of the old military post at Fort Bragg. In 1885 he moved the Kibesillah mill machinery to Fort Bragg and the whole town followed. The little town with the funny name died after less than 20 years and Fort Bragg, the future commercial center of the coast was born.

When Kibesillah was the queen of the north coast, only a rugged pack trail continued further north up the coast. Even today the Shoreline Highway turns to a twisting, cliff-hanging route, soon forced inland by the rugged terrain. A winery, seemingly misplaced, has recently been established on the very edge of the Pacific just north of the site of Kibesillah. The **PACIFIC STAR WINERY** has a few acres of vineyards here, planted in 1988. The owners intend to prove that the damp and chilly north coast weather provides an ideal climate for the grapes that grow so successfully in northern Europe.

The highway climbs toward the flank of rounded Kibesillah Hill. Watch for the **VISTA POINT** on the left (milepost 74.1), opposite a row of large cypress trees. The paved parking lot overlooks a broad sloping promontory rimmed with extensive rocky tidal shelves and tidepools, **BRUHEL POINT**. A pleasant and easy trail system allows you and your dog to walk down to and along the shore.

Place names left over from the aboriginal residents reflect the importance of this jutting headland at Bruhel Point. Kibesillah is a Pomo word, probably meaning "flat rock." Lilem was the Coast Yuki name for this place. They both refer to the jutting tidal shelves here, rich in intertidal life with a corresponding abundance of fish in the deep waters offshore. At least six different tribes of native people came here each year to collect and dry the sea's bounty. All these people, some of them traditional enemies, considered this place a neutral ground, the bounty of which was available for all.

Bruhel Point is still a popular fishing and tidepooling spot. Be extremely careful if you go near the water's edge. The tidal shelves are very exposed to wave action.

Shoreline Highway corkscrews for the three miles into Westport, traversing one of its most dangerous stretches along the top of steep ocean cliffs. The coastal marine terraces are completely absent here, where steep cliffs plunge right to the sea. Slow down, pull out for those rushing log trucks and enjoy this spectacularly rugged section of highway.

The highway soon descends steeply to Chadbourne Gulch, where a dirt road on the left offers daytime access to a mile-long dark sand beach backed by high cliffs. The beach, a fine place for bird-watching and surf-fishing, is expansive when the tide is out, virtually inaccessible when it's in.

Climb by tight, serpentine curves to cross the western flank of Bell Mountain (1050 feet), with steeply rolling Bell Point between you and the Pacific. These geographical features, named for early settlers of the Beall family, got misspelled somewhere along the way. Grand views invite a stop at one of several gravel turnouts.

When the sky is clear to the north, you can see the towering King Range of the Lost Coast rising 4000 feet above the ocean. The western end of the range ends at Punta Gorda (Fat Point), a rounded bluff only two miles south of Cape Mendocino, the westernmost point in California. The King Range and the 25 miles of wilderness beach at its base are public lands, centerpieces of the 60,000-acre King Range National Conservation Area run by the federal Bureau of Land Management.

The Coast Highway straightens out to descend into Westport, the last outpost of civilization before the Lost Coast. Look for the stately pioneer Switzer House, circa 1884, on the west as you descend toward town. The coast road turns left, then right to deposit you on Main Street, where the town's commercial enterprises cluster in a two block area.

Westport
(POP. 327, EL. 120)

*W*ESTPORT IS CIVILIZATION'S NORTHERNMOST OUTPOST on the Mendocino Coast. Westport's down-home charm is reminiscent of the rest of the Mendocino Coast 20 or 30 years ago, before it became such a destination for travelers. Most visitors speed by Westport as they hurry north or south. But you might enjoy stopping for a few minutes or a few days to sample the rugged natural beauty that graces this sleepy town, investing it with a slower pace and off-the-beaten-track quality that makes Mendocino or Gualala seem like life in the fast lane.

The commercial establishments that remain in downtown Westport can be counted on the fingers of one hand. The **BLUE VICTORIAN INN** offers shopping for eclectic antiques.

The main activity for visitors here is loafing as you soak in the dramatic natural setting where the wild Pacific meets the rugged edge of the continent. But here are a few suggestions for those bent on doing something. **ABALONE DIVING** and **SURF FISHING** bring more visitors here than everything else combined. You can buy a license at the Westport Store, but you need to bring your own snorkeling gear and pry bar or fishing gear. **WESTPORT-UNION LANDING STATE BEACH** to the north and **BRUHEL POINT HEADLANDS** three miles south offer beachcombing, bird watching and tidepooling in marvelous settings. The Nature Conservancy's **ANGELO RESERVE**, about 15 miles inland near Branscomb, offers daytime hiking and nature study. The rugged 7520-acre enclave of old growth forest straddles the upper reaches of the South Fork Eel River and its tributaries, surrounded by the rugged Coast Range. Please call first, 984-6653.

On about three weekends every year Westport comes alive with bustle approaching its nineteenth century heyday. The **OPENING WEEKEND** of abalone diving season (first weekend in April) brings divers from all over Northern California. In May, the Mother's Day **GREAT RUBBER DUCKY RACE** is capped off by a beef barbecue. In July, the **ANNUAL CHICKEN BARBECUE**, a benefit for the volunteer fire department, brings another overflow crowd to this otherwise sleepy burg.

Westport c. 1890

History

Westport started out as Beall's Landing around 1864, settled by Samuel and Lloyd Beall, formerly of Little River, Bridgeport and Mendocino. While very little information exists about Westport's early days, we know that E. J. Whipple of Ten Mile and Lloyd Beall were partners, acquiring land here by 1860. Beall built a loading chute around 1864. Alfred Wages settled along the creek to the north about the same time.

We also know that Captain M. C. Dougherty, an employee of the Mendocino Indian Reservation, started cutting timber on the hill east of town in the last half of that decade. He apparently used the timber to build a chute for shipping potatoes. While potatoes were an excellent cash crop in those days, the town's future was not to be in spuds.

Other men attempted to build more elaborate chutes to load ships beyond the dangerous rocks offshore. But only after James T. Rogers moved to the area in 1877 and built the town's first wharf, did this part of the coast begin to prosper. Constructed at great cost and requiring considerable engineering, Rogers' wharf was 380 feet long, with a chute at the end. By the end of 1877 Rogers named the landing Westport because the area reminded him of his home town of Eastport, Maine, on the New England Coast. Rogers soon constructed a second (north) wharf 610 feet long, capable of handling

150,000 board feet of lumber each day, turning Westport into a boomtown. A hotel, saloon, post office and general store soon joined the blacksmith shop and ranches that had already grown up here. By 1881 Westport sported two mills on Wages Creek, three hotels, six saloons, two blacksmith shops, three stores, two livery stables, two shoe shops, a barber shop, butcher shop, post office and telegraph office. By 1883 a stagecoach ran between Ukiah and Westport, with stops at Kibesillah (later at Fort Bragg) along the way. The coach left at sunrise and took all day to traverse the rugged country on rough roads. Westport soon boasted a population of 400, with around 65 ships loading at the chutes each year. One account claims Westport had 14 saloons in its heyday.

Tanbark, shingles, wool, oats and railroad ties rounded out the town's early exports. The wharves and chutes needed constant repair in winter, the price of their exposure to the brunt of coastal storms. Ship captains were at first reluctant to call at Westport because of the treacherous seas among the many offshore rocks. The south wharf, abandoned by 1900, was down Omega Street from today's store, while the north wharf was at the north end of Omega Street.

While Westport's timber enterprises struggled through boom and bust in the last two decades of the nineteenth century, the area's ranches continued to prosper.

Everyone struggled through the Great Depression of the 1930s. While some sold out and moved on, many others stayed to run the proud, isolated community. By 1952 many buildings had been consumed by fire, others died of neglect. The mills had closed as trucks and improved roads allowed the cut timber to be hauled to the big Union Lumber Company mill at Fort Bragg.

Westport today may be only a shadow of its heyday, but at least the town survives, unlike a dozen other lumber towns up and down the coast, where nothing but a leaning barn or ranch house mark the days of prosperity and tight-knit community.

Westport Lodging

Listings are organized from the most expensive to the least expensive

☆ HOWARD CREEK RANCH
$75–160
40501 N. Hwy One/Box 121
Westport 95488
964-6725/www.howardcreekranch.com

This 60-acre oceanfront farm, a designated historic site, borders on miles of beach and mountains. Views, fireplaces, skylights, antiques, flower gardens, handmade quilts, a 75-foot swinging foot bridge over Howard Creek, cows, sheep, llamas and horses add country charm and sophistication, all near Sinkyone Wilderness.

15 rooms, 3 w/ shared bath; full breakfast; 2 nights min. wknds & holidays; MC/V/AE/checks; private cabins; microwave, mini-fridge in cabins; some ocean views; pets by prior arrangement; jacuzzi/ hot tub/sauna; adj. to hiking; piano/guitar/books; massage; gardens

DEHAVEN VALLEY FARM COUNTRY INN & RESTAURANT
$89–144
39247 N. Hwy One
Westport
961-1660

Enjoy a restful, relaxing and thoroughly comfortable stay at this quiet and elegant getaway.

10 rooms; full breakfast; V/MC/checks; 1 suite w/ Franklin stove & wet bar; 2 shared baths; adj. restaurant (dinner by reservation); hot tub; ocean views; fireplaces; bathtubs; gardens; adj. to hiking; phone; horseback riding; special events

LOST COAST INN $70–100
38921 N. Hwy One/Box 418
Westport
964-5584/www.lostcoastinn.com

Scenic coastal surroundings showcase 19th-century architecture and intriguing Westport lore. Sample local wines and brews, or sip an espresso by the fire in their funky period saloon. Friendly hosts, comfortable rooms, ocean views and a tasty breakfast await.

4 rooms; continental breakfast; V/MC/checks; ocean views; wood stoves; adj. to hiking

WESTPORT INN $60
34070 Hwy One/Box 145
Westport
964-5135

Basic motel in a quiet coastal town, 300 feet from the ocean.

6 rooms; continental breakfast; closed occasionally in winter, call ahead; V/MC/Disc/checks; compl. coffee; bathtubs; small pets ok w/advance notice; adj. to hiking

Eateries

DEHAVEN VALLEY FARM RESTAURANT

39247 N. Hwy One,
Westport 95488
961-1660
$25 prix fixe

Serves superb five-course meals. Guests dine in the cozy, intimate dining room of the house, or outside when weather permits. A good selection of Mendocino County wines are featured.

Dinner by res. only, 7:30 pm seating; MC/V/checks; beer/wine; seats 50

WESTPORT COMMUNITY STORE & DELI

24980 Abalone, Westport
964-2872
B, L, D: $1.50–6

Full service grocery has a delicatessen with many choices: bagels, croissants, pizzas, soups and sandwiches. Since there is only one dinner restaurant around Westport, they will help you assemble a picnic for indoors or out. Established 1918.

Daily 7 am–9 pm during daylight savings, 'til 8 in winter; all CCs; beer/wine; grocery; gas pumps; a few outdoor tables; take-out; ঌ by arrangemnt via back door

CONTINUING ON . . .

Stock up on gasoline and whatever else you might need before leaving Westport. Other visitor-serving facilities in the next three miles north include private and public campgrounds and two charming and remote country inns. Beyond that, the next services of any kind are 30 twisting miles north at Leggett.

As the Coast Highway heads north from the sleepy little town, a dirt parking area on the left offers a stairway to ¼-mile-long **PETE'S BEACH**, the southern end of **WESTPORT-UNION LANDING STATE BEACH.**

You then pass the historic Westport Cemetery, also on the left. Next door, ½ mile north of Westport, is privately run **WESTPORT BEACH RV CAMPGROUND** 964-2964, 37700 N. Hwy One, Westport 95488. Seaside camping in a willow-sheltered canyon only a stone's throw from a large, wild beach. 175 sites, full RV hookups, closed Dec–Feb. $19–32.

8. Westport to Leggett & Highway 101 — 30 miles

THE ROUTE

NORTH OF WESTPORT, THE SHORELINE HIGHWAY makes a final skip-jump survey of the Pacific's rugged edge, then climbs inland over ridges and through verdant canyons on one of the most rugged winding portions of the entire coast road. This stretch of highway is so remote it remained unpaved until around 1960. Highway One's final 30-mile lunge to its northern terminus at Leggett on Highway 101 makes nearly 400 curves, perfect for gymkhana drivers but a bit much if you are in a family-filled station wagon. If you have never driven this northernmost leg of the highway before, it is strongly recommended that you begin fresh and rested in the early part of the day. This is not the place to race the setting sun to your night's resting spot, or to plunge headlong into a pitch-dark night, dodging deer and other nocturnal critters dashing across the pavement in fear of their lives. If you decide not to push on, Westport and the three miles of highway to its north offer four lodging choices and large public and private campgrounds where you might spend the night.

THE DRIVE

After the road winds through Wages Creek Canyon, it rounds a bend for a view of a long, gentle marine terrace backed by another razor ridge topped with ragged forest.

The Branscomb Road forks right 1½ miles north of Westport. It reaches Highway 101 at Laytonville in just 26 miles, but the route is slow and winding especially on the west half (see CHAPTER II.Back Roads).

Shoreline Highway crosses DeHaven Creek and passes, on the right, **DEHAVEN VALLEY FARM COUNTRY INN**, homesteaded by the Gordon family in 1875. It became an inn and restaurant in 1972.

Just beyond on the left, you come to the southern end of the developed portion of **WESTPORT-UNION LANDING STATE BEACH** (47 acres), with picnic tables and pit toilets above spacious DeHaven Creek Beach.

Highway One straightens out across the marine terrace. Watch for abundant deer crossing the road here to scavenge in the nearby campground. The main entrance to the Westport-Union Landing State Beach appears soon on the left. It offers 100 wind-prone blufftop campsites ($11/night) and access to sheltered Howard Creek Beach, where the sands are streaked with pink grains. Another entrance to the state campground lies ¼ mile north.

Howard Creek blacksmith shop

On the east side of the highway look for the entrance to **HOWARD CREEK RANCH**, homesteaded by the Howard family of Missouri in 1867, an inn since 1978.

Highway One pushes north past a **VISTA POINT** on the left, a superb spot to survey the dramatic meeting of land and sea.

Union Landing

This flat seaside expanse was the site of Union Landing, where a loading chute and wharf opened in 1899. The enterprise was begun by Charles McFaul, who had previously lived at Little River and Bridgeport. Union Landing withered away quickly after the sawmill at Howard Creek burned in 1924. Today it is hard to imagine the bustling enterprise and stately home occupying this windswept point.

The coast road winds along the base of steep, slide-prone cliffs. In the middle of these is another deep canyon carved by Juan Creek, named for Juan Alviso, who settled here in 1875.

Passing a few more cliffs at the base of towering Hardy Ridge, take advantage of the ample space to pull over on the left, your last chance to admire the grandeur of this rugged coast. Visible to the north is Cape Vizcaino, with sheer cliffs plunging 600 feet to the breakers. The King Range and the rest of the Lost Coast have now disappeared behind the nearby cape, but the towering cliffs and offshore rocks give this place a profound edge-of-the-world feeling.

At Hardy Creek the Coast Highway suddenly veers away from the coastline to climb up wooded Hardy Creek Canyon. Another lumber company and mill town sprang up here in 1896, managed by McFaul

Hardy Creek Hotel

Rockport on Highway One, 1958

before he started Union Landing. Highway One climbs by hairpin turns to 747 feet where it crosses Cottaneva Ridge, which plummets west into the sea at Cape Vizcaino. The highway drops back nearly to sea level at Rockport, where the Pacific is only ½ mile down Cottaneva Creek. You won't see the ocean from the road again, except for distant, enticing vistas from the high ridges farther inland.

Rockport is truly a ghost town now, but it was another lumber town in its heyday, its history typical of the boom-bust nature of such tiny burgs. In the 1870s, W. R. Miller built a sawmill here. To facilitate loading the cut lumber onto ships, in 1877 he built a 250-foot suspension bridge from the cliffs north of Rockport Beach to Sea Lion Rock offshore, the first suspension bridge constructed on the Pacific Coast. The ships were loaded by wire chute from the offshore rock. The original mill burned in

1890. Mammoth storm waves demolished the suspension bridge in a winter long forgotten. When Smeaton Chase rode through Rockport in autumn 1911, it was nearly as quiet as it is today: "I saw nothing alive but a few pigs rooting under the old pear and apple trees." His previous stop at Hardy Creek had offered lodging and three bustling saloons. The tiny mill town and doghole port went boom and bust through several successive owners. In 1924 a Mississippi company built an electric mill, logging railway and new suspension bridge. Rockport shut down completely for ten years during the Great Depression, then reopened in 1938. Rockport Redwood Company rebuilt the wire chute. Though they only used it twice, this was one of the very last chutes in operation on the entire redwood coast. Lumber was hauled out by truck until the mill burned in 1942. The Rockport Hotel still stood in the 1970s.

Mendocino Redwood Company owns the land today. They offer a **PICNIC AREA**, on the left at milepost 88.7, where you can take a short walk in an enchanting remnant of the original virgin forest and use their pit toilet.

Highway One rambles up Cottaneva Creek for the next six miles, following its lush dark canyon jammed with ferns, alders and redwoods. You are not only leaving the coastal zone, but also departing the ancestral lands of the Coast Yuki people for the territory of the Sinkyone tribe, who inhabited the coast north to Shelter Cove and nearly all of the South Fork Eel River watershed to the east. Only at the remote headwaters of the South Fork does the Sinkyone territory give way to that of the Kato people.

After the Cottaneva Creek bridge, watch on the left for County Road 431, the Usal Road (milepost 90.88). This steep and twisting, narrow dirt track follows the shoreline north into the Lost Coast, and arrives six miles later at the logging ghost town of Usal, which began around 1890, and the southern end of **SINKYONE WILDERNESS STATE PARK**. Usal Road is only safe for street vehicles during the summer season when the county maintains it, usually from Memorial Day until after Labor Day and the first big storm. Usal Road is never safe for trailers, vehicles with bad tires, brakes or transmissions, nor for drivers who suffer vertigo on steep terrain.

Author Jack London and his wife Charmian drove their wagon over the Usal Road in 1911 on their way to Eureka. Long before that, in 1869 the Humboldt Trail followed essentially the same route north to Eureka. Usal Road was the only road north until 1933 when the state took over the Mendocino coast road from the county. State engineers, daunted by the rugged, unforgiving nature of the Lost Coast to the north, planned and built Hollow Tree Road to meet Highway 101 at Leggett.

You may have found the Shoreline Highway to be a long and

Off Track on the Lost Coast

From Rockport north, 70 of the California Coast's most gorgeous miles hunker in a wilderness of wooded canyons and jagged ridges reachable only by trails and rough dirt roads. California's Lost Coast possesses such intractable force that it turns the Pacific Coast Highway away from the shore, something even the rugged Big Sur coast couldn't do.

The last decades of the nineteenth century brought stabs at civilizing this uncharted territory.

Sawmills and doghole ports sprang up at Needle Rock, Bear Harbor and Usal first, and later at Shelter Cove and Wheeler. The isolated towns boasted hotels, schools, churches and even railroads for a while. Then the wilderness conspired with hard times to wipe the towns away. Nothing remains but a few overgrown foundations, sagging fences, crumbling chimneys and escaped garden plants.

If you're a hardy and

winding road, but the most difficult stretch of the entire route may well be this final 15-mile run to Leggett. This steep, twisting ride makes about 250 turns as it crosses three rugged, wooded ridges before descending to cross the South Fork Eel River and join Highway 101. Take a short break to stretch your legs and settle your mind and stomach, then press on. Please remember to watch for bicyclists (especially April through October) and pull off at turnouts for faster traffic at the earliest opportunity.

Soon after passing the Usal Road you climb steeply over a ridge as North Fork Cottaneva Creek gathers in its headwaters below. Highway One descends briefly into tiny Hales Grove, where you might be able to buy a burl, but will no longer find any gas or food. The town of Hales Grove originally sprang up around the turn of the century. Then called Hollow Tree or Monroe, depending upon which company you worked for, today it is seldom called anything, except by its handful of residents.

State Route One climbs along a ridge with the South Fork Usal Creek far below on the left, the tributaries of Hollow Tree Creek on the right. This being the heart of

Usal Wharf, 1892

north coast lumber country, you pass many gated private logging roads as you wind over ridge and through canyon. One of them is the WRP (Willits Redwood Products) Road, once part of a network of private logging roads that stretched from Fort Bragg to the Oregon border. After a few dozen more curves, you pass one final turnout at the top of a ridge before the highway plunges into the canyon of the South Fork Eel River. At the bottom of one more steep, twisting descent you cross a bridge over the South Fork.

Highway One makes a brief, spiralling climb to Leggett, where the romantic road ends as it meets Highway 101, 12 miles south of Mendocino County's northern border, in the deep, rocky, slide-strewn canyon of the Eel River, California's third largest. The vast wild forests of Humboldt County lie to the north.

While you must be miles from home (nobody lives around here, do they?), you have completed the amazing odyssey of a journey along Highway One, America's most romantic road. If you are truly an incurable romantic you may choose to turn around and retrace your tire tracks south along the Shoreline Highway. Otherwise you must remember to come back and do it again some day.

Whether you followed California Highway One for all or part of its 106-mile traverse of Mendocino County or have just completed all 711 miles of the coast road from Dana Point to Leggett, you have plenty to write home about. Which of the

intrepid explorer, you can find the Lost Coast by a few remote roads. Twisting dirt tracks lead to the 7567-acre Sinkyone Wilderness State Park, reaching Usal from Highway One near Rockport, and Needle Rock and Bear Harbor from Garberville. The north half of the Lost Coast, the 60,000-acre King Range National Conservation Area, much of which is now being considered for wilderness area status, is even more remote, with winding roads from Garberville and Weott gaining only its edges. The whole area offers remote camping with pristine forests, jagged ocean-facing ridges, and hidden coves and beaches.

Nearly all the Lost Coast lacks commercial facilities, but the few exceptions are worth noting. One crooked paved road runs west from Garberville to Shelter Cove, where a campground, lodgings and seafood cafes have been carved from the wilderness. Here you can sample the Lost Coast's wild beauty without hitting the trail. In the Shelter Cove subdivision immense elk often wander the streets and bears may invade at night. Further north, the pastoral Mattole River Valley forms the Lost Coast's northern edge. Tiny Petrolia and Honeydew provide a few more places to eat and relax without sleeping with the bugs and snakes. Call 923-2613 for information.

Saving the Last Old Growth

For eons the vast redwood forest stood intact, growing. Then the loggers came, cutting great trees to supply booming California. For 80 years they harvested slowly, requiring a large crew to handsaw each giant and bring it to earth.

When technology reached the remote forest, the harvest quickened as steam donkey engines, railroads and finally chainsaws and bulldozers each replaced the work of ten men. By 1950 the lumber production from Mendocino County mills was 50 times what it had been only 30 years before. With all the machines and new mills, the remaining ancient forests fell fast, leaving only four percent of the original redwood forests by 1980.

In 1979 I hired on as a timber cruiser for Georgia-Pacific at Fort Bragg. They sent us to inventory their last virgin stands, north of Usal on the Lost Coast. I naively hoped those remnants of the primeval forest would remain. We walked all day beneath the immense cathedral forest, rubber-necking at trees towering 300 feet overhead.

Within four years nearly all that forest of several thousand acres was cut. The

countless coastal vistas did you find most inspiring? Was it the sweeping blond beaches and striated cliffs near Point Arena? The towering sea stacks, convoluted coves and peninsulas around Elk? The tall ridges soaring above the placid Navarro River? The rocky headlands topped with Victorian buildings rising from the churning surf at Mendocino Bay? The windswept dunes backed by ragged green forest at Ten Mile? Or perhaps that last glimpse of the wild Pacific where the road turned inland at Hardy Creek, the emphatic edge of the continent punctuated by rocky spires and towered over by slide-torn ridges?

LEGGETT
(POP. 192, EL. 932)

FINDING YOURSELF AT THE END of the Shoreline Highway might be a bit of a letdown, but despair not. You need not rush home unless duty nags insistently. The little known Leggett Valley offers its own gentle charms, as well as being the gateway to the heart of the Redwood Empire that lies to the north.

Right beside the junction of Highways One and 101, Drive-Thru Tree Road (Hwy 271) leads to downtown Leggett, where you'll find a cafe, gas station and . . . **LEGGETT MARKET** 925-6000, 6 to 8:30 daily, 'til 9 in summer. At **DRIVE-THRU TREE PARK** 925-6363 you can drive through the historic 315-foot-tall Chandelier Tree and picnic amidst a pleasant 200-acre grove of redwoods. Daily 8:30 to 8, close earlier in winter.

Nearby along Highway 101 in Leggett, (north of Highway One junction), look for **PEG HOUSE DELI** 925-6444. Built entirely without nails by pioneer Danish carpenters, it serves as the unofficial visitor center for the Leggett Valley, doing double duty as deli and grocery. Daily 9 to 9. Across the highway is **STANDISH-HICKEY STATE PARK** 925-6482, fee. This 1200-acre redwood park has 161 campsites, picnicking, with campfire programs and swimming in summer. ♿.

land was preserved as Sinkyone Wilderness State Park, but its grandest forests were gone.

Today we debate whether one or two percent of the original redwood forest remains. Fortunately parks preserved most of these remnants long ago. But some of the ancient trees still sing their death chants each day, falling to the screaming chainsaws to let you and I live the good life on redwood decks.

Cutover forests do grow back. Sustained yield harvesting can be a reality. Silt-choked rivers, where salmon struggle to reproduce, can be renewed if we take the initiative.

But when an ancient forest is gone, it will never return. The Northwest's ancient rain forests hold more biomass than even the celebrated tropical rain forests, with genetic diversity nearly as rich. Saving the remaining ancient forests represents far more than saving a few owls or fish; they are the web of life that weaves our environment into a whole cloth.

Don't toss out your redwood souvenir (it's from a young tree anyway), but support preservation of the remaining old growth forests of the world. Trees are the lungs of our planet, and when the earth can no longer breathe, how will we?

Not far north along Highway 101 are **HELEN'S BEER GARDEN**, open afternoons, and the **WORLD FAMOUS TREE HOUSE**, which appeared in *Ripley's Believe It or Not* in 1934 as the "tallest one-room house in the world." The still healthy tree now serves as the entrance to a much larger gift shop. Leggett concludes with **REDWOODS RIVER RESORT** (see Listings) and **CONFUSION HILL** 925-6456. At this gravity defying location, water apparently runs uphill.

Leggett Lodging

Listings are organized from the most expensive to the least expensive

REDWOODS RIVER RESORT

$49–115
75000 Hwy 101, Leggett 95585
925-6249

Family resort on the Eel River with cabins and A-frame motel with kitchens, barbeques, all dishes supplied. All are housekeeping rooms, sleeping from 1 to 8 people. Beautiful 21 acres of redwoods, many old growth. Wild blackberries and huckleberries.

15 rooms; Disc/V/MC/checks; smoking on balcony only; lower winter rates; suite w/loft, sleeps up to 8; all units have complete kitchenette; coffee in room; heated outdoor swimming pool; wood stoves in cabins; adj. to hiking, fishing; special facilities for children; recreation room; &

STONEGATE VILLA MOTEL

$32–79
65260 Drive-Thru Tree Road, Leggett
925-6226/888-925-6226

7 rooms; MC/V; no-smoking; off-season rates; queen beds; some kitchens

REDWOODS RIVER RESORT RV PARK

925-6249

7 miles north of Leggett, Hwy 101, has 60 sites, hookups, hot showers, pool, laundry and store. $14–30

CONTINUING ON . . .

The shortest route back to the San Francisco Bay Area is south along Highway 101. The 186-mile trip from Leggett takes about four hours. If you choose to head north, you'll find plenty to see.

The Redwood Highway (Highway 101) north to the Oregon border was another great road engineering achievement. Pre-dating the coast highway by 15 or 20 years, the challenged redwood-route engineers had to contend with the steeply rugged, slide-prone canyon slopes of the South Fork Eel River, a mild alternative compared to the river's immense main canyon to the east.

Not far north of Leggett is a pretty and convenient pit stop, **SMITHE REDWOODS STATE RESERVE**, which has flush toilets, big redwoods, and good swimming in summer. The next 20 miles offer . . .

RICHARDSON GROVE R.V. PARK & CAMPGROUND 247-3380, has 91 sites, hookups, hot showers, laundry, store and propane. $15–28.

RICHARDSON GROVE STATE PARK 247-3318, fee. The 1500-acre park offers the first stands of really big redwoods for travelers heading north. 170 campsites, picnicking, swimming in summer, plus a nice little visitor center.

BENBOW INN 923-2124, 445 Lake Benbow Dr, Benbow 95542, is an historic resort in the grand country hotel tradition: 55 rooms from $125-300. Good restaurant too. Closed January to March.

BENBOW LAKE STATE RECREATION AREA 946-3238, fee. This 1000-acre park has 76 campsites in a bend of South Fork Eel River.

Just north is a pleasant picnic area, which in summer sits beside seasonal Benbow Lake, a popular spot for swimming, canoeing and wind-surfing. In summer, music concerts happen beneath the stars here, and **SHAKESPEARE AT BENBOW LAKE** happens during the second half of August. Call Matteel Community Center for concert information, 923-3368, and 923-1060 for Shakespeare information.

BENBOW VALLEY RV RESORT & GOLF COURSE 923-2777, 2 miles south of Garberville, Hwy 101, has 112 sites, hookups, hot showers, pool, hot tub, cable tv, laundry and store, $36–40, plus 5 cottages and trailers at $125/night.

GARBERVILLE (pop. 1350, el. 532) offers full services, plus access to the Lost Coast via neighboring **REDWAY**. Contact the Chamber of Commerce at 923-2613, 773 Redwood Drive, Suite E. Mon–Fri 9:30–

5:30, Sat 12–4. ☆**WOODROSE CAFE** 923-3191 in Garberville is great for breakfast and lunch, while ☆**MATEEL CAFE** 923-2030 in Redway has delicious lunches, dinners and pizzas.

From Garberville Highway 101 offers freeway for the 65 miles north to **EUREKA** (pop. 25,500, el. 13), the largest city on the coast between San Francisco and Seattle. You might call the Chamber of Commerce at 800-356-6381 (www.eurekachamber.com) for more information if you are heading there. The **AVENUE OF THE GIANTS** provides a wonderful scenic alternate route through giant redwood groves for 33 miles.

Highway 101 continues north to **REDWOOD NATIONAL PARK** and Crescent City, then into Oregon, following the coast all the way to the Olympic Peninsula and Olympic National Park in Washington. You may also leave the coast route by heading inland via Highway 299 north of Arcata to Redding (on I-5), or northeast from Crescent City on Highway 199 to Grants Pass, Oregon (also on I-5, near Ashland).

9. HIGHWAY 128 TO HIGHWAY ONE — 58 MILES

THE ROUTE

*T*O REACH THE HEART OF THE MENDOCINO Coast by a route more direct than following serpentine Highway One up the coast, take Highway 128 west from Cloverdale, 89 freeway miles north of San Francisco on Highway 101. This portion of Highway 128 offers the most direct route to the section of the Mendocino Coast between Elk and Mendocino. As a bonus it explores one of the most pastoral wine producing regions anywhere. (If you are going to Fort Bragg or points north, see CHAPTER 10.)

Highway 128 was traditionally known as the McDonald-to-the-Sea Highway. When the modern road was constructed in the 1920s, it began at McDonald, then the name for the traditional community of

Mountain House seven miles north of Cloverdale. At that time the Redwood Highway, predecessor to Highway 101, followed today's Highway 128 to McDonald, then descended to Hopland.

The 58 miles of Highway 128 between Cloverdale and Highway One near Albion twist, turn, climb and dip like all the routes to reach this magical coastline. Expect at least two hours for this stretch if you have never driven the road before, about 1½ hours otherwise. The route traverses rolling sheep country, drops into Anderson Valley to wind through vineyards and orchards, then plunges through dense redwood forest along the normally placid Navarro River. The highway follows the river so closely that floods close this route periodically during the winter rainy season. Highway 128 ends at Highway One, a climactic approach to the Pacific Ocean where the Navarro River empties into it.

A Scenic Option: For an even more scenic and circuitous route through the oak-studded hills of Northern California, consider following Highway 128 north from the resort/hot springs town of Calistoga at the northern end of the famous Napa Valley. But don't go via Napa and Calistoga if you plan to hurry. The winding curves and rough terrain are meant for touring, not making time. From Calistoga plan at least 2½ hours of driving time (not counting stops) to travel the 90 miles to Highway One.

Gas Up & Get Out: Before you pass **CLOVERDALE** (POP. 5400, EL. 333), Citrus Capital of Sonoma County, you might want to gas up and use the facilities. While the two hours to the coast is nothing compared with the two day stagecoach journeys made on this route in the 1800s, supplies and accommodations are scarce until Boonville and limited between Boonville and Fort Bragg. If you want to stop, use the first or second Cloverdale exit.

THE DRIVE

Take the third Cloverdale exit from busy Highway 101 for the quickest access to Highway 128 west. You head northwest on Highway 128, ascending through pastoral Oat Valley. To the north, Redwood Mountain towers 1000 feet overhead. Your road climbs Fairbanks Hill by switchbacks, quickly leaving Sonoma County for Mendocino

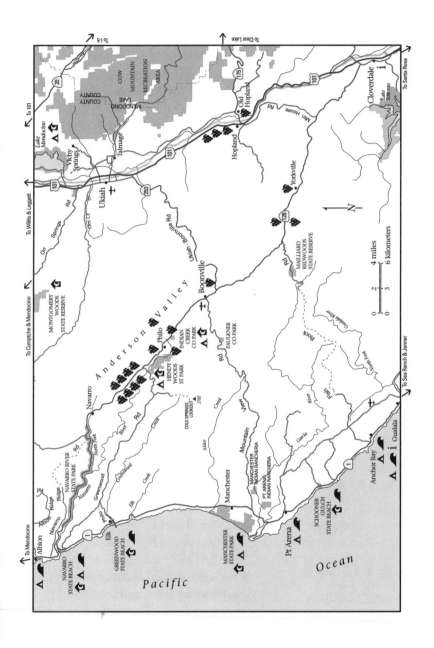

KZYX & KZYZ
90.7 FM & 91.5 FM

Mendocino County's only public radio station, the "mighty midget" offers National Public Radio and Pacifica links, plus a tangy taste of the locale. Tune in to "K-ZYX in the sticks" for bluegrass, blues, classical, jazz and rock around the clock. If you have trouble picking up the signal at 90.7, they also broadcast to the inland areas as KZYZ at 91.5 FM.

Christmas Tree Farms

What better way to find the holiday spirit and your perfect manicured Christmas tree than in the country where it grows in the sparkling fresh air on a rolling, dewy hillside? These slopes shelter choose and cut farms where you'll find fragrant fir, spruce or pine. The cool but usually snow-free coastal hills provide a great place for such a family adventure. Choose and cut your gem near Yorkville at Lawson's 894-2749 or Copper Queen Ranch 895-3317.

County. You leave cultivated fields for steep wild grasslands with scattered oak forests and chaparral, the predominant look of the idyllic country you will pass through on the way to Anderson Valley.

The highway drops down to Mountain House, an old stagecoach stop on the left, where Mountain House Road enters on the right, having climbed from Hopland.

Stagecoaches ran three days a week from Cloverdale to the coast via Anderson Valley beginning around 1860. At Navarro Ridge one could connect with the daily coast stage to go north to Mendocino City or south to Point Arena. Even in the 1880s city folks came to Anderson Valley for a week of hunting, fishing or relaxation by the river.

Drive up and over a small summit, then descend into a canyon where the road straightens somewhat, with one good turnout, to follow the headwaters of Dry Creek, which flows south into Sonoma County's Dry Creek Valley, highly regarded for its wine appellation. You might spot some bamboo growing along the creek.

At the very head of this stream sits the tiny community of **YORKVILLE** (POP. 25, EL. 945) towered over by Ward Mountain (3044 feet) to the north and Big Foot Mountain (2089 feet) to the south. Yorkville offers rural charm, a few Christmas tree farms and:

☆SHEEP DUNG ESTATES $95-250
P.O. Box 49, Yorkville 95494
894-5322/www.sheepdung.com

This hilltop hideaway offers heaven on earth for city dogs and their owners, with 320 acres to roam, a pond for swimming, trails, and modern, self-contained solar-powered cabins designed to be dog friendly. Most anyone else looking for an idyllic rural escape will also find it heavenly.

5 cottages w/ full kitchens stocked w/ brkfast, beverages; res. essential; min stay 2 nights; checks; midwk discount; woodstoves, barbecues, hammocks; adj. to hiking; families, pets welcome

LINDA VISTA B&B $130-155
33430 Hwy 128
Cloverdale 95425
894-2591
www.lindavista.com

Enjoy large bedroom suites with queen bed end views of vineyeards and rolling hills. Private bath has whirlpool tub and seperate shower. Breakfast is served in the formal dining room or on the veranda in season.

2 suites w/private bath; full breakfast; res. essential; checks; satellite tv; whirlpool in suite; phone; heated pool, gardens, adj to hiking; families welcome; pets ok in kennel by arrangement

YORKVILLE MINI MARKET & DELI
26701 Hwy 128, Yorkville
894-4091
L/D:$3–8

Custom-made sandwiches and burgers, homemade chili, soups, salads, plus local wine, beer and gifts.

Daily 9–6; ATM/V/MC; some seating

A little farther along you encounter the first of the region's wineries, **YORKVILLE VINEYARDS & CELLARS** 894-9177, with tasting daily 11–6.

Highway 128 tops a saddle west of Yorkville and descends along Rancheria Creek, a tributary of the Navarro River. Many valley oaks grow here, with scattered cottonwoods, redwoods and madrones.

Boontling

Anderson Valley's own dialect began around 1880 and thrived in the early twentieth century. It's almost impossible to tell how Boontling got its start. Some say the valley's hops workers cooked it up. Others argue the sheep shearers harped it first. Most agree the men started it to exclude the women from their talk, but the women caught on quickly and Boontling evolved into a way to exclude strangers. After 1920 it was used more to amuse visitors than exclude them.

At its height Boontling contained a basic vocabulary of more than 1000 words, plus 300 specialized names for local residents. While only a few old-timers harp it fluently today, you'll see or hear many examples as you pass through. Some examples: bahl gorms are good food, buckey walter is a telephone, horn of zeese is a cup of coffee, bright-lighter signifies city slicker, briney means the coast, eeble is to scrutinize, jape is to drive, and shark means to put (someone) on.

You pass **FISH ROCK ROAD** on the left at milepost 36.65. Fish Rock winds tortuously west for 30 miles to drop to Highway One at Anchor Bay. While the drive is scenic, the several miles of dirt road discourage most people from using it as a thoroughfare. If you long for a side trip, consider taking Fish Rock Road just 3½ miles to tiny **MAILLIARD REDWOODS STATE RESERVE.** This undeveloped state park of 242 acres preserves a couple of virgin groves of immense redwoods beside the road at the headwaters of the Garcia River. It offers a fine spot for a blanket picnic on a warm day.

Soon you'll encounter another winery. **MAPLE CREEK WINERY** 895-3001, 20799 Hwy 128 is on the right, with wine tasting, picnic grounds and a gallery, open daily 10:30–5. In about one mile **MEYER FAMILY CELLARS** 895-2341, 19750 Hwy 128 on the left features port.

Highway 128 turns north-northwest, soon leaving Rancheria Creek to descend along the rocky canyon of Robinson Creek. You climb over one more big hill, then descend by some nasty curves where big rocks hang incongruously suspended in a barbed-wire fence beside the road. A local rancher uses the stones to keep his fence taut.

Suddenly you pass the state fire station and enter Anderson Valley, an outpost of civilization famed for its locally created Boontling language and more recently for sparkling wines. Highway 128 bisects the valley for the next 16 miles, between here and Navarro.

You pass Highway 253 on the right, a 17-mile lateral that connects to Highway 101 at Ukiah, about 30 minutes away.

Boonville
(pop. 715, el. 400)

𝓗ighway 128 traffic slows to 30 mph to pass through Boonville, the unofficial capital of Anderson Valley.

The upper valley of the Navarro River supported a large population of Northern Pomo people, who thrived on abundant acorns, game and fish in the mild climate. The Pomo named the area Taa-bo-tah, meaning "long valley." Most of the native population was forced onto the Mendocino Indian Reservation near Fort Bragg in 1856. In 1851 the first white settlers came, naming Anderson Valley for their leader,

Picking hops in Anderson Valley

Walter Anderson. After he first saw the valley, Anderson announced his intention to move to "the Garden of Eden." In the next six years 20 more families settled in Anderson Valley, many of them of Scottish or Irish descent. One was W. W. Boone, a relative of Daniel Boone. The valley's largest town was named for W. W. after he bought the principal store (from early San Francisco merchants Levi and Strauss). The burg had previously been called Kendall's City. Boonville and Philo sprang into existence around 1862. The downriver settlements of Christine, Wendling and Navarro soon followed. By 1900 about 100 families had settled in these parts.

Modern Boonville has gasoline available at the **REDWOOD DRIVE-IN.** You will also find **ROOKIE-TO GALLERY** 895-2204, 14300 Hwy 128, art and fine crafts by regional artisans, daily 10–5:30, closed Tues and Wed, Jan–March. The **ANDERSON VALLEY BREWING CO.** 895-2337/ www.avbc.com has a new facility at 17700 Hwy 253, with tours daily at 1:30 and 4 pm. Their **OFFICIAL BOONVILLE BEER GIFT STORE** 895-2769 is downtown at 11141 Hwy 128. For wine tasting in town, visit **MENDOCINO SPECIALTY VINEYARDS** 895-3993 which pours wines of **CLAUDIA SPRINGS, EAGLEPOINT** and **RAYE'S HILL WINERIES,** plus tasting of Stella Cadente Olive Oil. Also downtown is **ALL THAT GOOD STUFF** 895-3638 cards, games, toys. The **BOONVILLE FARMERS MARKET** happens at the Boonville Hotel, June–Oct, Sat 9:45–noon.

For more information, contact **ANDERSON VALLEY CHAMBER OF COMMERCE** 895-2379, Box 275, Boonville, 95415.

At the west end of town **MOUNTAIN VIEW ROAD** is on the left. It heads west for 25 twisting miles to Manchester (see CHAPTER 11. BACK ROADS), but first leads to **ANDERSON VALLEY NURSERY** 895-3853. 18151 Mountain View Road. Specialists in native and Mediterranean plants, open Friday, Saturday and Sunday 10–4, and by appointment. **BOONVILLE AIRPORT** is nearby, off Mountain View Road by the high school.

Boonville Lodging

Listings are organized from the most expensive to the least expensive

☆THE OTHER PLACE $175–300
Off Hwy 128 .2 mile from Boonville
Boonville 95415
894-5322/ www.sheepdung.com

Imagine 550 acres of pastoral hills to roam, shared only with the guests at two other cottages. Each cottage has sweeping views and is furnished with modern dog-friendly furniture, creating a comfortable yet sophisticated atmosphere.

3 cottages w/ full kitchens stocked w/ brkfast, beverages; res. essential;, 1 2-bdrm cottage; 2 nights min; checks; woodstove/phone/tv/vcr in rms; adj. to hiking, pond; 1 unit ৬

ANDERSON CREEK INN $100–180
12050 Anderson Valley Way
Boonville
895-3091/800-552-6202

www.andersoncreekinn.com

A quiet, gracious ranch-style inn on 16 acres with outstanding valley and hill views. Five spacious rooms have king beds and private baths, three have fireplaces.

5 rooms; full breakfast; V/MC/Disc/checks; min stay 2 nights on wkends, holidays May-Oct; offseason rates; outdoor pool; fireplaces; bathtubs; adj. to hiking

BOONVILLE HOTEL $85–250
14040 Hwy 128/Box 326
Boonville
895-2210

Simple yet elegant comfort abounds throughout this lovingly restored hotel. Decorated throughout with freshly cut flowers, the hotel offers a gracious respite from the city, as well as exquisite dining.

10 rooms; continental breakfast; closed in Jan; 2 nights min. holiday wknds; V/MC/checks; 4 suites; adj. restaurant; bathtubs; gardens; ৬

Eateries

☆ BOONVILLE HOTEL RESTAURANT & BAR
14040 Hwy 128, Boonville
895-2210
D: $16–26

Serving excellent food, from fresh and local ingredients whenever possible. The presentation is simple but elegant in the bright, casual dining room of Shaker-like decor. Bar open daily.

Thur–Mon 6–9 pm; closed Jan; res. advisable; V/MC/checks; beer/local wines; seats 45; ৬

☆LAUREN'S
14211 Hwy 128, Boonville
895-3869
D: $8.50–15

A casual place serving simple meals inspired by flavors of the season. Comfort food influenced by American, Asian, Mexican and Mediterranean cooking. Local musicians sometimes.

Tues-Sat 5-9; checks; beer/wine; seats 60; take-out; ৬

BUCKHORN SALOON
14081 Hwy 128, Boonville 95415
895-3369
L/D: $9–17

Legendary Boonville beer on tap plus a local wine list. Pub fare, plus fresh seafood on weekends. Outside seating available during summer months. *Bar opens 10:30 am, food from 11 am–8:30 pm or later, daily in summer, closed Tue–Wed Oct–June; V/MC/AE; beer/wine; seats 75 + outside; take-out;* &

LUMBERJACK PIZZA
14161 Hwy 128, Boonville
895-2480
$8.50–19

Fresh brick-baked, handmade pizza, plus pasta, soups, salads. *Wed, Thur 4–9,Fri 4–10, Sat 12–10, Sun 12–9; seats 40; take-out*

HORN OF ZEESE
14025 Hwy 128, Boonville
895-3525
B: $3–7, L: $6.50–9

Breakfast all day kind of place harps Boont, makes food from scratch. Charbroiled chickenburger and ahi specialties, omelettes, soups and pies too. *Daily from 7 am–3 pm; closed Thur in winter; ATM/checks; seats 42+ outside; take-out;* &

CAFE GLAD
14111 Hwy 128, Boonville
895-3038
B: $2–5, L: $5–10

This small bakery/cafe bakes all their pastries from scratch daily. Lunches feature sandwiches made on their fresh focaccia, plus soups and salads. Espresso bar with organic coffees and teas. Special desserts by order. *Mon–Fri 7 am–3 pm (close at 2 in winter), Sat 8–12; checks; seats 20; take-out;* &

Anderson Valley Events

Held at Boonville Fairgrounds unless noted otherwise.

Legendary Boonville Beer Festival: *3rd Saturday in April.*

Spring Wildflower Show: *Last weekend in April, free.*

Anderson Valley Pinot Noir Festval: *3rd weekend in May, tasting, winery open house and more.*

Wild Iris Folk Festival: *Last weekend in May.*

Old Time Fourth of July Celebration: *Parade, chili Cook-Off, music & more*

Woolgrower's Barbecue & Sheep Dog Trials: *3rd weekend in July.*

Wine Tasting Championships: *Last weekend in July at Greenwood Ridge Vineyards near Philo. Competition for novices and experts, with food, wine and live music.*

Mendocino County Fair & Apple Show: *mid-September. Great old-fashioned county fair features rodeo, midway, sheep dog trials, animal judging, music and Sunday parade.*

Christmas Crafts Fair: *First two weekends in December, Anderson Valley Grange. Sponsored by KZYX, this event brings a large variety of local artists out of the hills so that you can find some truly original gifts.*

BOONVILLE GENERAL STORE
Hwy 128 at Farrer Ln., Box 525
Boonville 95415
895-9477
B/L/D: $4–12

Features handmade organic gourmet foods—sandwiches, soups, pizzas baked on stone, breads and pastries baked daily. They sell artesanal cheeses, olives, picnic fare and local wines. They also carry durable goods and gifts for home, garden and kids.

Daily May-Oct: 9 am–5 pm, Thurs-Mon: Nov-Apr; V/MC/Checks; beer/wine; families welcome; seats 15; take-out; &

REDWOOD DRIVE-IN
13980 Hwy 128, Boonville
895-3441
B: $2–8, L/D: $3–10

Full breakfast, freshly made sandwiches, lunch specials, many varieties of hamburgers, salad bar, and at least 12 flavors of old-fashioned milk shakes.

Daily 6 am–8 pm; close 1 hour earlier in Jan, Feb; V/MC; seats 50; take-out; &

☆ BOONT BERRY FARM
13981 Hwy 128, Boonville
895-3576

L/D: $2.50–10

A small and welcoming store with natural food products. They serve delicious and wholesome food, healthy with international influences.

Mon–Sat 10-6, Sun 12-6; checks; seats 25; take-out

MAGGIE MAE'S
14111 Hwy 128, Boonville
895-3994
L/D: $3–8

Tiny eatery has ice cream and delicious shakes, plus coffee drinks and hot dogs: Polish, veggie and Caspar footlongs. They also encourage impromptu acoustic music jamming—the instruments are waiting!

Daily 11 am–6 pm; shorter hours in winter; seats 12; take-out

TAQUERIA DEL TACO
14161 Hwy 128, Boonville
895-9035
L/D: $1.50–7

Good Mexican food made fresh daily, from ala carte to combination plates. Family run for all families.

Daily 10:30–10; seats 40; take-out

CONTINUING ON . . .

Leaving Boonville, Highway 128 straightens out across the valley floor, heading northwest toward Philo as vineyards begin to dominate the landscape. In one mile, look for the little red Con Creek schoolhouse on the left. This one-room affair

Traveling Emporium

houses **ANDERSON VALLEY HISTORICAL SOCIETY MUSEUM** 895-3207. Friday through Sunday 1–4 pm, may open earlier in summer: if the flag is flying, it's open. Nearby, also on Anderson Valley Way (the old highway) is **ANDERSON CREEK INN B&B** (see Boonville Listings). Highway 128 winds gently into Philo, Anderson Valley's second city.

PHILO
(POP. 473, EL. 290)

*A*FTER YOU PASS the KZYX studio, the highway dips across Indian Creek. On the left is . . .

INDIAN CREEK COUNTY PARK Fee. Turn left for picnic ground, camping ($10/night) in 10 shady sites beneath big redwoods beside a small stream, and short walks in a redwood grove.

Philo was named by early settler Cornelius Prather, who arrived in 1862 and named the community for a favorite cousin. Agriculture dominated until a sawmill was established in 1878.

As you pass the Philo sawmill, slow down as you enter the town of Philo's central district, with a gas station and . . .

LEMON'S PHILO MARKET 895-3552, 8651 Hwy 128. Daily.

PACIFIC ECHO CELLARS 895-2957/800-824-7754, 8501 Hwy 128, has a pleasant tasting room occupying a remodeled farmhouse, where rotating art exhibits add a refined air to the sipping of sparkling wines. In 1981 John Scharffenberger was the first vintner here to make champagne-type wines in Anderson Valley. (He now makes red wines at Eaglepoint Winery and gourmet chocolate outside the valley.) Daily 11–5.

Philo Lodging

Listings are organized from the most expensive to the least expensive

HIGHLAND RANCH $285/PERSON
PO Box 150, Philo 95466
895-3600/www.highlandranch.com

Uniquely personal, this is a private and congenial retreat for individuals, couples or groups. Relax in a hammock, fish for bass in the pond, or take an excursion on foot, bike or horseback through the redwoods or along the river. With delicious meals featuring local bounty, the ranch is a true getaway.

12 rooms; all meals, wine & spirits included; 2 day min. stay; V/MC/AE/Disc/checks; families, pets welcome; children under 13: $190/day; swimming pool; fireplaces; bathtubs; gardens; tennis; phone in room; tv in lodge; mountain bikes; fishing; conference room; ठ

Valley Agriculture

Ever since early settlers carved farms and ranches out of the wilderness, agriculture has kept the wheels of valley commerce turning. Sheep have been the most numerous livestock since the early days. Mendocino County grazed more than 75,000 head in 1880, and sheep still number about 12,000 today, fourth among county agricultural resources behind timber, grapes and pears. Apples and hops dominated the valley harvest, but wine grapes took over in the 1980s as Anderson Valley established a reputation for growing superior cool weather grapes.

☆PHILO POTTERY INN $110-165
8550 Hwy 128/Box 166
Philo 95466
895-3069/www.philopotteryinn.com

The only historic B&B in Anderson forest beside the Navarro River. Wander through the organic garden, swim in emerald-green swimming holes, or hike year round. Hendy Woods State Park borders the center, offering trails to Valley, built in 1886 entirely of redwood. Five comfortable and cozy rooms surrounded by large oaks and a beautiful garden. Lavish breakfast starts your day. Visit local wineries, bicycle back roads, picnic under redwoods or enjoy the front porch and garden.

5 rooms, 2 w/ shared bath; full breakfast, aperitifs; min. stay 2 nights wknds; MC/V; winter discounts; wood stoves; bathtubs; common room/library; families welcome; gardens; adj. to hiking

PINOLI RANCH COUNTRY INN $125
3280 Clark Rd, Philo
895-2550

A unique and peacefully secluded inn nestled on 100 acres with incomparable views of the valley, offering privacy, warm hospitality and excellent service to make your stay enjoyable.

2 rooms with private baths; full breakfast; res. essential; V/MC/ checks; fireplaces/wood stoves; bathtubs; complementary wine; suite avail; gardens; adj. to hiking

INDIAN CREEK INN $115-130
9050 Hwy 128, Philo
895-3861

5 rooms; closed Christmas; checks; gardens; adj. to hiking; families welcome; ♿

HOLLY HILL FARM B&B $110
2151 Hwy 128, Philo
895-2269/www.hollyhillfarminn.com

Passive solar design guest house with large decks has two bedrooms on 12 acres.

1 private 2 bedroom guest house; cont. brkfast; res. essential; checks; kitchen/phone/vcr in house; hammocks, deck; families welcome; ♿

ANDERSON VALLEY INN $55–99
8480 Hwy 128/Box 147,
Philo 95466
895-3325/www.avinn.com

Tastefully decorated motel rooms just minutes from wineries, Hendy Woods State Park and Navarro River. Helpful and friendly innkeepers.

7 rooms w/priv baths; V/MC/AE/checks; families welcome, pets ok some rooms; 2 room suites avail.

WELLSPRING RENEWAL CENTER
$30–100
Box 332, Philo
895-3893/www.wellspringrenewal.org

On 53 acres of sunny meadows and redwood forest beside the Navarro River. Wander through the organic garden, swim in emerald-green swimming holes, or hike year round. Hendy Woods State Park borders the center, offering trails to giant redwoods.

9 cabins & lodges; will cook for groups of 14 or more; indiv. may join existing groups for meals; V/ MC/checks; camping: $14/person & kids' rates; off-season midweek disc, holidays excluded; cooking facilities; 4 cabins share bathhouse; wood stoves; ৬

VAN ZANDT REDWOOD VIEW RESORT $70–80
Philo
895-3174

This traditional family resort built in 1930 offers old river charm and country comfort for a vacation "just like in the good old days."

5 cabins + tent house; closed Oct 1–Apr 30; res. essential; checks; smoking rms; kitchens; tent house shared bath; swimming hole; adj. to hiking; playground; hammocks

Eatery

LIBBY'S
8651 Hwy 128, Philo
895-2646
L/D: $6–12

The place to get affordable, home style Mexican food plus burgers is this friendly family-run business.

Tue–Sun 11:30–2:30, 5–8:30; beer/wine; take-out; seats 45;

Sparkling Wines

Italian immigrants to Anderson Valley produced the first local wines around 1880, but it was not until Husch Vineyards opened in 1968 that the modern age of wine making came to the valley. During the 1970s Edmeades, Lazy Creek, Navarro and Handley joined the local scene. Then in 1981 John Scharffenberger started to make sparkling wine (champagne) from Anderson Valley grapes. By the end of the decade French champagne makers had invested heavily in Anderson Valley, seeing similarities in climate and soil to the fog-shrouded champagne region of France. The results have been excellent, producing healthy prospects for the valley's wine producing future and great fun for any traveler who likes wine.

CONTINUING ON . . .

Strung out over the next mile, look left for: **ANDERSON VALLEY FARM SUPPLY** 895-3655, 7050 Hwy 128. Nursery and propane. **BRUTOCAO CELLARS** 895-2152, 7000 Hwy 128, tasting 10–6 daily. **GOWAN'S OAK TREE** 895-3353, 6600 Hwy 128. The white clapboard roadside stand has been a valley fixture for more than 60 years. Buy homegrown produce and picnic beneath giant oaks, looking across the river to the virgin redwoods of Hendy Woods State Park. Daily 8–6. Just up the road the Gowan family sells firewood for people planning to camp.

After the big bend at Gowan's, Highway 128 climbs to its junction with **PHILO-GREENWOOD ROAD.** For a delightful short side trip, turn left to visit **THE APPLE FARM** 895-2333, 18501 Philo-Greenwood Road. Delicious organic apple products, jams, jellies and chutneys, plus cooking classes and cabins, daily. **HENDY WOODS STATE PARK** 895-3141. Fee. Entrance on left, ½ mile from Hwy 128. This 845-acre park, where trails explore 100 acres of immense virgin redwood groves, has camping, picnicking, hiking and wheelchair access. (See CHAPTER 11. BACK ROADS, for more about 18-mile Philo-Greenwood Road.)

Back on Highway 128, continue northwest through the heart of Anderson Valley's wine belt, with nine tasting facilities in the next 2½ miles. **NAVARRO VINEYARDS** 895-3686, 5601 Hwy 128. This attractive winery has a solid reputation for quality, specializing in Pinot Noir,

Chardonnay, Gewurztraminer and Alsatian-style wines. Daily 10–5, 'til 6 on weekends. **GREENWOOD RIDGE VINEYARDS** 895-2002, 5501 Hwy 128. This small winery pours its wines in a distinctively modern building with grand pastoral views. They excel at White Riesling, Zinfandel and Pinot Noir, plus Merlot and Sauvignon Blanc. Daily 10–5.

The highway passes a handsome weathered old apple drier on your right, one of many that once prospered in the region. **LAZY CREEK VINEYARDS** 895-3623, 4741 Hwy 128. Tasting daily 10–5. This cozy little winery excels at Gewurztraminer, with good Chardonnay and Pinot Noir rounding out the line. **ROEDERER ESTATE** 895-2288, 4501 Hwy 128. The esteemed 200 year-old French champagne maker chose this area for its U.S. operation because the climate is most similar to France's Champagne region. The first release of their California Brut in 1988 put Anderson Valley on the international vintners' map. Their Brut Rosé and L'Ermitage are exquisite. Informative tours give a good picture of the complexities of producing traditional sparkling wines. The tasting room features a zinc-topped, antique French bistro bar and 200-year-old terracotta tiles. Tasting daily 11–5, tours by appointment.Right across the road is **HUSCH VINEYARDS** 895-3216, 4400 Hwy 128. At the valley's oldest winery, climbing roses cloak the tiny rustic tasting room hosted by a friendly, informed staff. Their good wines reach their peak with Chardonnay, Gewurtztraminer and Sauvignon Blanc, with good Cabernet Sauvignon and Pinot Noir. Picnic under the vine-draped arbor. Daily 10–5, 'til 6 in summer. **ESTERLINA VINEYARDS & WINERY** 895-2920, 1200 Holmes Ranch Road. This tiny winery on a back road perches high in the valley's rolling hills, producing Pinot Noir, Riesling, Cabernet Sauvignon, Merlot and Chardonnay. Tasting 11-5 daily by appointment.

Picnickers on the Albion RR, Flynn Creek

CHRISTINE WOODS VINEYARDS 895-2115, 3155 Hwy 128. Named for the early community here, this tiny vintner produces Chardonnay, Pinot Noir and Cabernet. Daily, 11–5. **HANDLEY CELLARS** 895-3876, 3151 Hwy 128. Well-made wines, including an excellent sparkler, are poured in a charming, sunny tasting room, with a garden courtyard for picnics. Daily 11–5.

As the highway continues towards the coast, notice that the valley has narrowed, becoming more wooded on this lower end. The pioneer community here was called Christine after the first white child born in Anderson Valley. Your road soon returns to its winding ways. Cross Floodgate Creek, which got its name from a practical setup here in the early days. When the Navarro River overflowed its banks, some of the flood waters would be diverted into the nearly level canyon of Floodgate to ease the flooding downstream.

After a series of curves the road comes to **NAVARRO** (POP. 67, EL. 272).

John Gschwend built Anderson Valley's first sawmill in this area in 1856. The first town here, called Wendling, was established around 1860, when the town of Navarro was located on the coast at the mouth of the Navarro River. Wendling grew into a booming lumber company town with more than 1000 employees and seven saloons. When the coastal Navarro withered away in the early 1900s, Wendling changed its name to Navarro. The mill closed in the 1930s. Later most of the town was destroyed by fire. Navarro Hotel, the last grand remnant, burned to ground in 1974.

Now nearly a ghost town, especially compared to the town's heyday as a lumber town first, then as a mecca for steelhead fishermen, one of the few retail businesses is **NAVARRO GENERAL STORE & DELI** 895-9445.

Highway 128 straightens out briefly as it leaves Navarro and Anderson Valley behind to follow the Navarro River to the coast. You follow the North Fork Navarro River for the next few winding miles. Soon Flynn Creek Road forks right, winding over two passes to reach tiny Comptche in 7½ miles. The original pioneer route to the coast climbed over Navarro Ridge from the west side of Flynn Creek. The rough dirt road remaining today is not recommended for driving, but offers a fine mountain bike route.

Highway 128 continues along the river canyon, winding through forest. A corridor of redwoods along the road and river between here and the coast has been protected in **NAVARRO REDWOODS STATE PARK**. The 650-acre park is mostly undeveloped, but at milepost 8.0 on the left is **PAUL DIMMICK CAMPGROUND**, with 30 campsites near the confluence of Navarro River with its North Fork. The first-come, first-serve sites have water and flush toilets in summer, only pit toilets in winter.

Now the road parallels the Navarro River, much larger than its North Fork. In summer a number of popular swimming holes draw locals and visitors alike. You might try parking at the following mileposts and taking the short walk down to the river to test the waters: 7.35, 6.7, 6.4, 5.25, 3.8, 3.65.

Amidst another onslaught of tricky curves, the highway passes Hop Flat where high water markers show where the river crested 15 feet above the road in 1955, 1964 and 1983. The flood of 1995 crested nearly as high.

Highway 128 straightens out briefly before ending at milepost 40.28 on Coast Highway One, right beside the broad, now-tidal Navarro River, about one mile before it empties into the Pacific Ocean. Continue straight on Highway One to reach Albion, Mendocino and points north (see CHAPTER 5). Turn left and cross the bridge if you are going south to nearby Elk or Point Arena and Gualala (see CHAPTER 4).

10. HIGHWAY 20 TO HIGHWAY ONE — 33 MILES

THE ROUTE

*H*IGHWAY 20, WHICH HEADS WEST FROM WILLITS,
139 miles north of San Francisco on
Highway 101, offers the shortest and easiest
road access to the Mendocino Coast,
meeting Highway One at the south end of
Fort Bragg. Expect the 33 miles of Highway
20 from Willits to Highway One to take at
least one hour, however. These 33 miles,
anything but straight and level, challenge
the driver with dozens of curves twisting
over seven major hills. Many trucks and
recreational vehicles use this route, further
slowing traffic. Diligent use of the eight
paved and numerous dirt turnouts heading
west (21 paved going east) is, as always,
highly recommended. Incidentally, the
western-most leg of Highway 20 was not
paved until about 1960. Until World War II, long

and winding Sherwood Road, the original stagecoach route, was the main road between Willits and the coast. Fort Bragg used a horse-drawn hearse into the 1940s, even when the dear departed had to be taken to Willits for burial.

Highway 20 also serves as a main east-west artery to reach the Mendocino Coast from Clear Lake, the Sacramento Valley and even Lake Tahoe. In the east, Highway 20 originates at Interstate 80, west of Donner Summit and east of Emigrant Gap. To reach Fort Bragg from Interstate 5 expect 3 to 4 hours; from I-80 plan at least 5½ hours for the 236 miles of primarily two-lane, winding asphalt.

WILLITS (POP. 5175, EL. 1377) offers ample lodging and services. Consider staying here when the coast is full on busy weekends and in summer. During those periods don't leave Willits without your room or campsite on the coast already reserved. Mendocino County's third largest town offers twelve motels and two campgrounds, numerous cafes and other services. The **CHAMBER OF COMMERCE** 459-7910, 239 S. Main (Highway 101), may be helpful. Mon–Fri 10 to 4.

Recommended lodging:

ETTA PLACE B&B 459-5953, 909 Exley Lane, on 17 acres. 2 rooms, $65–95.

BAECHTEL CREEK INN & SPA 459-9063/800-459-9911, 101 Gregory Lane, 43 rooms, $59–105.

OLD WEST INN 459-4201/800-700-7659, 1221 S. Main, 18 rooms, $45–150.

HOLIDAY LODGE 459-5361/800-835-3972, 1540 S. Main, 16 rooms, $55–79.

SUPER 8 MOTEL 459-3388, 1119 S. Main, 44 rooms, $59–109.

Recommended eateries:

☆ **PURPLE THISTLE** 459-4750, 50 S. Main. Dinner: $6–19. Non-traditional Japanese, Mendonesian and international cuisine, all carefully prepared from scratch using only the finest natural ingredients. *Tues–Sat 4:30–8, later in summer; res. advisable; V/MC/AE/Disc/checks; beer/wine; families welcome; take-out; seats 36 inside, 50 on patio;* &.

ARDELLA'S KITCHEN 459-6577, 35 E. Commercial. Breakfast, Tue–Sat 6am–noon, $2–8.50.

EL MEXICANO 459-5702, 166 S. Main. Lunch & dinner. Daily except Sunday 11–8:30, $4–12.

☆**BURRITO EXQUISITO** 459-5421, 42 S. Main. Lunch & dinner daily 11–9, $3–9.

MENDOCINO COUNTY MUSEUM 459-2736, 400 E. Commercial, has Pomo and pioneer artifacts, revolving history exhibits, a community art gallery and a display of old steam engines outside. Wed–Sun 10–4:30

THE DRIVE

From Willits, Highway 20 climbs steadily to its 2040-foot summit near Two Rock in just 5½ miles. If the weather is clear, use the turnout on the left at the summit for a panoramic view over the wild terrain between here and the coast.

From the crest the road turns winding and steep. Descend, then climb to a second summit (1800 feet) at Three Chop Ridge. Here the forks and tributaries of the Noyo River are to the north, with Big River's headwaters to the south. Several miles west on Three Chop was the site of an important archaeological discovery in 1984.

The road begins its steepest, windiest stretch as it descends Seven Mile Grade. About half way down the treacherous hill the road enters 50,000-acre Jackson State Forest. You pass some big redwoods beside the road. Jackson State Forest offers free camping in two designated campgrounds. This largest state forest in California was created in 1947 when California bought the lands of the Caspar Lumber Company. Caspar had logged the forest by railroad from 1903 to 1946.

You cross James Creek at the bottom of

Discovery on Three Chop Ridge

At an archaeological dig north of Highway 20 in 1984, Professor Thomas Layton and his students hoped to find evidence of a prehistoric camp of native people. When the group found pieces of pottery instead, they were dismayed, thinking the dig contaminated by a recent logging camp.

The real story unfolded slowly, revealing the site as a Northern Pomo village inhabited into the 1850s. The potsherds proved to be nineteenth century Chinese porcelain, salvaged by the Pomo from the schooner Frolic when it shipwrecked near Caspar in July 1850. Further digging revealed other booty from the wreck: oriental ginger jars and pieces of glass from bottles of Edinburgh ale.

Several more years of archaeological sleuthing led Dr. Layton to the remains of the ship and an enthralling story of the shipwreck*—the incident that brought commerce to the Mendocino Coast when San Franciscans came looking for salvage goods and instead found the north coast's immense and precious redwood forests.

*See "Wreck of the Frolic,"
Chapter 6.

Seven Mile Grade, then parallel the pretty North Fork of Big River on your left. Dogwood Picnic Area sits between road and stream on the left at milepost 18.5. The lovely spot offers picnic tables and pit toilets.

Chamberlain Creek, at milepost 17.3, marks the halfway point between Willits and Fort Bragg. The sunny clearing left of the highway, the site of Caspar Lumber Company's Camp 20 logging camp from 1939 to 1955, has pit toilets, sheltered picnic tables and historical displays of old logging equipment. Interpretive loop trails of one and two miles climb through forest north of the highway. The old Caspar Woods Schoolhouse, moved here by rail in 1939 from an earlier lumber camp, stands just across the creek to the east. A sturdy footbridge spans the creek, allowing you to explore around the historic school and walk under the highway to the new arboretum on the north side of the highway. The latter paths are wheelchair accessible.

Highway 20 generally follows the old Caspar Lumber Company railroad grade as it pushes west over Dunlap Pass. Before the summit, watch on the left for the entrance to Dunlap Campground, one of the last remaining places you can camp free near the coast. After the summit the highway drops to the headwaters of South Fork Noyo River in the deep valley occupied by Camp

Locomotive "Daisy" with load, 1904

19 Ranch. Caspar Lumber Company's Camp 19 hummed with activity beside the big pond here from 1929 to 1939.

The route then rises over McGuire Hill only to drop to Whiskey Springs, site of another span of logging railway and of an illegal distillery during Prohibition. The highway climbs steeply again, the hill ending with the only short passing lane on this twisting stretch of road. At milepost 8.08 you cross the Mendocino Hiking & Equestrian Trail, a rugged 44-mile path connecting Mendocino and Willits. To the south it follows Little Lake Road, the historic route between those two towns.

As you descend once again, look for State Forest Road 350 on the

Laying track at Camp One, 1904

right (milepost 5.9). The dirt track descends three miles to the Noyo
Egg Collecting Station on the South Fork Noyo River, where migrating
salmon are stripped of their eggs for hatchery use.

This was the site of Camp One, Caspar Lumber Company's biggest
and longest lasting backwoods camp. The small town at the camp,
occupied from 1904 until the railroad was abandoned in 1945,
provided bunkhouses for single men, bungalows for families, a store,
a cookhouse, an ice plant, an engine house and switching yard for the
engines used in the woods. Camp One was the original site of the
Caspar Woods Schoolhouse now at Camp 20.

Today the area offers free car camping and access to several
hiking trails, but one needs a trail guide or detailed map of Jackson
State Forest to properly explore the maze of narrow dirt roads
beyond Camp One.

On nearby Kass Creek another community flourished in the 1930s.
Members of the north coast's Finnish population homesteaded
Sointula in response to the desperate financial climate of the Great
Depression.

Back on Highway 20 you leave Jackson State Forest and climb
through a residential community atop Noyo Hill. The old Finnish

Bigfoot

The steep, wooded terrain along Highway 20 presents nothing but wild and remote country to travelers zipping along on the asphalt. One should not be surprised, therefore, that bigfoot was seen here in 1962.

According to the weekly Fort Bragg Advocate-News, *a relative visiting Bud Jenkins at his home on Highway 20 saw a shadowy figure staring over a low fence in the fog. He figured it was a bear until the beast stepped over the fence and stood up next to him. The man screamed and ran inside, with the creature pursuing him, then trying to open the door. Three people saw the giant before it ran off. They found a footprint, measured at 18 inches, and a hand print, and said the visitor had a pungent odor. The local Pomo called these beasts Ka-mets, describing them as eight-feet-tall and fond of human flesh. That was the last bigfoot reported in Mendocino County, probably because the region has become so civilized in the last 30 years. Today one has to go farther north, deep into Trinity or Siskiyou counties to have any hope of spotting bigfoot.*

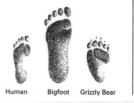

Human   Bigfoot   Grizzly Bear

Dance Hall, now a private residence, still stands south of the route.

It was beneath Noyo Hill near the turnoff for Road 350 that hundreds of Chinese laborers dug the railroad tunnel that allowed the Caspar Lumber Company trains to reach the Noyo River in 1903. While the tunnel was being built, dozens of unemployed workers threatened to run the Chinese out of town until the sheriff diffused the incident by challenging the protestors to take over the dirty, dangerous job.

After this last hill the highway makes a corkscrew descent called Thirteen Turns. As the road straightens out, look on your left for **LEISURE TIME RV PARK** (see Fort Bragg Listings).

When you see the boat-building yard to the right of the highway, you know you are finally getting close to salt water. On your right South Harbor Drive leads to a public boat ramp and **DOLPHIN ISLE MARINA**. In another ¼ mile Highway 20 meets Boatyard Drive on the right, which leads to **BOATYARD SHOPPING CENTER: HARVEST MARKET**, **RITE-AID**, and clothing and crafts stores, laundromat and pizza parlor. Also on Boatyard Drive is **TRAILER COVE RV PARK**, which looks over Noyo Harbor.

Highway 20 ends at Highway One. Turn right for Fort Bragg and points north (see Chapter 6), left for Mendocino and points south (see Chapter 5).

11. Back Roads of the Mendocino Coast

*T*HESE BYWAYS SHINE FOR THOSE WHO LIKE SLOW travel and exploring out of the way places. They are not for large recreational vehicles or people who expect broad, white-lined pavement, guard rails and ample warning signs. Please explore them slowly and with respect for the private people whose neighborhoods they are, or explore them not at all. Stagecoaches travelled most of them long before asphalt came to Mendocino County.

Fish Rock Road
30 miles Anchor Bay to Yorkville

This scenic byway leaves the coast near its namesake offshore sea stack, climbing steeply up a lush canyon and over the flank of Gualala Peak (2210 feet) for grand views over wild wooded terrain. Turning to dirt, it dips and soars along ridges, then drops to

Point Arena Hot Springs

the headwaters of the Garcia River (Point Arena Hot Springs was once a few miles downstream), where the pleasant groves of **MAILLIARD REDWOODS STATE RESERVE** straddle the road. Pavement resumes for the final four miles into the Navarro River watershed to meet Highway 128 north of Yorkville.

MOUNTAIN VIEW ROAD
25 miles Manchester to Boonville

This steeply winding roller-coaster pike plies numerous canyons and ridges of the outer Coast Range where the unpeopled views seem to stretch forever. Not for the squeamish or incautious, the track's original stage journey took two days, with a stop at the long-gone wayside inn called Mountain View House. After twisting steeply down to the lovely canyon of Rancheria Creek, tributary to the Navarro, the road climbs one more ridge to pretty little **FAULKNER COUNTY PARK** (picnicking) before dropping to Boonville.

PHILO-GREENWOOD ROAD
18 miles Elk to Philo

Exiting downtown Elk, this most residential of south coast back roads soars quickly to Greenwood Ridge, then saunters along past numerous homesteads and apple farms high above Greenwood Creek. After dipping through the headwaters of Elk Creek, the stage route climbs again to Signal Ridge, then wiggles down to meet the Navarro River where the big ancient redwood groves of **HENDY WOODS STATE PARK** flank the new vineyards of Anderson Valley's wine region. Highway 128 and a dozen wineries lie right across the river.

COMPTCHE-UKIAH ROAD
45 miles Mendocino to Ukiah

The old stage road makes a coiling ascent from the mouth of Big River, then straightens out across the now-residential pygmy prairie before winding through the high country overlooking Big River State Park and timberlands. The community of Comptche (pronounced comp-chee),

Ukiah Stage on Ukiah Street, Mendocino

named for a local Pomo chief, lies 14 winding miles up the road, offering only a general store for visitors, plus occasional homegrown festivities.

The byway narrows, climbing through homesteaded valleys and over ridges. The track makes a winding one mile descent, then starts a meandering climb along South Fork Big River, bringing you to **MONTGOMERY REDWOODS STATE RESERVE**, where a primordial and majestic redwood grove offers a refreshing walk. This virtually undeveloped 1484-acre park straddles the South Fork Big River, offering the finest stand of

Orr Hot Springs Resort

virgin redwood forest in the county and some of the world's tallest trees. Two miles of trails explore the groves, a popular summer retreat for early settlers from all over the county. Well shaded picnic tables, vault toilets.

One mile up the road, **ORR HOT SPRINGS RESORT** 462-6277, 13201 Orr Springs Rd, Ukiah, offers rustic baths and overnight accommodation in a beautiful setting. $40–185. Reservations are required for day use or overnight; call before leaving if you plan to stop.

Your byway, now called Orr Springs Road, corkscrews steeply out of the redwood canyon into oak-spattered grasslands, then, with grand views of valleys and mountains to the east, descends a winding ridge to Ukiah. Plan at least two hours from Mendocino to Ukiah, slightly more round trip from the coast to Montgomery Woods or Orr Springs.

BRANSCOMB ROAD
26 miles Westport to Laytonville

This meandering turn-of-the-century stage route ascends along narrow Packard Ridge, providing grand views south over the forks of Ten Mile River and north into lesser watersheds. In the first 10 miles , the many blind curves require attentively hugging the road's right shoulder and frequent toots on the claxon. At 10 miles Wilderness Lodge Road forks left, winding with the South Fork Eel River past homesteads for 3½ miles to the Nature Conservancy's pristine and remote 7520-acre **ANGELO RESERVE**, 984-6653, where you might want to take a hike.The Preserve offers great hiking through old growth forests and meadows along the river to old homestead sites. It doesn't allow vehicle access beyond the entrance, mountain biking, dogs, camping or smoking.

The Branscomb Road picks up a white stripe and shoulders as it rambles east up the river to **BRANSCOMB** (POP. 101, EL. 1540), where the **BRANSCOMB STORE** feels like a flashback to another era. The byway continues upriver nearly to the source, passing big redwoods in tiny **ADMIRAL WILLIAM STANDLEY STATE PARK**. The route rolls gently over a divide and descends to Ten Mile Creek and Long Valley, ending at bustling Laytonville on Highway 101.

FAREWELL MY BRETHREN,
Farewell O earth and sky, farewell ye
neighboring waters,
My time has ended, my term has come.

Along the northern coast,
Just back from the rock-bound shore and the
caves,
In the saline air from the sea in the
Mendocino country,
With the surge for base and accompaniment
low and hoarse,
With crackling blows of axes sounding
musically driven by strong arms,
Riven deep by the sharp tongues of the axes,
there in the redwood forest dense,
I heard the mighty tree its death-chant
chanting.

        — Walt Whitman,
    from *Song of the Redwood Tree*

Coast Media

*Y*OU MAY THINK YOU'RE IN THE BOONIES, BUT THE RADIO airwaves are alive and well here. TV coverage is a bit thin unless you tap into the cable. Print journalism also thrives to varying degrees, but if you crave a daily the *Santa Rosa Press Democrat* offers the only coverage that even acknowledges the Mendocino Coast.

RADIO FM:

KZYX/Z 90.7, 91.5, Philo. Public radio for Mendocino County offers National Public Radio and Pacifica links, local news, and diverse music for a tangy taste of the locale. Sometimes 6 am to midnight, sometimes round the clock. 895-2324.

KOZT 95.3, 95.9, Fort Bragg. Adult rock 24 hours a day, plus local news. 964-0095. Winner, Rock Station of the Year Award, 2002-2003.

KMFB 92.7, Mendocino. Golden oldies, plus eclectic evening variety, jazz, blues reggae and Late-night Liz Tues-Thur. S. F. Giants, Raiders and 49ers games. 964-4653.

KMUD 91.1, 88.9, Garberville. Public radio for southern Humboldt County. 923-2513.

KHUM 104.3, 104.7, Ferndale. Radio without the rules. 786-5104.

KUKI 97.1, 103.3, Ukiah, Fort Bragg & Willits. Country. 969-5868.

KSAY 98.5, Fort Bragg. Adult contemporary, light rock. 964-5729.

KTDE 100.5, Gualala. Music 24 hours, news, weather. 884-1000.

RADIO AM:

KDAC 1230, 1250, Fort Bragg. Spanish, Mexican. 964-3250.

KPMO 1300, Mendocino. Talk radio,Oakland A's games. 964-4653.

PRINT MEDIA—WEEKLIES:

Independent Coast Observer, Thursday, Gualala 884-3501.

Mendocino Beacon, Thursday 937-5874. Since 1877.

Fort Bragg Advocate-News, Thursday 964-5642.

Anderson Valley Advertiser, Wednesday, Boonville 895-3016.

PERIODICALS:

A&E — Local arts and entertainment; quarterly of Mendocino Art Center. 937-5724.

New Settler Interview — In-depth interviews; monthly. 937-5703.

Campgrounds South to North

Gualala Point Regional Park 785-2377, ½ mile south of Gualala. 19 campsites, 6 hike/bike. ♿ For reservations call 565-2267 at least 10 days ahead.

Anchor Bay Campground 884-4222, Box 1529, Gualala 95445. 52 sites, hookups, day-use access to beach.

Rollerville Junction 882-2440, 22900 Hwy One, Point Arena 95468. 55 sites, hookups, pool, spa, store. ♿

Manchester Beach KOA 882-2375, 43800 Kinney Rd, Box 266, Manchester 95459. 77 sites, hookups, pool, spa, store. ♿

Manchester State Park 937-5804, Kinney Rd, Manchester 95459. 46 primitive sites, 10 walk-in, 1 group camp.

Hendy Woods State Park 937-5804, Philo-Greenwood Rd, Philo 95466. 92 sites. ♿

Dimmick Campground, Navarro Redwoods State Park 937-5804, Hwy 128, Navarro. 28 primitive sites.

Navarro Beach Campground, Navarro Redwoods State Park, Hwy One, 937-5804. Primitive sites, no water, 7-day limit.

Schooner's Landing 937-5707, Albion River and Hwy One, Albion 95410. 41 sites, hookups.

Albion River Campground 937-0606, Albion River and Hwy One, Albion 95410. 100 sites, hookups. ♿

Van Damme State Park 937-5804, Hwy One, Little River 95456. 74 sites, 10 walk/bike-in, 1 group camp. ♿

Mendocino Campground 937-5322, 9606 Hwy One, Mendocino 95460. 60 tent sites, hot showers. April to October.

Russian Gulch State Park 937-5804, Hwy One, 2 miles north of Mendocino 95460. 30 sites, 1 group camp. April to October. ♿

Caspar Beach RV Campground 964-3306, 14441 Pt Cabrillo Dr, Caspar 95432. 89 sites, hookups, store. ♿

Woodside RV Park 964-3684, 17900 Hwy One, Fort Bragg 95437. 104 sites, hookups, store.

Pomo Campground 964-3373, 17999 Tregoning Lane, Fort Bragg 95437. 120 sites, hookups, store. ♿

Hidden Pines Campground 961-5451, 18701 Hwy One, Fort Bragg 95437. 50 sites, hookups.

Leisure Time Campground 964-5994, 2½ miles east on Hwy 20, Fort Bragg 95437. 83 sites, hookups. ♿

Camp One and Dunlap Campgrounds, Jackson State Forest 964-5674, off Hwy 20 near Fort Bragg. Primitive sites.

Dolphin Isle RV Park 964-4113, 32399 Basin St, Fort Bragg 95437. 83 sites, hookups, deli. ♿

Harbor RV Park 961-1511, 1021 S. Main, Fort Bragg 95437. 83 sites, hookups.

Green Acres RV Park 964-1435, 23600 Hwy One, Fort Bragg 95437. 100 sites, hookups. ♿

MacKerricher State Park 937-5804, Cleone 3 miles north of Fort Bragg 95437. 143 sites, 11 walk-in. ♿

Larson's Cleone Campground 964-4589, 24400 Hwy One, Fort Bragg 95437. 30 sites, hookups, store.

Westport Beach RV Campground 964-2964, ½ mile north of Westport 95488. 175 sites, coastal access. Closed Dec-Feb.

Westport-Union Landing State Beach 937-5804, 3 miles north of Westport 95488. 100 primitive sites. ♿

Usal Camp, Sinkyone Wilderness State Park 986-7711, 6 miles north of Hwy One at Rockport. 15 primitive sites.

Standish-Hickey State Park 925-6482, Hwy 101, Leggett. 164 sites. ♿

Redwoods River Resort 925-6249, 7 miles north of Leggett, Hwy 101. 40 sites, hookups, store.

Richardson Grove Campground & RV Park 247-3380, Hwy 101, Piercy. 91 sites, hookups, store.

Richardson Grove State Park 247-3318, Hwy 101, Piercy. 169 sites, store. ♿

Benbow Lake State Recreation Area 946-3238, Hwy 101, 2 miles south of

Garberville. 76 sites. ౬

Benbow Valley RV Park 923-2777, 2 miles south of Garberville, Hwy 101. 112 sites, hookups, store, golf. ౬

Dean Creek Resort 923-2555, 3 miles north of Garberville, 4112 Redwood Drive, Redway, 64 sites, hookups, store.

Vacation Home Rentals

These home-like accommodations generally require advance booking & longer stays than other lodgings. They are often more comfortable and may be more affordable for large families or groups.

Beach Rentals, Box 246, Gualala 95445, 884-4235. 56 units.

Coast Retreats, Box 977, Mendocino 95460, 937-1121. 5 units.

Irish Beach Rentals, Box 337, Manchester 95459, 882-2467. 37 units.

Kennedy & Associates, 39040 S. Hwy One, Box 900, Gualala 95445, 884-9601/800-773-8648. 25 units.

Mary Cesario-Weaver, Box 1395, Mendocino 95460, 961-0937, 3 units.

Mendocino Coast Reservations, 1000 Main, Box 1143, Mendocino 95460, 937-5033/800-262-5801. 63 units.

Ocean View Properties, S. Hwy 1, Box 1285, Gualala 95445, 884-3539. 42 units.

Point Arena Lighthouse Keepers, Box 11, Pt. Arena 95468, 882-2777. 4 units.

Robison Properties, 18901 Bald Hills Road, Comptche 95427, 800-359-4649. 15 units.

Ram's Head Vacation Rentals, Box 123, Sea Ranch 95497, 785-2427/800-785-3455. 130 units.

Sea Ranch Escape, Box 238, Sea Ranch 95497, 785-2426/800-732-7262. 80 units.

Shoreline Properties, 18200 Old Coast Hwy, Ft. Bragg 95437, 964-1444. 30 units.

Further Reading

If you want to delve deeply into the history of the Mendocino Coast, two nonprofit, privately funded organizations offer the best collections of historical resources.

Mendocino Historical Research, Inc., Box 922, Mendocino 95460, 937-5791, operates the Kelley House Museum in Mendocino, with an extensive library of historical documents available for research by appointment.

The Mendocino County Historical Society, 603 W. Perkins Street, Ukiah 95482, 462-6969, operates the Held-Poage Research Library at that location, also by appointment.

Most of the books below are still in print, a few are out of print (o.p.) and will be difficult to locate.

Adams, Charles C., *Boontling: an American Lingo*, Mountain House Press, Philo, Ca., 1990, reprint of 1971 edition.

Adams, Rick and Louise McCorkle, *The California Highway 1 Book*, Ballantine Books, New York, 1985. (o.p.)

Alt, David D. and Donald W. Hyndman, *Roadside Geology of Northern and Central California*, Mountain Press Publishing Co., Missoula, Montana, 1999.

Bear, Dorothy and Beth Stebbins, *Mendocino Book One*, Mendocino Historical Research, Inc., Mendocino, Ca., 1973.

Bear, Dorothy and Beth Stebbins, *A Tour of Mendocino*, Bored Feet Press, Mendocino, Ca., 1992.

Brown, Vinson and Douglas Andrews, *The Pomo Indians of California and Their Neighbors*, Naturegraph Publishers, Happy Camp, Ca., 1969.

Buchanan, Flora and Yerda Matson Dearing, *Memories of Cuffey's Cove and Early Greenwood, 1850-1930*, Greenwood Hobbyists, Elk, Ca., 1977.

California Coastal Access Guide, Sixth Edition, University of California Press, Berkeley, 2003.

California Coastal Resource Guide, University of California Press, Berkeley, 1987. (o.p.)

Carpenter, Aurelius, *History of Mendocino County*, Pacific Rim Press, Mendocino, Ca., reprint of 1914 edition. (o.p.)

Chase, J. Smeaton, *California Coast Trails*, Narrative Press, Santa Barbara, Ca., 2001, reprint of 1913 edition.

Collins, Walter G., *Tales from the Redwood Coast*, Mendocino County Historical Society, Ukiah, Ca., 1979.

Collins, William and Bruce Levene, *Black Bart: The True Story of the West's Most Famous Stagecoach Robber*, Pacific Transcriptions, Mendocino, Ca., 1992. (o.p.)

Hayden, Mike, *Exploring the North Coast*, Chronicle Books, San Francisco, 1982. (o.p.)

Hyman, Frank, *Historic Writings*, self-published, Fort Bragg, Ca. 1966. (o.p)

Jackson, Walter A., *Bridgeport*, Mendocino County, California, Mendocino County Historical Society, Ukiah, Ca., 1976.

Jackson, Walter A., *The Doghole Schooners*, Bear & Stebbins, Mendocino, Ca., 1977. (o.p.)

Jenny, Hans, *The Pygmy Forest Ecological Staircase*, Nature Conservancy, 1973. (o.p.)

Konigsmark, Ted, *Geologic Trips: Sea Ranch*, GeoPress, Sea Ranch, Ca., 1994.

Kroeber, A.L., *Handbook of the Indians of California*, Dover Publications, New York, 1976.

Lane, Becky, *Evolution of Glass Beach*, Lane Family, Mendocino, Ca., 1996.

Layton, Thomas, *The Story of the Frolic*, Stanford University Press, 1997.

Layton, Thomas, *Voyage of the Frolic*, Lightning Source, 1999.

Layton, Thomas, *Gifts from the Celestial Kingdom*, Stanford University Press, 2002.

Levene, Bruce & Sally Miklose, *Fort Bragg Remembered: a Centennial Oral History*, Fort Bragg Centennial, Fort Bragg, Ca., 1989.

Levene, Bruce, *Mendocino & the Movies*, Pacific Transcriptions, Mendocino, Ca., 2001.

Levene, Bruce et al., *Mendocino County Remembered, an Oral History*,

Volumes One & Two, Mendocino County Historical Society, Ukiah, Ca., 1980. (o.p.)

Matson, Walter, *Reminiscences of a Town with Two Names: Green-wood, Known Also as Elk*, Greenwood Hobbyists, Elk, Ca., 1980.

Mendocino County Historic Annals, Volumes One and Two, Pacific Rim Press. (o.p.)

Mendocino Historical Review, Volumes One through Thirty-five, 1975–1994, Mendocino Historical Research, Mendocino, Ca.

Parks, Annette W., *Qhawalali, "water coming down place," a history of Gualala*, Mendocino County, California, Freshcut Press, Ukiah, Ca. 1978. (o.p.)

Reminiscences of Early Days: a True Account of Fort Bragg, Kibesillah & Vicinity, Mendocino County Historical Society, Ukiah, Ca., 1970.

Ryder, David W., *Memories of the Mendocino Coast*, Taylor & Taylor, San Francisco, 1948. (o.p.)

Sholars, Robert, *The Pygmy Forest and Associated Plant Communities of Coastal Mendocino County, California*, self-published, Mendocino, Ca., 1982. (o.p.)

Stebbins, Beth, *The Noyo*, Bear & Stebbins, Mendocino, Ca., 1986.

Sullenberger, Martha, *Dogholes and Donkey Engines*, California Dept. of Parks and Recreation, Sacramento, 1980.

Wurm, Ted, *Mallets on the Mendocino Coast*, Trans-Anglo Books, Glendale, Ca., 1986. (o.p.)

Photograph Credits

MCHS= Mendocino County Historical Society, Ukiah
MHR= Mendocino Historical Resarch, Inc, Kelley House, Mendocino

Page	Description	Source
14	Old coast road at Flumeville	John Biaggi
22	Dust tracks on coast road	Cal. Transportation Library
32	Pomo people with baskets	MHR
36	Gualala Ferry, c.1890	Robert J. Lee collection, MCHS
40	Gualala House, c.1872	" " " " "
51	Collins Landing, c. 1875	" " " " "
52	*Brilliant* under sail	MHR
54	Nip and Tuck slide chute	"
56	Point Arena, c.1890	"
57	Point Arena after 1906 quake	Robert J. Lee collection, MCHS
65	Manchester topiary	Liz Petersen
69	"vicious bulls"	Bob Lorentzen
	Bridgeport Ranch	Liz Petersen
71	North Fork Elk Creek trestle	Robert J. Lee collection, MCHS
72	Elk milepost	Bob Lorentzen
74	Greenwood from south, c.1900	MHR
	Union Hotel Bar	"
80	Cuffeys Cove, c.1885	Robert J. Lee collection, MCHS
81	Frank Farnier in his saloon	MHR
83	Navarro, c.1899	"
89	Albion by Edward Weston	"
98	Little River—first dam & bridge	"
99	Peterson's shipyard	"
107	Hotels on Main Street, c.1862	MHR, Carlton Watkins
109	Pomo basket weaver at Big River	MHR, Carlton Watkins
	Second mill, Bever at incline	"
111	Three schooners loading, Mendocino	"
	Passengers unloading	"
117	Mansions on Little Lake Street	"
140	Caspar mill, 1910s	Robert J. Lee collection, MCHS
142	Jughandle trestle, 1884	MHR
144	Military post, Fort Bragg, c.1860	"
146	Noyo, 1863	"
147	Wooden dolls	Robert J. Lee collection, MCHS

149   Women watching ships, Noyo Landing MHR
150   Fort Bragg barrel race, c.1900   "
174   Chute at Laguna Point   MHR
175   Cleone, c.1890   "
176   Yuki dwellings on reservation, c.1860   "
177   Inglenook post office   Robert J. Lee collection, MCHS
178   Fred LeValley's stage at Ten Mile   MHR
179   Kibesillah, c.1879   Robert J. Lee collection, MCHS
183   Westport, c.1900   MHR
188   Howard Creek Blacksmith   "
189   Union Landing   "
189   Hardy Creek Hotel   "
190   Rockport Bridge, C.1880   "
190   Rockport 1958   Cal. Transportation Library
192   Usal Wharf, 1892   MHR
194   Fred Freathy, scaler   MHR
205   Picking hops, Anderson Valley   Robert J. Lee collection, MCHS
208   Traveling Emporium, Mendocino 1903   "   "   "   "   "
213   Excursion on Albion River RR   Robert J. Lee collection, MCHS
220   "Daisy" with log load, 1904   "   "   "   "   "
221   Laying track at Camp One, 1904   "   "   "   "   "
224   Point Arena Hot Springs Resort MHR
225   Ukiah Stage on Ukiah Street, c.1880   "
        Orr's Hot Springs Resort   "

Front & Back Cover   John Birchard

INDEX

About Bored Feet

We began Bored Feet Press in 1986 to publish and distribute our first book, *The Hiker's hip pocket Guide to the Mendocino Coast.* Our publishing company has grown by presenting some of the most accurate guide books for California.

We like to hear your feedback about our products! And if you would like to receive updates on trails we cover in our publications, send us your name and address, specifying your counties of interest.

We also offer www.boredfeet.com, our lightning-fast mail order service offering books and maps about the West. Your purchases directly from Bored Feet support our independent publishing efforts to bring you more information about travel, outdoor recreation, nature, history, food and wine in the Western United States. Thanks for your support!

If you would like more of our guides please send check or money order, adding $3 shipping for orders under $30, $5 over $25 ($6/8 for rush).

A FEW OF OUR BEST SELLING TITLES:
(You'll find many more books and maps at www.boredfeet.com)

Hiker's hip pocket Guide to Sonoma County, 2nd edition	$15.00
Hiker's hip pocket Guide to the Humboldt Coast, 2nd edition	14.00
Hiker's hip pocket Guide to the Mendocino Coast, 3rd edition	15.00
Hiker's hip pocket Guide to the Mendocino Highlands	16.00
Gift Set: Hiking the California Coastal Trail: both volumes	37.00
Great Day Hikes in & around Napa Valley, 2nd edition	15.00
Mendocino Coast Bike Rides	16.00
A Tour of Mendocino: 32 Historic Buildings	7.00
Geologic Trips: Sierra Nevada	17.50
Geologic Trips: San Francisco & the Bay Area	13.95
Trails & Tales of Yosemite & the Central Sierra	16.00
Mendocino Coast Glove Box Guide: Lodgings, Eateries, Sights, History, Activities & More, 3rd ed.	17.50

For shipping to a California address, please add 7.25% tax.
PRICES SUBJECT TO CHANGE WITHOUT NOTICE

BORED FEET · www.boredfeet.com. P.O.Box 1832, Mendocino, CA 95460
Phone 707/964-6629 · 888-336-6199. Fax 707/964-5953